AIDAN'S SONG

A Year in

the Life of

a Parish

Priest

AIDAN WILCOXSON

CONCILIAR PRESS ✠ CHESTERTON, INDIANA

Published by   Conciliar Press
                A division of Conciliar Media Ministries
                1550 Birdie Way
                Chesterton, IN 46304

Printed in the United States of America

ISBN 978-1-936270-03-3

For Cynthia,
Whose eyes, for me, have always been
"Love's best glasses."

CONTENTS

FOREWORD

The Archpriest Alexander Elchaninov kept a diary that has allowed his words to serve as a type of spiritual father to a multitude of people who have now read his words in the book, *A Diary of a Russian Priest*. In the section of the book taken from his letters to young people, he advised them to keep a diary, noting that:

> This helps one to study oneself, saves one from making the same mistakes, keeps the past alive. It is worth while noting every great joy, sorrow, every important encounter, every book which has impressed us, our tastes, hopes, desires.[1]

In *Aidan's Song: A Year in the Life of a Parish Priest,* the advice of Fr. Alexander, a pastor of pastors, has been taken, and the result is a most revealing story, exposing the blessings and struggles of every faithful priest. The Priest Aidan Wilcoxson opens his heart and shares his thoughts as he does what St. Gregory the Great has called the "art of arts," which is pastoral care.

In a real sense, this book is something like a *Far Side* cartoon that could well be titled, "What the Priest Is Really Thinking." Fr. Aidan is bold to give us insight into what it means for the priest to love and to admonish those whom he has been given the task of shepherding. When the priest is catechizing, baptizing, serving the divine services, burying the dead, preaching, hearing confessions, and all that is part of his charge through ordination, how does he allow Christ to be seen and heard?

In these pages, a Texas priest, who recognizes that he is an earthen vessel, gives us an answer to both what the priest does and what he thinks. More

---

1. Alexander Elchaninov, *The Diary of a Russian Priest,* trans. by Helen Iswolsky (St. Vladimir's Seminary Press, Crestwood, NY, 1982), p. 190.

importantly, we discover what he prays, and this is the foundation stone for every good priest. It is all done with good Texas humor.

Fr. Aidan is one of hundreds of Orthodox priests who have become Orthodox Christians through conviction and who have usually done so, along with their families, through a sacrifice of worldly comfort and security. For this reason it is also important that we see, through this record of daily life, the priest's wife and family. This is the story that is lived daily by the many Orthodox clergy who are planting Orthodoxy in places where it has never existed. It is in the words from Philippians 3:8 that we can find what sustains this one priest, who pastors the people of St. John the Forerunner Orthodox Church, Cedar Park, Texas, and those for whom he has become an advocate:

> Yet indeed I also count all things loss for the excellence of the knowledge of Christ Jesus my Lord, for whom I have suffered the loss of all things, and count them as rubbish, that I may gain Christ.

The Very Reverend Chad Hatfield, D.D.,
Chancellor, St. Vladimir's Seminary, Yonkers, NY

PREFACE &
ACKNOWLEDGMENTS

I hesitate to call this a journal. The word implies that I have been a witness to historic events or that I am an especially insightful person. You won't have to look far into these pages to discover that neither of those things is true.

But what I am is an Orthodox priest. And basically, what I have tried to write is a hymn of gratitude. I am grateful for many things: for my calling, for the wonderful parish I serve, for the family that loves me far more than I deserve. But what I am most thankful for is the services of the Church—because it is my participation in those services that allows me to fully appreciate my calling and my parish and my family. It is my participation in the Church's prayers that enables me to see the light which—in the lovely words of Galway Kinnell—"heavens the earth."

So what I have tried to do in these pages is to bear witness to that light. I have attempted to describe the joy that I experience just about every day of my life. And speaking of joy: Yes, that's me on the cover. It's a painting that was done by a young man in our parish community who is a gifted artist. His name is Baker Galloway. You can read about the circumstances that inspired him to portray me doing a cartwheel in the entry for March 19. He captured the delight and silliness that characterize a great deal of my life.

As to the other circumstances surrounding this journal, the entries are themselves, I hope, self-explanatory. For those readers who might not be familiar with Orthodox liturgical terms, I have also included a brief glossary at the end of the volume. The journal was written from November 2006 to October 2007, so the timing of the movable feasts reflects that year.

This journal is dedicated to the one great love of my life, my wife Cynthia. But there are also a number of people who helped me turn the journal into a book: Khouria Frederica Mathewes-Green and Father Joseph Huneycutt read the manuscript early on; Katherine Hyde, editor at Conciliar Press, did the nitty-gritty work of actually making the manuscript readable; and my brother and concelebrant, the Very Reverend Chad Hatfield, and my father in Christ, His Grace, Bishop BASIL, were encouraging at every step along the way. I would also like to express heartfelt appreciation to my two wonderful children, Brendan and Katie, and to the remarkable people of St. John the Forerunner parish in Cedar Park, Texas. May the Lord God remember them all in His Kingdom, always, now and ever, and unto ages of ages.

An unworthy priest,
Aidan

"In Thee continually is my singing of praise."
Psalm 70:6

NOVEMBER

When I pulled into the parish parking lot this morning, there was just enough light to see. I think it was about 6:30. I sat in the car and went through my sermon. Then I got out of the car and walked into the trees that cover the back of the lot. I stood in the middle of one of the open spaces and went through the sermon again.

I like preaching to the trees. It's not like they listen—at least, not the way we do. It's more like they absorb. Anyway, a squirrel was active up in the tops of the trees. Also, I could hear some deer snorting and moving about over in the scrub cedar.

I went over a couple of rough spots in the sermon. When I got done, I just stood there for a few minutes. The sunlight was starting to break through the low, dark clouds. A trace of fog mingled with the waist-high grasses. I started to turn back toward the building, and that's when I saw what I'm now going to try to describe. I can still see it even now, but I'm not at all sure I can put words to it.

Most of the trees on our lot are live oaks. They stay green pretty much all year 'round. What I saw when I turned to go was a corridor of these live oaks, and at the end and in the center of this corridor, a slightly smaller tree. I don't know what kind of tree it was, but its leaves were changing color: they were light yellow and a ruddy gold. Then the sun hit those leaves and the tips of all that waist-high grass, and I looked down that corridor of trees, and for a moment—for just a brief moment—I saw what Adam must have seen in that garden on the world's first morning. I saw the Tree of Life.

Of course, for a long time now, that tree has been a cross, but I got to see what that wood looked like before it was all about suffering and sacrifice and victory. I got to see what it was like in the beginning when the First Man looked on that tree and saw blessing and beauty without end.

We had a joyful and peaceful liturgy this morning. Everyone was singing well, and I didn't quite get the sermon the way I wanted, but folks were still attentive. When all the visiting was winding down and I was walking to the car, I thought briefly about walking out into the trees to see if I could somehow recapture that moment. But I stopped myself. I knew I probably wouldn't even be able to find that exact corridor of trees again. And if I did, the tree with the colored leaves wouldn't look the way it had just a few hours earlier. So I offered a thanksgiving and drove home, and Cynthia and I had hamburgers for lunch.

But even now, in my heart, the tree still gleams through the early morning mist, and the wonder of Adam rests ever so quietly on my soul.

Monday, November 6
✣ *Paul the Confessor*

In the upper-right-hand section of our holy doors is an icon of St. John the Theologian. Actually, it's a reproduction of a famous icon, but I get to look at it a great deal when I stand before the doors during the daily services. And there's something just a little different about this particular icon: St. John is obviously smiling. It's a quiet and gentle smile—almost a suppressed grin. But I never quite knew what to do with that smile until I reread *A Canticle for Leibowitz*—a novel we're using as part of our Wednesday night theological seminar. We've been studying apocalypticism, and in the *Canticle* there's a statue of the martyred St. Leibowitz, who has the same kind of smile St. John is wearing in the icon:

> He . . . found the face of the saint again. It was such a small grin— sad, understanding, and something else. Laughing at the hangman? No, laughing *for* the hangman. Laughing at the *Stultus Maximus*, at Satan himself. It was the first time he had seen it clearly. In the last chalice, there could be a chuckle of triumph.

The *stultus maximus*, the greatest foolishness. Since St. John is the author of the Apocalypse, since he has already been present at the End, since he was the last surviving apostle, he has indeed Seen It All. And It All brings a smile to his face.

I think he is also smiling at me. As priests go, I'm the most maximus of all stultuses. But I'm glad he smiles at me, because that quiet little grin is the key to my humility, and, Lord willing, the key to my salvation.

Tuesday, November 7
✠ Thirty-three Martyrs of Melitene

I went to see Mrs. O this morning. She is the only member of our parish who is currently in a nursing home. The past few times I've seen her, she was fast asleep. Rather than try to wake her, I just sit by her bed and go through several prayer ropes. But this time, she was wide awake and cheerful, having just made a fairly substantial dent in a fairly substantial breakfast tray. She greeted me, told me to sit down, and started to talk about her kids in high school and college and her husband traveling on business. Of course, all of that was many years ago, but since Christ Jesus is the same yesterday, today, and forever, I don't think it matters one bit. We even talked about some of her worries from that time, so perhaps they were finally resolved. We at least offered them up in prayer, and then she sent me off after obtaining a promise that I would "say hi to Matushka" for her. So I did a little time travel today; I got to carry greetings across thirty years or more. Who else gets to do such wonderful things? In what other line of work would you encounter such marvels?

Thursday, November 9
✠ Nektarios of Pentapolis

I'm sitting outside the cafeteria of the Intermediate School in Bastrop. Cynthia is doing a training event for child-care workers. The program's not over until nine PM; I drove out here with her so she wouldn't have to be on the road late by herself.

I just finished Vespers and Small Compline and the Midnight Office. Of course, it's not anything at all like doing the services in church—basically, I just read through the texts. And it's definitely a pain having to haul all the different books around (tonight I have five and a thin pamphlet). But the services are always a blessing, and there are even benefits to doing them this way.

For one thing, you can linger over a line from a hymn or a passage from a psalm. You can't do that when you're singing in church. Also, taking the services on the road gives me the chance to pray in all kinds of places—parking lots, fast food restaurants, airports. I get to speak the Name of the Most Holy Trinity in places where it may never have been spoken—or at least, not reverently or for a long time.

Last night at the theology seminar, we talked about what it means to sanctify this creation and how only those parts of this creation that have been sanctified will be part of the New Creation—the New Heaven and Earth. I think that's a big part of what happens when I pray on the road: through the prayers of the Church, I'm helping sanctify all of Central Texas.

This intermediate school is fairly new, and it's surrounded by brand new housing developments and commercial buildings. But out behind the school, someone had the good sense to leave a nice big grove of pecan trees. They're pretty old trees, too. Someone has loved them and cared for them a long time. So I spread out all my books on a picnic table out back of the school, and the pecan trees and I started the new day together. I did my prayers, and they did their prayers. They even did some liturgical dancing as the wind rocked their branches back and forth: "Then shall all the trees of the forest rejoice at the presence of the Lord, for He cometh, He cometh to judge the earth."

So it's not just me being compulsive about my "personal devotions." It's about being a priest wherever I happen to find myself. It's about doing the basic work of the Church and offering prayers on behalf of every part of this planet, from wherever I happen to be on the planet.

I love my job.

Monday, November 13
✠ *John Chrysostom*

It was a long, but good weekend.

Fr. MK and his wife, Khouria AK, flew into town for our women's retreat.

So Cynthia and I did a lot of house-cleaning, gift-bag-assembling, meal-preparing, and trip-coordinating. Thankfully, Katie was in town, and she helped a lot.

Just a few observations: I was genuinely impressed with Khouria AK; she is intelligent, very observant, and unbelievably at peace with her life and its limitations (several years ago, an accident during an operation left her a paraplegic, so she can only get around in a wheelchair). Fr. M remains Fr. M: He is deeply compassionate, but in a direct, "let's get on with it and, please, no whining," kind of way.

The retreat itself went well. People seemed responsive to what Fr. MK and Khouria AK had to say. There were lots of conversations between sessions, and many people went to confession once it was all over. At one point, Fr. MK observed that he is always amazed how much crud people carry around with them. That is true. But the women of our community do it with such strength and simple elegance.

The liturgy Sunday morning was filled with light: the light through the shaded windows in the altar, the light reflecting off the holy vessels and the fans, the light that glowed in the golden vestments, the light that burst upon us when we were all singing.

That evening we had Fr. MK and Khouria AK over for dinner. In the morning I took them to the airport. As we parted, Fr. MK said to me, "It looks like things are going very well here." That is his version of high praise, and it made me feel very good.

But as we were leaving the hotel, something happened that I think is much more representative of my life as a priest.

I went up to their hotel room, and Fr. MK gave me the suitcases and said he and Khouria AK would meet me at the car. I loaded the suitcases and waited outside. A few minutes later, Khouria AK came out; she said Fr. MK would be down shortly. I helped her into the car. When she was situated in the front seat, I pushed her wheelchair aside and handed her a bag she had been carrying. However, the wheelchair began to roll down the steeply sloped driveway. When I finally turned around and saw it, it was about halfway down the drive and headed for the highway.

So somewhere in greater Austin, any number of people are telling their co-workers and family members about the weird thing they saw on their morning commute: a guy in a black dress racing after an empty wheelchair.

(Another snapshot: Just as Fr. MK stepped out of the elevator and into the lobby, he glanced out the windows and saw his wife's empty wheelchair roll by; later, he told me he thought to himself, "OHHKaaaaay . . .")

But that's pretty much my life as a priest. It may look as if things are going well, but truth is, most of the time, I'm chasing after things I should have been keeping track of all along.

Wednesday, November 15
✤ *Guria, Shamuna, Habib, Martyrs*

Today we began the Nativity Fast. Reader MT's parents are in town for some medical testing, so I changed the altar cloths to purple and got out our huge bag of purple incense. No kidding. It really is purple. And I think that purple incense may well turn out to be our first bona fide miracle, because no matter how resolute we are in trying to use up the stuff—and we've been trying ever since I've been here—the bag never seems to get lighter. The incense itself is only a shade or two away from being a perfect match with the altar cloths, but when it's burned, it has an oddly sweet smell—like something you might get a whiff of at the State Fair. It certainly prevents us from taking ourselves too seriously during fasting seasons. So I did Vespers by myself and was there alone again this morning—quiet prayers as the purple incense filled the altar, and the angels smiled.

Friday, November 17
✤ *Gregory of Neocaesarea and Hilda of Whitby*

My left knee refuses to bend. I must have jammed it somehow when I was chasing Khouria AK's wheelchair. So no prostrations until it heals up. That's a major bummer. It sounds odd, but I really do love to make prostrations during the Lenten services. It makes the prayers more substantial.

Cynthia, on the other hand, is really sick. She was taking a steroid for her wrist pain, which helped a great deal; unfortunately, the steroid also kept her up at night. The doctor told her to stop taking the steroid, but that gave her a severe headache which, at this point, appears to have become a sinus infection, complete with fever. We've made several trips to the doctor this week without seeing much in the way of results. She is very tired and getting very discouraged.

Saturday, November 18
✠ *Plato and Romanus, Martyrs*

This has been a movie weekend. Last night, Brendan came through on his way to his Air Force Reserve weekend in San Antonio. We went to see the new Bond film. I'm not a real fan, but it wasn't too bad. All the women kept their clothes on, and, on top of that, the ending didn't take place in some vast, remote compound where Bond tries to escape from the fiendish contraption that's supposed to kill him while an electronic voice on the PA system counts down to the end of the world.

Cynthia had fever again when we got home. Brendan left for San Antonio, and I sat up with her until she was finally able to get to sleep.

This afternoon I heard RJ's life confession in preparation for her chrismation in the morning. I taught the catechumen class and was impressed once again with how eager and engaged and involved this latest group is. Vespers was subdued and a bit raspy since Reader MT and I were the only voices; also, we messed up the timing of the Entrance and the Theotokion. When I got home, Cynthia's fever had returned.

Sunday, November 19
✠ *Prophet Obadiah*

This morning I'm out among the trees behind the building. The sun hasn't come up yet, and it's pretty cold—even with a T-shirt, my clergy shirt, my cassock, and a sweater. I'm going through my sermon, and the sky starts to glow orange like a fire on a crisp morning. Out in the tall grass, a deer breaks cover and bounds off into the trees. But after a few minutes, the deer walks back out towards me. It's a doe, and she's got her neck stretched out, and she's looking straight at me. I can see her brown eyes. I go through the sermon again, and she stays right there, listening. After I'm done, she wheels, her white tail flashes, and she leaps—once, twice, three times—back into the trees.

Orthros was bright and clear. At the end of the Praises, RJ came forward to be chrismated. She is a strong and honest young woman, and when it came time for the tonsure, as I was clipping some hair from her forehead, I caught sight of her eyes—brown eyes, as it happens—and it was as if I were back out among the trees face to face with the doe.

We started the liturgy. The service moved with a natural speed and organic rhythm, and when it came time for the homily, as I looked out across the nave, face after face held the same attentiveness, expectancy, and grace that I had already witnessed twice that morning.

"O Heavenly King, O Comforter, the Spirit of Truth, who art in all places and fillest all things . . ."

Monday, November 20
✠ *Forefeast of the Entry, Gregory of Decapolis*

Katie got up early yesterday morning and drove up from San Antonio for liturgy. Brendan came back through later in the afternoon. Since they both have to be at work later in the week, we had our Thanksgiving dinner last night.

Cynthia was still feverish off and on, so we propped her up on the couch, and she supervised as the rest of us finished putting together the meal: turkey, mashed potatoes, fruit salad, rolls, dressing, and gravy, with pie and brownies for dessert. It was great to have everyone sit down and eat together. Afterward, we watched *Mission Impossible III* (we all agreed that since Tom Cruise has just gotten married, he probably needs the revenue). The movie was all right, and the Scientology jokes made it even better.

Later, when everyone was asleep, it was a special blessing to read the prayers with everyone under the same roof. I love these people so very much.

It's now 6:45 AM, and I'm sitting in a gas station in Westlake grading papers (I teach composition at a local community college). I'm scheduled to do a house blessing early this morning, and I don't want to get stuck in traffic. Brendan has to leave this morning, but Katie is going to be able to stay a few more days.

Tonight we will do Great Vespers for the Entrance.

Tuesday, November 21
✠ *Feast of the Entrance of the Mother of God*

Cynthia went to work for a few hours this morning, but she's still pretty weak. I'm glad Katie is here to help—it is nice having a nursing student around.

Vespers last night was a blessing. This morning was colder than it has been so far this fall. The blue cloth on the altar and my blue vestments matched the temperature in our converted porch/sanctuary. But Orthros and Divine Liturgy were quietly joyous. I used some of the incense EH brought back from Greece this summer, and I spoke on contemplation and noetic prayer at the homily. I was the only one in the altar, since Fr. Deacon BL had to work and none of the servers were able to arrive on time. But the liturgy was focused and peaceful, and I know it was a special gift from the Mother of God.

Wednesday, November 22
✠ *Philemon, Apphia, Archippus, Onesimus, Apostles*

On Monday I got an email from VP that her mom, Mrs. O, isn't doing well, so this morning after Orthros, I drove up to Georgetown to see her. She was pretty sleepy. We tried to talk some, but mostly I just sat and prayed with her. After I left the nursing home, I drove over to the community college to meet my class. I recited the Hours in the car and managed to get lost on all the new highway and tollway overpasses in Round Rock. So for a while, I was flying through the air, high over Central Texas, racing the angels and chanting psalms.

I got to class and ended up working on my sermon, since only three students showed up, and it didn't take long to look at their papers. Afterwards, I drove home, finished my sermon, and then went to Vespers.

When I ran home between Vespers and the Paraclesis, there was a message on the machine from Subdeacon TW. He said his daughter HM's baby had died, and that she would have to wait until next week to deliver it. I went back to church and stood in front of the icon of the Mother of

God. During the Paraclesis, I prayed for HM and for her husband, TM, and for their baby, and for all the suffering children in this suffering world.

Saturday, November 25
✠ *Catherine the Great Martyr*

It has been a nice holiday. Cynthia is still very tired, but she's not sick anymore, and I took two days off, so we had lots of time together. It was nothing spectacular, but then, you know you're really in love when unspectacular is something you can look forward to and even cherish. On Thursday, we went for a drive, did some reading, and took a long nap. On Friday, I mowed the lawn, and then we went out and got some lunch and saw a movie. (*The Queen*—it was all right. Cynthia and I agreed that the main character was much like my maternal grandmother—right down to the omnipresent purse.) This morning we went to the grocery, and I changed the filters on the air vents. I guess some would see all that as boring. I see it as golden.

Today is Katie's nameday. We called and sang a bad version of Happy Nameday to her answering machine. I can't think of St. Catherine except with red hair and a passport and a willingness to go anywhere there's adventure to be had or work to be done or injustice to be addressed or swing dancing in progress.

Sunday, November 26
✠ *Alypius the Stylite*

This morning I was standing at the altar just after the liturgy started, and I had a flashback to when I was a United Methodist pastor. In the early 1990s I somehow started listening to John Michael Talbot; he had several mass settings I really liked. I remember thinking how wonderful it would be to worship in a setting where the service just flowed, and no one had to stop to give directions or offer explanations. How great it would be if everyone knew the words to the hymns, and everyone sang for all they were worth. I remember thinking that could never actually happen in a Methodist setting—at least, not on a weekly, consistent basis.

All those recollections made me very thankful for the people of this parish. When it comes to worship, they have made my dreams come true. They provide such a beautiful setting for worship, there's just no excuse for not praying well.

Subdeacon TW called yesterday evening to say that his daughter HM was back in the hospital with fever. This morning I called the hospital before Orthros. The baby—they named him Ian—had been delivered a few hours earlier. I prayed with HM over the phone, and at the end of the liturgy, we did the first trisagion prayers for Ian.

After coffee hour, we had our second play rehearsal. This year's St. Nicholas play is a medieval pageant called *Noah's Flood*. The kids and young adults are hamming it up, but the real show-stoppers are going to be the music (courtesy of the Fallen Angel Band) and the dancing thunderclouds (who put together some impressive choreography, thanks to SM).

That's life in the Church. That's life just this side of the Kingdom. Sadness that will break your heart and laughter that brings tears to your eyes, and it's all part of the one song we offer up together in praise of the Most Holy Trinity.

Monday, November 27
✚ *James the Persian*

The leaves have been more colorful than usual this year. Light yellow and deep orange and rich red up against the dark green of the scrub cedars. The last few mornings, the sky has stayed dark, and the air has been misty, and the colors have been especially delicate.

There's a window that reaches high up the wall in our dining room. As you walk into the room, you can see across the street to where our neighbors have installed an inflatable Christmas display on their roof. It's a reindeer pulling Santa out of a chimney (or shoving him down into it; Cynthia and I are not quite sure). Anyway, the contraption actually moves, and they're keeping a spotlight on it until late at night.

I'm really thankful for the leaves.

Tuesday, November 28
✛ *Stephen the New*

My knee is a lot better. That means I can do the prostrations (I have to keep a chair close by to grab when I stand up, though), and that means the services feel complete. I love doing the Mid-Hours during Nativity Lent. This morning a phrase from Psalm 31 stuck with me: The Most Holy Trinity is addressed as "my Rejoicing." I really like that, and it helped me make a decision about what to call this journal.

I initially thought about calling it *Metanias Give Me Wedgies*. I decided against that, not because it isn't true, but because it isn't the full truth. Metanias do give me wedgies. And I trip over my exorasson. I burn holes in my endorasson. My phelonion and my epitrahelion never line up. My prayer rope gets caught in the car door; I can't sing, and my sermons are the homiletic equivalent of macaroni and cheese. That's the kind of priest I am.

Which is why I think I have the patron saint that I do. Aidan of Lindisfarne was a hard-working bishop who loved his people. But, like me, he lived and worked far from the great cultural centers of his time. Like me, he was a Christian only a few generations removed from barbarism, and he ministered in the midst of a culture of barbarism. For all those reasons, I have a great love for him, and that is why I'm going to call this journal *Aidan's Song*. Because, bumbler that I am, I've got a great Celtic Spirit-bearer singing on my behalf before the throne of the Father, Son, and Holy Spirit. And what I hope to do with this journal is, every once in a while, catch a few lines of that music and hum along in praise of the One who has made me a priest and who is my Rejoicing.

Thursday, November 30
✛ *Andrew the First-Called*

Yesterday after Orthros, I drove to Georgetown and saw Mrs. O in the hospital. She was sound asleep by a big window full of fall colors. I sat there amidst the splendor and prayed for her.

Then I drove up to Temple for Ian's funeral. By then the day had turned windy and muddy, but there was a nice group of family and friends at the graveside. And it was a tiny little grave. Ian's brothers (who are both still very young) kept wandering over to look into the grave. A Lutheran pastor who was there for one of the other family members spoke to me after the service. He said that he was "moved" by how the service "just allowed the presence of God to fill that little shelter we were in" (the funeral home had provided a portable metal awning). I'm praying that the presence of the Most Holy Trinity will fill the hearts of Ian's parents, as well. They were so desperately sad.

Lord, have mercy.

DECEMBER

Fr. TM called to check on me the other day. It's always good to talk with him, but I never can remember all I need to tell him on the spur of the moment. So yesterday I sent him an email detailing all the junk I've got stacked up in my soul, and he sent me back a few observations. I'm going to get Fr. DB to hear my confession later this month, but I'm so thankful I have a spiritual father and that he calls me from time to time. Just that brief contact can make a huge difference in my ability to keep going and stay faithful.

I try to remember that difference when I'm hearing confessions. I try to remember how desperate I often feel, and I do my best to focus intently on what people tell me. In fact, when folks come to me for confession, what I most often feel like is a corner man in a boxing match. It's not a very pious image, I know, but it sure reflects what I experience: People stagger in all tired and banged up; in the few minutes we have together, I do my best to give them a few pointers ("Watch out for the jab!" "Just cover up and stay on the ropes a while!"); then back they go, out into the ring.

The ones that bring tears to my eyes are the people who are getting the stuffing knocked out of them because of some bad habit or difficult relationship. I know, and they know, they're probably going to get clobbered when they go back out there, but when the bell goes off, they're back on their feet. I also know that one day it's all going to come together, that grace is going to guide their hand, and they are going to knock the devil on his ass, but in the meantime, it's really hard to watch them get beat up.

Like I said, it's not a conventional way of thinking about confession, but truthfully, I have a hard time identifying with the way many people talk about the mystery. For example, people often think being a father confessor means that you carry around with you all these deep, dark secrets. From time to time, they'll even ask, "Father, doesn't that get to you after a while, having to hear all that stuff?"

I hurt for people when they talk about their pain and when they describe the wreckage in their lives, but I never remember it. It's not that I don't care—I really do—but the suffering doesn't stay with me. When I first started hearing confessions, I figured it was just one of my many shortcomings; I thought perhaps I should be burdened with all these deep, dark secrets, and that after a while, I would be burdened because I would become more sensitive. But now I realize it's a special grace that father confessors receive. I've usually forgotten most of what people tell me by the time they reach the door of the nave.

Christ Jesus knows that my heart is already layered over with plenty of gunk, and I don't need to add any more. And, besides, what is true about the people who come to me for confession is not their sins. After the prayer of absolution, none of those things even exist anymore. What's true about all of those people is the simple and shining fact that Christ Jesus loves them.

Sunday, December 3
✤ *Zephaniah the Prophet*

Today was one of those non-stop days. The services went well, but the nave was packed out. Then we had a Meal for Missions (we're raising money to send our high school seniors on mission trips), and then we practiced the St. Nicholas play. It was cold, which made it uncomfortable to be outside. But since we hold services in a remodeled ranch house, we count on folks being able to go outside after the services. I mean, just about all of us can take being cooped up for a hour and a half in a space the size of a two-car garage, but afterwards we need some relief. And that didn't happen this morning.

The end result is that over one hundred people (about half of them kids) were eyeball to eyeball throughout the meal and the play rehearsal. Even in the midst of all that, everything ran smoothly, but after it was over, I walked out to the end of the parking lot and got in the car. During the night a big branch had fallen out of one of the trees right next to the lot. After I started the car, I sat there for a moment staring at that branch, and I thought to myself, "That's what I feel like."

Monday, December 4
✠ *Great Martyr Barbara and John of Damascus*

We honor so many wonderful saints this time of year, but my favorites are the Palestinian fathers. Yesterday we commemorated John the Hesychast, and tonight at Vespers we sang the service for Sabbas the Sanctified. I don't know why I feel such a strong connection with these men. *The Desert a City* is one of my all-time favorite books, but the attraction goes beyond that. I think what speaks to me is their desire for holiness, their desire for the life of the Most Holy Trinity, and how the beauty of that desire can transform this world and everything in it.

Like tonight when I was coming home from Vespers. It was already dark, and I was in the car, sitting in a long line of other cars, waiting for the light to change at the 183 intersection. The sky was completely clear except for a huge full moon that was rising behind a light ridge of clouds. The clouds were far away, and yet, sitting in the car, it was almost as if I could have reached through the windshield and touched them. It was almost as if that bright horizon were the boundary between this world and the land of the Most Holy Trinity. At least, I'm certain that for John and Sabbas, the edge of the Kingdom would often have been just that close.

And perhaps it's that way for me, too—at least, to a certain extent, because when the light changed and the line of cars began to move, the guy behind me had to tap on his horn a couple of times to get me going.

Tuesday, December 5
✠ *Sabbas the Sanctified*

The inflated Christmas display over on our neighbor's roof—the one that is framed in our dining room window—has fallen over. I think the wind must have toppled it. However, the mechanical portion of the display is still moving, and the lights are still on, so now it looks like Santa and the reindeer are wrestling or doing something mildly obscene on the roof across the street.

Wednesday, December 6
✠ *Nicholas the Wonderworker*

Last night we had Great Vespers for St. Nicholas, and this morning we had Orthros and Divine Liturgy. The service last night was deeply festive, and the services this morning were filled with a sharp joy.

I love the feasts that fall on weekdays. And I'm glad we do the full services. Not just because it's liturgically proper, but because it's so very subversive. On a Tuesday night, ten of us get together and pray for an hour while the rest of the world does Really Important Things. On a Wednesday morning, twenty-four of us get together and pray for another four hours while the rest of the world continues to rush around and do Really Important Things. But what we are doing is making a beautiful, direct, and quiet statement: *This*— this right here—is what is Really Important. This is the one thing needful. This is the transforming heart of the world.

Of course, that's the same thing we do on Sunday morning, but the world still allows that it is all right—perhaps even useful, in some ways—to be religious on Sunday morning. But being religious on a Tuesday night and Wednesday morning is a face-on challenge to the rulers of this age.

Thursday, December 7
✠ *Ambrose of Milan*

This morning after Orthros I worked on my sermon, and then I headed downtown for lunch with KR, a young woman who's been visiting our parish.

On the way, I stopped off at Best Buy and did a little Christmas shopping. I like buying gifts for people, but it's almost painful to do it at this time of year. Every store you step into has Christmas music blaring over the sound system, and so much of that music is sacred music. It was intended to be used in worship; it was never meant to accompany the kind of uber-consumption we Americans typically engage in. "Santa Claus Is Coming to Town" and

"White Christmas" I can handle—in fact, I actually like those songs. But when I hear "Hark, the Herald Angels Sing" or "Joy to the World," it makes me want to cry.

Lunch with KR was good. She had a lot of good questions, and she's working hard at thinking it all through. It's such a blessing—such a great blessing—to be able to simply answer questions and get to know people without having to worry about "closing" some sort of deal. When I was a United Methodist pastor, there was a constant emphasis on growth. Some of it was evangelically motivated; some of it was entrepreneurial in nature. But to me, it was always distasteful. It colored—I should say, it stained—every relationship and every contact with people outside the parish. So it feels great—it feels terrific—not to have anything to sell.

Friday, December 8
✠ Patapius

Thinking about lunch yesterday caused me to remember something good that happened last Sunday: We made RT a catechumen. RT is a friendly and talented young man who started visiting our services early in the fall. He is also very tall—I had to stretch, and he had to bend down slightly, so that I could get my hand on his head during the first blessing prayer.

Whenever we make someone a catechumen, I always think of the closing scene from the movie, *The Bridges of Toko-Ri*. The old admiral has just received word that William Holden and Mickey Rooney have died in an irrigation ditch in North Korea, and he starts to think out loud. He wonders how it happens that men are willing to fly off the decks of carriers and hurtle through the air at supersonic speeds and risk their lives in battle, and he ends with two profound questions: "Where do we get such men? Where do they come from?"

That's what runs through the back of my mind as we are doing the catechumen service: "Where do we get such people?" I mean, good grief, it is not easy to be Orthodox. There's all the new stuff that people have to learn, and then there's the standing and the fasting and the liturgical schedule, and you pile on top of all that the history and the different jurisdictional customs, and then you toss in the fact that they would have a much easier time joining just about any other Christian group, and the wonder is not that, every once in a while, one of our catechumens drops out of the process; the wonder is that any of them persevere.

Where do we get such people? Where do they come from? Christ Jesus sends them to us; the Holy Spirit sustains them and guides them—but that doesn't make it any less amazing.

Saturday, December 9
✤ *The Conception of the Mother of God*

Eugene Peterson defines contemplation as "becoming aware of the total surrounding context—reflecting on human presence in a divine atmosphere." He adds, "virtually all children up to the age of three to five years are contemplatives."

I think he's right on target. One of my earliest memories of being contemplative comes from being in worship. My mother had taken me to an evening service—most likely a Sunday evening. During the congregational prayer, when everyone else had their heads bowed and their eyes closed, I got up in the pew and looked around. This was before I had started school, so it's not like I was very tall. But I distinctly remember looking around at all those people, and I specifically remember thinking—or just somehow knowing—that I was in the presence of Someone great and wise and strong. I also tacitly understood that this Someone could be trusted completely.

I didn't feel the exhilaration that accompanied being "naughty," and my mother (who was right beside me and was undoubtedly aware of what I was up to) didn't try to make me "behave." I just felt this profound sense of freedom. The freedom that comes from being loved and nurtured and then turned loose in the cosmos.

That was my first full-blown contemplative experience—at least the first I fully remember. There are other snatches of memory that I might sometime describe here, but hardly a week or a day goes by that I don't run into the same kind of experience. Not that those moments somehow make me a mystic. Peterson rightly remarks that "contemplative is not a term of achievement. . . . It is not a badge of merit." And that is certainly true. But Peterson also implies that contemplation is almost entirely a natural phenomenon, and I think that's overstating our contribution to the whole thing.

To me, contemplation is almost entirely an experience of grace. And when you're talking about grace, you have to talk about the Mother of God. She is the icon of contemplation, because she is the icon of the human response to grace. And I now know that she has always been at the center of my contemplative life.

After all, it was no accident that I was sitting next to my mother that night in the service. Later, when I was an unhuggable teenager, my mom would grab my face in her hands and look straight into my eyes as if to say, "Oh yeah, just try to make me stop loving you." And on the day I was ordained a priest, when I stepped out onto that vast solea at the cathedral in Wichita to begin my last few litanies as a deacon, I looked up into the apse, and there was that massive icon of the Mother of God with her arms stretched out to me. It was as if she were putting my face in her hands.

That's grace. That's contemplation. Suddenly remembering that you are in the presence of beauty. Suddenly realizing that you are being sustained by love. The daily task is simply to keep that remembrance and to live in that realization.

Sunday, December 10
✠ *Eugraphos, Menas, Hermogenes, Martyrs*

I'm sitting in the bathtub. I guess I should add that I'm fully clothed and there's no water in the tub. Anyway, it's the only quiet spot in the house since Brendan and Katie are both home.

It's been a fast-paced weekend, but it has also been filled with the deep-down kind of joyful contentment that can only come from doing things that are right and true and real.

Yesterday morning, after I did my prayers and wrote in this journal, I got up in the attic and brought down all the Christmas decorations. Then I put the Pogues on the stereo and assembled our fake tree (which is looking more and more fake with each passing year).

Cynthia put some of our other decorations out, and then we left the house to continue our quest for a Really Good Chinese Restaurant. The quest has become something of an epic undertaking, since it is now entering its fifth year. Anyway, we ended up at a noodle house on Lamar. The place was hopping, and it was authentic—in fact, we were the only Westerners to be seen. The food was all right, but both Cynthia and I had to admit that we actually prefer the faux Oriental atmosphere of more American establishments (and the kind of service you get there). So we might have to revise the name of our quest to the search for a Really Good Chinese Restaurant That Isn't Too Chinese. At any rate, the epic continues . . .

The services this weekend were wonderful. It's gotten to the point where they are just a regular part of our lives. Vespers is not some special religious thing we do on Saturday; it's as natural as putting out the Christmas decorations. Orthros is a deeply spiritual experience, but the joy we experience there is the same joy that made us smile when we were eating Chinese food. And the liturgy—what can you say about the liturgy? It's this glorious mixture of chaos and structure, of authority and freedom, of being intensely focused and completely relaxed.

Which is precisely what our evening at home was like. Katie was at liturgy this morning; Brendan drove in later this afternoon. Cynthia cooked a great dinner, and when we ate together, there was a lot of gentle teasing and a lot of talk about holiday plans and presents. Then we did the dishes and put on some Christmas music and finished decorating the tree.

So there's the liturgy we do at church and the liturgy we do at home. There are the services we do in the temple, and there's the service we call our lives. Speaking of services, I need to put this journal down and get started on the Ninth Hour and Vespers. I brought all the books with me into the bathroom. Probably should get out of the tub . . .

Monday, December 11
✣ *Daniel the Stylite*

Today has been bright and clear. I drove down to the community college, and the sun flashed through the windshield in great golden sheets. The last leaves are starting to fall.

While I was sitting at a stoplight, I couldn't help but smile thinking about yesterday's St. Nicholas play. The kids had their lines down well; the music was fabulous, and the dancers were even more outrageous than expected. What really made the whole production, though, was the preschool and elementary kids as animals—they had great costumes and great zoo moves. Their procession into the ark was the highlight of the show.

Afterwards, Cynthia told me that during the play she was thinking about the sort of productions other Christian communities do: There's the traditional shepherd/wise men/baby Jesus pageant with a narrator and the choir and the whole thing strictly supervised by the same person who has overseen the play year after year. Then there are the professional productions that larger parishes now offer, complete with lights and orchestra and live animals. Then there's our show: a 900-year-old script, lots of silliness, a cast that includes half the parish, and "Ghost Riders in the Sky."

Cynthia prefers our approach. I couldn't agree more.

Tuesday, December 12
✣ *Spyridon the Wonderworker, Herman of Alaska*

A couple of weeks ago, VK asked me what I thought the next step in her spiritual disciplines should be. I suggested that she come to Orthros a couple of mornings each week. She has started doing that, and it is a real blessing. Just having a woman there on a regular basis makes a difference. When it's all guys, the services eventually and invariably take on a kind of locker room feel—especially early in the morning. Nothing profane, mind you, just a kind of masculine roughness. But a feminine presence adds propriety and elegance and a special grace.

And the services are so very important. I was reminded of that this morning as we sang about St. Herman. He is the spiritual father of the entire American Church, but most of his "ministry" was just him on an island praying. But from those prayers, the Church took root, and it continues to grow. And that is how the Church grows today. This morning six people were at the service. We prayed for two hours, until the sun came up, and then we all left and went to work. But it is in that hidden striving, that work which is unseen by the world, that the Church flourishes.

When I got home this morning, I found a reminder of just how badly the Church is needed. In the mail was a glossy brochure from a large local Protestant community. The print was boldface; the text exploded with exclamation marks: Life-Changing Messages! High-Quality Children's Ministry! Live Music! Casual Atmosphere! Five Christmas Services!

Holy Father Herman, pray for the Church in this land.

Wednesday, December 13
✠ *Eustratius, Eugene, Mardarius,*
Auxentius, Orestes, Martyrs

Every day I'm in the car, I read a page or two out of the *Philokalia*. I keep a volume on the seat next to me, and I pick it up when I'm stuck in traffic or sitting at a long light. Right now, I'm working my way through St. Peter of Damascus. Back when I first read through the *Philokalia* (fifteen years ago, before I was Orthodox), I thought St. Peter's writing was formless, repetitive, and not very original. Now I can't get enough of him. And I'm especially enjoying his wry sense of humor. Like this priceless paragraph:

> I marvel at God's wisdom, at how the most indispensable things—air, fire, water, earth—are readily available to all. And not simply this, but things conducive to the soul's salvation are more accessible than other things, while soul-destroying things are harder to come by. For example, poverty, which anyone can experience, is conducive to the soul's salvation; while riches, which are not simply at our command, are generally a hindrance. It is the same with dishonor, humiliation, patience, obedience, submission, self-control, fasting, vigils, the cutting off of one's own will, bodily enfeeblement, thankfulness for all things, trials, injuries, the lack of life's necessities, abstinence from sensual pleasure, destitution, forbearance—in short, all the things conducive to the spiritual life are freely available. No one fights over them. On the contrary, everyone leaves them to those who choose to accept them.

Friday, December 15
✠ *Eleutherios, Hieromartyr*

Yesterday, when Cynthia got home, we drove downtown (through a lot of traffic) to St. Elias. They held a Vesperal Liturgy for St. Eleutherios, the patron of our young diocese. Not many people were there since this was the first time we've had such a liturgy. But I like serving at St. Elias. The whole place is made of aging wood. The altar is cramped, but it is high above the nave, and the floors creak whenever you move, so the overall effect is like praying on the quarterdeck of an old sailing ship.

And it was a lovely voyage. Before we began, Fr. JK heard my confession, and I heard Fr. DB's confession. Fr. DB then did the chanting (he has such a rich voice), and Fr. JK handled the liturgy (he serves with great command and energy). Fr. Deacon GB from the Greek parish was with us, and he served as well. I was left alone to pray, and that was joy.

On the way home, we got a call from Cynthia's half-brother. Their mom is in the hospital, and it appears she has had another stroke.

Saturday, December 16
✠ *Prophet Haggai*

We got up this morning at 4:30 AM. After prayers, we hit the road and were in Dallas shortly before 9:00. We had breakfast with my parents and visited with my sister and her boys. My parents gave us some of their best guidebooks for England and Scotland—we hope to travel there next summer—and we gave them two rosaries we had bought with money that came to us after my great-grandmother died. We purchased the rosaries when we were trying to figure out ways to supplement our Methodist spirituality. But we didn't use them for long, since shortly after that we stumbled on Holy Orthodoxy. Now that my parents are part of a Western Rite parish, we figured they could make good use of them. And since they were purchased with money that came from my mom's grandmother, it was a fitting bit of Kingdom symmetry.

At 10:45 we headed over to see EH, Cynthia's half-sister, who lives close to Carrollton. EH's husband, WH, has emphysema, and he has been declining for some time now. This week the nurses told EH that he would do well to make it into the new year. We didn't see WH, as he was asleep—and he hasn't wanted visitors recently, anyway. But we got to talk a bit with EH down in the lobby of their apartment building. She has always been a cheerful person, but she looked really tired. Nevertheless, she was as upbeat as ever, and it sounds like she's doing a good job of hanging in there with WH.

At 11:45 we were back on the road and headed for Bedford. Mrs. E,

Cynthia's mom, was still in the hospital, but we had already received word that she was rapidly improving, and when we arrived, she appeared to be doing well. We talked about all that had happened (actually, Cynthia's mom is almost deaf, but she refuses to get hearing aids; so she talks in a normal voice, but everyone else shouts). When her lunch arrived, Cynthia helped her with it. Afterwards, a nurse stopped by, and Cynthia went out into the hall to get an update. Mrs. E and I made small talk, which, sadly, has been pretty much the extent of our relationship these last 28 years (of course, I'm not sure that small talk is the appropriate term when one person is bellowing).

At 2:00 we started back for Austin. The nurse told Cynthia that her mom had indeed suffered a stroke, but that it was a small one. The nurse said that Mrs. E is recovering well, but she added that another stroke was likely at some point in the future. It was good for Cynthia to actually get to talk to one of the nurses. Cynthia has six half-brothers and sisters, but, oddly enough, having that many family members often makes it harder, not easier, to get accurate information when something like this happens.

We drove non-stop and arrived back home just in time for me to get to Orthodox Instruction. Then came Great Vespers and quite a few confessions, and now it's about 8:45 PM, and I'm ready for bed.

Tuesday, December 19
✠ *Boniface, Martyr*

Talked for a good long time on the phone with my friend DT. As we were catching up with each other, I happened to ask him how his kids are doing. He said that his daughter is just about to finish nursing school, but she's also living with a guy. DT talked briefly about how painful that is for him and his wife. I told him I would be praying for them and for his daughter and her boyfriend.

Of course, I really mean that. And DT knows I mean that. In our theological seminar, we've been reading through the Apocalypse, and I've been deeply impressed by the graphic and concrete ways in which St. John the Evangelist describes the efficacy of prayer: When the faithful persevere in prayer, suddenly, plans are unveiled, announcements are made, angels spring to action, and history narrows to the edge of a sickle that is being wielded by the Lord of the Harvest. And when I tell my friend that I'm going to engage in that kind of activity on his behalf, then that creates a bond between us that renders the telephone superfluous.

It's hard, though, when you can't tell people you're praying for them. Mrs. E, Cynthia's mom, is that way; there are also a number of people like that on my side of the family. They just wouldn't know what to do with that information, and it would be almost impossible to explain it to them. Talking to these folks about spiritual issues is like calling across a great chasm. And what frightens me—what truly frightens me—is the thought that this chasm could well be a reflection of the one Father Abraham refers to in his exchange with the rich man: "And besides all this, between us and you a vast gulf has been fixed, in order that those who might pass from here to you may not be able, and none may cross from here to there."

Wednesday, December 20
✠ *Ignatios the God-Bearer*

Today we begin the services of the Forefeast. And with the Forefeast, time starts to take on that special elastic quality. In the middle of a busy festal cycle, when there are lots of special services and weekday liturgies, and folks are off work, and the kids are out of school, it is easy to lose track of what day of the week it is, since all the normal markers have shifted. But I think that when time takes on that kind of pliancy, there's more to it than just the rearranging of schedules. I think that, during a feast, we actually have greater access to the Kingdom, and the more we are in the environs of the Kingdom, the more flexible time becomes.

I experience that a great deal after prayer and during the services. The other day, after I was done with the Hours and the Typika, I walked around the corner to the mailbox, and it was like I was stepping in between the sunbeams. During the Divine Liturgy, Fr. Deacon BL will ask me something or one of the servers will need some help, and it's always just a bit startling. It probably looks like I'm waking up, but it's just that moment of readjustment when the gears of chronological time kick in and take over once again.

I think that's why I took so readily to being a hospice chaplain— and why I was happy doing that job for over a decade. The dying frequently just slip in and out of time, and if you're going to stay up with them on that journey, you need to be able to flex right along with them.

At its best, I think that kind of experience is what Holy Scripture calls the "fullness of time." It's the clear, true sense that there is something solid and permanent and shining just beyond the quick succession of moments our clocks are designed to measure. And the feast gives us a precious opportunity to abide in that fullness.

Thursday, December 21
✠ *Juliana, Martyr*

This morning I got home early from Orthros, and Cynthia reminded me that we hadn't prayed together all week. Bummer.

So we stood together in front of the icon of the Mother of God that hangs in our front hallway—the one that is surrounded by all our family photographs—and we did our prayers.

Then we kissed, and she left for work. Now the thought keeps coming back to me: What did I ever do to deserve a woman like her?

Friday, December 22
✠ *Anastasia, Martyr*

Last night Reader MT was swamped in the bookstore, so I did Vespers by myself. I was alone in the temple throughout the service. It got dark quickly; in fact, by the time I did the censing on "O Lord, I have cried," you couldn't see from one end of the nave to the other. But after I censed the iconostasis, I turned into the nave, and as I did, a great shower of sparks flew out of the censer into the night. It looked like a new galaxy had suddenly burst into existence, bright stars and shining worlds cascading across space and time. And like some great angel I strode on through the fire, swinging the censer and singing the praises of the Most Holy Trinity, while all around me an entire universe briefly and brilliantly came to life.

Back in the sanctuary, I tripped over my cassock as I was stepping up to the altar. I didn't fall down, but I only managed to stay upright with some arm-flailing and some frantic foot moves. It was all very unpriestly, but I think Peter Sellers or Jerry Lewis would have been proud.

Monday, December 25
✠ *The Feast of Nativity*

I'm sitting in the altar. It's about 6:30 AM. Outside, it's raining, slow and steady, just as it has been all weekend. When I got out of the car, I thought I was going to race for the building, but I ended up walking through the rain, and I started thinking about all the blessings the Feast has showered on me.

Friday was filled with confessions and the Royal Hours and two trips downtown to pick up Cynthia's present. It's a large print, and I couldn't get the box in our car when I first went down there, but Reader MT graciously let me borrow his vehicle, and even though I got stuck in traffic on the way back, the extra time was just extra time to pray. So I sat in Reader MT's car along with all the other folks sitting in their cars, and I whispered the hymns of the forefeast until the love that burns at the heart of everything began to glow within me.

And I caught fire with that same love again on Saturday morning. Katie got in on Friday, and Saturday morning I drove her and Cynthia around as we finished up some last-minute shopping. I had brought along a book to read while they did their thing—I just figured I'd hang out in the car until they were done. But instead of reading, I just ended up watching all the people going in and out of the stores, and that watching led to praying. There were couples and families and folks who were all alone; some were obviously having a good time; some were determined and resolute; some were tired and distracted. But I sat there and prayed for them all. I didn't ask for anything; I simply watched them: the way a father watches his children as they play; the way a lover watches his beloved get dressed in the morning; the way, I think, Christ Jesus watches over this entire world.

The services Saturday night and yesterday morning were magnificent. All the chanters were able to participate, and everyone else was singing well, too. I got to serve the gifts to Cynthia and Katie and Brendan, who got in late Saturday. So far, though, the high point of the feast was last night at Great Vespers. When the chanters were reading through the eight Old Testament lessons, it was as if the Holy Spirit was kneading those passages into my soul, working the words down deep below my conscious mind, just folding my heart up and over and all around those living syllables.

So now I'm pregnant with Scripture. I'm sitting here in the altar waiting for the festal services to resume. I'm writing in this notebook and humming the hymns of the feast as some of the water that collected in my hair on my walk from the parking lot drips onto the page . . . or maybe those are just drops of joy.

Thursday, December 28
✠ *The Martyrs of Nicomedia*

Brendan was finally able to head out this afternoon. He had planned on leaving yesterday, but we discovered that his truck was leaking coolant, and when we took it to our mechanic, it turned out that he needed a new water pump. Then the whole thing was delayed further when the supplier sent the wrong part. So Brendan was not in a good mood.

It all finally culminated with a scene in the kitchen last night when he yelled and slammed a cabinet door, proclaiming that he should have just taken a chance and driven home and not listened to "our" mechanic.

I went to bed. Those few moments in the kitchen reminded me of life ten years ago, when we were all trying to learn how to be adults together, and the memory wasn't a pleasant one. But two moments of special grace came during the night. At some point, I woke up, and Cynthia touched me on the arm; leaning over, she whispered in my ear. All she said was, "I love you," but it was as if the Holy Spirit had touched my soul and whispered into my heart.

And then I had a dream. Brendan usually carries a little notepad around with him for lists and reminders and that sort of thing. In my dream I picked up his notepad. It was open, and a list was written on one of the pages. I don't recall exactly what was on the list, but I clearly understood that it was a list of things he was worried about. I stood there looking at the piece of paper, and then I thought, "I need to be praying about all this."

I remembered all of that this morning at Orthros. After I got home, I worked on two of the three sermons I need to have ready for this weekend. When Brendan got up, he was quiet; I could tell he was angrier with himself than he was with me. His truck was ready a little before noon, and he gave me a hug and apologized before he left. Just a few minutes ago he called to talk to Cynthia.

Saturday, December 30
✤ *Anysia, Martyr*

Tomorrow is the Leavetaking of Nativity. This year, for the first time, I started to genuinely listen to all those dialogues that involve the Mother of God. Most of them occur in the stichera hymns during "O Lord I have cried": there's one in which she's talking to St. Joseph and one in which she's talking to the wise men (I don't think there's a dialogue with the shepherds; I'll have to look into that). But my favorites are the ones in which she speaks to the infant Christ—because she just marvels; she is simply in awe. In those hymns, the Church gives us glimpses into all those things that the Mother of God kept and pondered in her heart.

I want my heart to be like her heart.

I want to learn how to marvel.

Sunday, December 31
✤ *The Leavetaking of Nativity*

Yesterday afternoon we got BG and RJ married. They chose to have the service over at Transfiguration parish since the crowd would never ever have fit in our space. They've got a whole lot of new iconography over there now, and that just made the event even more beautiful. BG and RJ were stressed and, I think, a little overwhelmed, but finally, there they stood—and they were just as straight and just as true, and they glowed just as brightly as the candles they were holding, and after a bit, they were able to leave behind all the wedding craziness and look on out into the future. And if that future is going to be anything like what I saw reflected in their eyes, then it's going to be filled with struggle and triumph and all kinds of blessings for all kinds of people.

Right after the wedding I headed back over to St. John's, arriving just in time to get ready for Orthodox Instruction. When the class was over and it was time for the ninth hour, I suddenly realized that Fr. Deacon BL and all the chanters were at the wedding reception. So I went ahead and did the services by myself. Even with the wedding, we had a good turnout for Great Vespers, but the poor people had to endure my singing as well as my attempts to figure out how the Sunday following Nativity and the Leavetaking of the Feast and the Resurrection material for Tone 4 all fit together. It wasn't at all pretty, but we got through it, and I only saw the figures on the iconostasis wince a few times.

JANUARY

We had a lot of folks at Great Vespers last night and a good group this morning at Orthros and the Divine Liturgy. I am really proud of my parish. Most of them work so hard to get to the services, and that's so important.

At the same time that I'm proud of my community, I also know that they deserve a better priest. For example, this morning we were serving St. Basil's Liturgy (which is actually my favorite), but I kept stumbling over the prayers: "heal the sick" came out "heal the spick," and several other moments were equally ridiculous and embarrassing.

But it's not just that I was having an off day. It's not something that could be taken care of by a few sessions with a locution coach. Those words should gush out of my heart like jetting water. They should blaze on my tongue like fire. Because those words are life. His life. My life. The life of the people in this parish. But when I get distracted or careless, when I get in a hurry or when I get excited, they just become words again. Words I'm reading off a page. Words I'm not even pronouncing correctly.

In the Prayers of Preparation before Communion and the Prayers of Thanksgiving after Communion, several times we request that we be able to receive the Holy Mysteries "unto our last breath." In my case, that translates to, "Let me keep at this until I get it right." Of course, I'll be fifty this year, so I'm not going to get just a whole lot more practice. But what I'm hoping is that there will be a Divine Liturgy where the prayers are like great comets falling upon the earth, and the homily is a song such as only the angels can sing, and when I step back and close the curtain to the altar, another curtain will open, and the Spirit will say, "Come!" and the Prayers of Thanksgiving will begin and never, ever, ever end.

That's when I'll be the priest I should be. That's when my people will have the priest they deserve.

Tuesday, January 2
✠ *Seraphim of Sarov*

Today we turn from Bethlehem to the Jordan as we begin the Forefeast of Theophany. Actually, the Jordan may just come to us if it continues to rain as much as it has been. All this water is fitting preparation for the feast.

I don't have to prepare a sermon this week. That's a blessing for me— and for the parish as well. Bishop Basil will be with us on Sunday. He's a wonderful homilist, and it will be good for the parish to hear some really good preaching for a change.

But I still have plenty to do this week. I've got thank-you notes to write, two OCMC applications to finish up and send in, the house blessing schedule to mail out, my parish council report to file, and I've got to put together the syllabus for this coming semester's college classes.

Today is also laundry day. Since I have my office at home, I can take a break from time to time and start the washer or take stuff out of the dryer or hang things up in the closet. I'm pretty good at it now; at least I don't shrink clothes anymore. For many years now, Cynthia and I have just divided up all the household chores: she does cooking and the insurance work; I do the grocery shopping and laundry, and I definitely think I got the better end of the deal. What I like best about laundry is the fact that when it's done, it's done. The basket's empty; everything's put away; there's a definite, definable, identifiable end. And there's not much in a priest's job that has a definite, definable, identifiable end.

That can get pretty discouraging. So when the horizon of the Kingdom keeps receding into the distance, I sort some clothes. When deification begins to seem like a mythological concept, I do a load of whites. When the timeline for the new building has to be revised one more time, I clean the dryer vent.

Come to think of it, that's probably why Christ Jesus did all that carpentry work. That's probably why the apostles did all that fishing.

Wednesday, January 3
✛ *The Prophet Malachi*

As I've been writing in this journal over the past couple of months, an image has begun to form in my heart, and that image has slowly been transformed into a clear insight: What I'm doing with this journal is what the ancient stylites did on their pillars.

The stylites were ascetics who lived on the tops of tall columns. Many of them stayed up there for decades. I've never understood how it all worked (logistically, at least; I mean, after all, where did they go to the bathroom?), but after posting these entries on our parish website, and after listening to so many people say such encouraging things about what I've written, I'm beginning to understand why those guys took to those pillars. A lot of popular writers suggest that the stylites wanted to get away from people, but if that is the case, then why did they choose a way of life that was so visible? I don't think they climbed up on those columns to get away from others; I think they chose that form of asceticism because they wanted to live a transparent life. They did not want any secrets between them and the Most Holy Trinity—or between them and anyone else, for that matter. And that's why I'm keeping this journal: I want anyone and everyone to be able to look into my heart.

Actually, I need to qualify that somewhat: I initially started writing this journal because I wanted one specific someone to be able to look into my heart. That someone is Cynthia. She is the most intensely honest person I've ever known, and the longer I know her, the more honest I want to be. Not that I've always followed through on that desire. We've been married twenty-eight years now, and I'm not a very communicative person—it would be more accurate to say that I'm just emotionally constipated. But she always makes me want to get out of myself, and so I figured that if I couldn't talk about what is going on in my heart, I could at least write about it.

So, in a real sense, what lies behind this journal is what motivates most men to do 94.5% of what they do: I'm trying to impress a woman. But then I got to thinking: If Cynthia doesn't have much insight into what goes on in my heart, the people I'm supposed to be loving, the parishioners of St. John, must really be in the dark. So I decided to simply share this journal with everyone else.

And now that I'm up here on this pillar, all sorts of people have been saying things like, "I never knew you felt that way," or "I was so surprised," or "I had no idea that's how you looked at things." Well . . . yeah . . . that's me. But being a literary stylite and not having any place to hide is kind of freeing. So I'll stay up here and keep writing, and try to be as accurate and as honest as I can about what life looks like from the top of this column.

But what about Cynthia? After all, she was the original inspiration for the whole project. How does she feel about sharing my heart with everyone else? Actually, in many ways, she doesn't even need this scribbling. Because she has always been able to see all the way through to the back side of my soul, and she knew—long before I even started writing this stuff—that she is married to a priest who, in the wry words of Padraic Fallon, can "keep no beauty to himself."

Friday, January 5
✠ *Paramon of Theophany*

It's 10:30 PM. I should be in bed. It's been a long day, and tomorrow's going to be just as long. Today we did Orthros and the Royal Hours. Then at noon, we served the Vesperal Liturgy of St. Basil with the First Sanctification of Water. At 7:00 this evening, we did Small Compline with the Second Sanctification of Water. Tomorrow morning, I'm supposed to pick up Bishop Basil at his hotel at 7:45, then we will go to St. Elias to do Orthros and Divine Liturgy for the Feast followed by the Outdoor Sanctification of Water at Barton Springs, and then the regular Saturday night/Sunday morning parish schedule with Bishop Basil joining us at St. John's Sunday morning for a hierarchical liturgy.

So, yeah, I should be in bed. But I'm just jazzed from all the services today—that and the fact that I had a bowl of Intense Chocolate ice cream about 9:00 PM, and I've got a little caffeine buzz going. But as good as the chocolate was, the services today were even better.

First of all, there were all those great lessons at the Royal Hours and the Vesperal Liturgy—a complete aquatic review of Holy Scripture. We splashed in the Jordan; we dashed through the Red Sea; we got to rest by the fountains of Elam, and we got to draw from the wells of rejoicing. And when we were all just completely drenched, soaked to the bone and dripping with righteousness, that's when we turned to that wondrous prayer, that long and beautiful poem St. Sophronius wrote for the sanctification of the water.

What makes that prayer so magnificent is the way it conveys the fullness of time. I got an email after I posted the most recent installment of this journal. The person who wrote the email was asking how time can become full. And there's no better answer than St. Sophronius' prayer:

> Today the Prophet and Forerunner approaches the Master but stands before Him with trembling, seeing the condescension of God toward us. Today the waters of Jordan are transformed into healing by the coming of the Lord. Today the whole creation is watered by mystical streams. Today the transgressions of men are washed away by the waters of Jordan.

Today . . . Today . . . In the presence of the Most Holy Trinity, it is always Today; it's always Now. So, in the fullness of time, the Father, Son, and Holy Spirit behold the entire history of humanity and my whole life—which means that Today I am born, and Today I have been forgiven, and Today I am dying, and "Today Paradise has been opened to me, and the Sun of Righteousness shines down upon us all."

But this experience of time's plenitude doesn't shield us from pain or sorrow. If anything, pain and sorrow are intensified by this experience. So Today as I was reading the prayer St. Sophronius wrote, I was mindful of the woman who stopped me before the liturgy and told me that her son was being taken to the hospital, and I remembered the couple who have to go talk to a bankruptcy advisor, and I remembered the person who emailed me earlier in the day to ask me to pray for an employee who was going to have to be terminated, and the couple who told me about the headaches they had suffered with all week long. And even after the services, when one person told me about their family problems, and another told me about a son who's due to be in Iraq in February, those prayers weren't somehow too late—because they are also part of the Most Holy Trinity's Today. A Today which we access through our prayers and the prayers of St. Sophronius, because, as St. Peter of Damascus writes, "the words of prayer are written once and for all."

So the fullness of time is not a refuge. It's not a pain-free zone that we step into in order to escape from this life. If anything, it's where we can take on the full significance of sorrow and the raw agonies of pain. And I think that is one of the greatest gifts we Orthodox can give to the world. We can take upon ourselves all the horrors and heartaches of this world without minimizing any of it, without attempting to explain it away, without holding it at arm's length through abstraction or argument. We can take it upon ourselves, and we can take it all, through prayer, into the fullness of time, into the presence of the Father, Son, and Holy Spirit, and it will all be healed. It will all be transformed just as surely as the waters were Today made holy.

Saturday, January 6
✤ *The Feast of Theophany*

This morning I picked up Bishop Basil at his hotel, and we drove down to St. Elias. Orthros started right when we arrived, and I don't think I have ever served in a more crowded altar. Five priests, three deacons, two subdeacons, four altar servers, and the bishop were all vested, all trying to move around and get things done in an area about the size of a small kitchen. Just before the Great Entrance, when His Grace was finishing the Proskomidia and trying to hand out things in preparation for the procession, we were all crammed into the north end of the altar, and it literally got to the point of gridlock. It was a liturgical traffic jam. We simply couldn't go where we all needed to go.

Being the kind of guy I am, I immediately thought about the stateroom scene from that old Marx Brothers' movie, *A Night at the Opera*: Groucho, Chico, Harpo, and their straight man are in a small room on board a ship along with a huge steamer trunk. Then other people start arriving: two maids, two guys to check the radiator, a manicurist, a hair stylist, a plumber, and a telephone repairman. Finally, a steward from room service opens the door, and everyone spills out into the passageway.

When it was time for the Great Entrance, we didn't all tumble out onto the solea, but during the procession, it was hard not to smile, because I kept thinking about what that would look like.

Sunday, January 7
✣ *The Synaxis of the Forerunner*

This morning's services were almost indescribable. All the chanters were present for Orthros, and they did their work flawlessly: clear reading, delicately phrased singing, all of which let the poetry of the psalms and hymns shine brightly and fiercely.

Bishop Basil just stayed in the altar and prayed with us during Orthros, and his presence gave the whole experience even greater depth and power. I would have thought having him there with us would have made me nervous or self-conscious, but it was just the opposite: the longer the service went on, the more peaceful and focused I became.

So by the time we got to the tonsure for JW and BG, it was like a family gathering—in the best sense of the word. We all knew what to do, and we all did it naturally and reflexively, but also with great joy and reverence. Then we started the Divine Liturgy, and the choir was magnificent, and everyone sang, and Bishop Basil preached a wonderful sermon, and it was a day taken straight out of the Kingdom, a day where this life became the life we were meant to live—the life we will one day live in the land of the Most Holy Trinity.

Monday, January 8
✣ *George the Hozevite*

I'm sitting in a Whataburger in South Austin. It's 5:45 PM; I've just finished Small Compline and the Midnight Office. I'm getting ready to hit the road for a string of house blessings, but I'm also still thinking about this past weekend. Three things have been making me smile all day long.

First of all, when I went to pick up Bishop Basil on Saturday morning, I knocked on the door of his hotel room, and he said, through the door, that he would meet me down in the lobby in 20 minutes. Later, he apologized for making me wait; he said he was finishing his rule of prayer. I'm so thankful I have a bishop who keeps a rule of prayer.

Second, at the lunch on Saturday, I made a fleeting reference to the old PBS show, *Fawlty Towers,* and Bishop Basil picked up on it right away. I'm thankful my bishop is a John Cleese fan.

Finally, at the kiss of peace during yesterday's liturgy, His Grace gave me a big hug, and then he kissed me on the forehead and whispered in my ear, "You're a good priest." I think he missed that call, but I'm really thankful I have a bishop who understands the desire of my heart.

Wednesday, January 10
✠ *Gregory of Nyssa*

Since Monday morning, I have blessed eighteen houses. That's a lot of driving and a lot of holy water and a lot of singing. This time of year, I end up hearing the troparion for Theophany in my sleep ("When Thou, O Lord, wast baptized in the Jordan . . ."). Of course, I've had some songs that were a lot less spiritual stuck in my head, but when I wake up and the first thing that slips into my consciousness is a line from the Theophany troparion, then I know it's January, and we're in the afterfeast of Epiphany.

But even with all the extra activity, I love this time of year. Each home I bless is a blessing for me, because I get to stand right where the folks in our community stand when they say their prayers. And the icon corners that can be seen in the homes of our parish are just as diverse as the people who live in those homes: Some folks have a whole wall of icons; others have only one or two. Some people have their icons carefully arranged in a symmetrical pattern; others have large icons and tiny icons and icon cards and family photographs all jumbled together. Some folks have neat icon corners: the hand censer and the prayer book and the matches and the Bible are each in a particular place. Some people have messy icon corners: wax and last year's palm frond cross and all sorts of prayer lists are piled up among bottles of holy water and saints' lives and prayer ropes.

But it's an honor to stand in those sacred places. Because those are the places where my people weep and cry out and kneel and make prostrations and offer prayers of hope and gratitude. Those are the spots upon which they are being made saints, and, by standing in those same spots for a few minutes each year, I get to share in that grace. I get to participate in that sanctification.

Thursday, January 11
✠ *Theodosius the Founder of Monasteries*

Actually, it's Friday morning. It's 1:45 AM. I just got in from San Antonio. Katie had day surgery down there, and I was going to stay the night with her and Cynthia, but since I've got so much to do here I decided to go ahead and drive back.

I should also go ahead and get some sleep, but I wanted to write at least something about what happened while I was driving.

I left a little before midnight. I-35 was surprisingly quiet. It was just me and the big trucks. But as I rode on through the night, the silence somehow became more tangible. It's not that there wasn't the usual kind of road noise, but I didn't have the radio on, and I was praying, and gradually the world just filled up with a deep, calm silence as a bowl fills up with water. And I was submerged in that stillness, though not in a way that made me groggy or disconnected. The trip went quickly, and I remember thinking, "This must be the kind of peace the angels inhabit."

Friday, January 12
✠ *Tatiana, Martyr*

I'm sitting in the waiting room at Discount Tire. I'd been meaning to replace two of the tires on the car I drive, and, what with all the extra road time this month, I figured I should go ahead and get it done.

I've also been sitting in waiting rooms quite a bit over the last twenty-four hours. This one isn't so bad; there's music playing, but it's not overwhelmingly loud. Yesterday, when I was with Katie for her surgery, I spent over eight hours in small rooms, each of which had at least two TVs going. The impact was oppressive and deadening. I had my liturgical books with me, and I read through a day and a half's worth of services, and that was still barely enough to keep my soul somewhat intact.

Katie did well with the whole thing. She had laparoscopic surgery for what they thought was endometriosis. They didn't find any, though, and Katie was her usual happy self: In the surgery prep area, she sat on the bed, and we played Skip-Bo.

Cynthia was the real hero in all this, though. She worked all day yesterday, taught a class until nine PM in Lockhart, and then drove down to San Antonio just to be with her daughter. She's a great mom—and like all great moms, she doesn't consider what she does to be any big deal. To her, it is just what a mom does; it's just who a mother instinctively is.

Saturday, January 13
✠ *Hermylas and Stratonicus, Martyrs*

This morning I drove to Temple, Killeen, and Burnet to do house blessings. It was raining the whole time. I did my prayers and practiced my sermon and thought about how blessed—how extraordinarily blessed—our community is to have people who regularly drive an hour one way just to attend services. Truly, God is wondrous in His saints!

Speaking of driving, I just called Cynthia and told her she should start driving back to Cedar Park. She was planning on staying with Katie at least through Sunday, but the weather is supposed to get bad tonight, and Katie seems to be doing pretty well.

Sunday, January 14
✠ *The Leavetaking of Theophany*

This weekend has been a slightly soggy ending to an otherwise great feast. It's cold, and it's still raining, and the weather has kept a lot of folks at home. The attendance at Great Vespers was comparable to what we have at the daily services. Sunday morning was better, but since Shamassy JL was traveling and the choir had the week off, it was rough going in spots. Reader DN and his daughter, MN, did a good job singing, but it's hard to sub in that way. I bobbled the homily in a couple of spots as well, but we managed to bring the whole thing in for a solid landing.

I caught a short nap before heading out to do five more house blessings. The freezing rain they keep forecasting hasn't materialized yet, but it's supposed to hit tonight. I stopped by the grocery store for a few things, and you would have thought the world was ending: people were racing around and grabbing things off the shelves as if it were their last chance to ever buy food.

Right after I got home, Katie called. She isn't feeling well. Nothing seems to be terribly wrong, but she's sore, she's lonely, and, at several points, she started to cry. She also said that she feels like we ran out on her. I offered to drive down to San Antonio, but she said she didn't want me to do that. By the time we hung up, Katie was pretty irritable. I thought I would go ahead and drive down there, but Cynthia talked me out of it. Cynthia feels terrible; I feel even worse, since I'm the one who insisted that she needed to come home.

Monday, January 15
✠ Paul of Thebes

We are not in control. Every once in a while, here in Central Texas, the weather reminds us of that fact. Sometimes it's a hurricane; sometimes it's a tornado; right now, it's freezing rain.

We finally got some icy rain early this morning, and so I did the services here at home. Later, I worked on my homily. Cynthia is also at home since it happens to be a federal holiday. Around noon, we ventured out to the drugstore and the video store and discovered that the roads weren't bad at all—at least in our neck of the woods. But the big storm is supposed to get here later tonight.

Yesterday, after Katie called, I phoned Fr. Deacon GN in San Antonio. I asked him and his wife, MN, to check on Katie for us. They called earlier today to say that she's going to spend the night with them. Katie called just a few minutes ago and apologized for getting cranky on the phone. I apologized for making Cynthia come back to Cedar Park. Both Cynthia and I are thankful that Katie's going to have someone with her for a few more days. She feels better now, and we both feel a whole lot better.

Wednesday, January 17
✠ Anthony the Great

He giveth His snow like wool,
The mist He sprinkleth like ashes.
He hurleth His ice like morsels.
Who shall stand before His cold?

Not Central Texas, that's for sure. Everything's been shut down for the past two days. As bothersome as the weather is, though, it's also beautiful. Just a while ago, I took our dog, Shelly, out, and everything was white and still. About a block away are some tall trees, and just beyond the trees are a number of streetlights. The trees were completely covered in ice, and backlit by the streetlights, they looked like they were surrounded by silver halos.

Thursday, January 18
✠ *Athanasius and Cyril, Patriarchs of Alexandria*

It's early. I think it must be about a quarter to five. I'm not going to church this morning, since I'm not sure about the road conditions. I'll just do the services here at home. But the ice and the quiet the ice generates have given me some extra time to think, and what I've been thinking about is a line from a hymn that we sang yesterday for St. Anthony.

The line goes like this: "Thou didst turn aside from flesh and blood and left the world, while remaining united to it through great abstinence and silence." What's particularly interesting to me is the fact that it was abstinence and silence that kept St. Anthony intimately connected to the world. Because he didn't participate in everything the world did, and because he didn't listen to everything the world had to say, he was able to develop an intimate and saving relationship with the world—in fact, his troparion states that he "sustains the world by [his] prayers."

This is precisely counter to the approach that most American Christians are advocating. According to these folks, in order to effectively reach out to the world, we have to stay up with it; we have to stay connected to it; we have to be able to address its needs and speak its language. I think that way of doing things generates a few minutes of media coverage every once in a while ("Pastor Develops Innovative Approach to Evangelism"; "Congregation Sponsors Creative Outreach Program"), but it isn't producing Christians that have a deep and abiding relationship with the Most Holy Trinity.

So what is going to produce that kind of Christian? The best way I can help produce that kind of Christian is to actually become that kind of Christian. And that will happen when I do what St. Anthony did, when I embrace great abstinence and silence. Of course, the key word there is "great." That means we're talking about abstinence and silence that go beyond inconvenience and actually move into the realm of sacrifice. But the emphasis must also always be an evangelical one. In other words, asceticism is not primarily about enhancing my own spirituality; it's how I can be united with the world as well as with the Father, Son, and Holy Spirit. So I guess I'm not talking so much about heroic asceticism as I am about heroic love.

Friday, January 19
✠ *Macarius of Egypt*

Yesterday evening, I met Cynthia in Round Rock for an early supper, and then I drove to Taylor and Elgin to do house blessings.

There's a lot of new construction out that way—subdivisions, strip malls, convenience stores, fast food restaurants. But there's also still a lot of farmland, and for several miles, the highway was flanked by plowed fields.

As I glanced from side to side, the dark furrows quickly alternated with the dull glare of the water that had pooled up between them. Lights started to appear in the windows of farmhouses that were set back from the road. At one point, the traffic was slow, and I watched as a bull and seven muddy cows walked in slow single file over to a gate where a man was standing by his truck, waiting.

That's when I thought about this passage from one of my all-time favorite books, *The Wind in the Willows*. Mole and Rat have been visiting Badger in the Wild Wood, and, as they walk back home, Mole realizes something important about himself:

> As he hurried along, eagerly anticipating the moment when he would be home again among the things he knew and liked, the Mole clearly saw that he was an animal of the tilled field and hedgerow, linked to the plowed furrow, the frequented pasture, the lane of evening lingerings, the cultivated garden plot. For others, the asperities, the stubborn endurance, or the clash of actual conflict that went with Nature in the rough; he must be wise, must keep to the pleasant places in which his lines were laid and which held adventure enough, in their way, to last a lifetime.

As the traffic picked up, and the night closed in around me, I thought about the Mole and how there's an awful lot of him in me. I am also a creature of routine, "an animal of the tilled field and hedgerow." There are many, many days when I end up walking along the same well-worn paths, just like that bull, just like those cows.

But, for a priest, I think that's a good thing. One of the most important decisions the Church ever made was to add stability to the threefold evangelical counsels of poverty, chastity, and obedience. Like the holy fathers say, you have to stay in one place a long time if you are ever going to grow and produce fruit. I would add that if you ever want to see the Most Holy Trinity at work, then you have to focus on one spot until the light begins to shine.

That's especially critical in this day and age. A few months ago, I read a short story by Wendell Berry in which he identifies one of the "characteristic diseases" of our culture as "the suspicion that [we] would be greatly improved if [we] were somewhere else." Cynthia and I have been in our house just a little over four years, and just about every other house in the neighborhood has changed hands during that time. And, in this part of Texas, people pretty much live in their cars. But this frenetic mobility, this constant movement also has a huge impact on the Church. Since I arrived at St. John's, seven families have relocated to other cities—and a few of those families have moved several times since then; six families have switched parishes within the Austin area (and three of those families have done that more than once). So it's important that someone simply stay put, and that's one of the basic things I can do as a priest.

Of course, it also fits my personality—I'm at my best when I can sleep in the same bed and pray at the same altar and daily look upon the faces of the people that I love. But in the midst of so much restlessness, so much clamor for something different, when so many people actually seek out and even create distractions, a simple and stable life can be a blessing in all sorts of ways for all kinds of different people.

Tuesday, January 23
✠ *Hieromartyr Clement*

I'm still thinking about the blessings of a simple and stable life. This is how my life begins just about each and every morning.

The alarm goes off at 5 AM. The first thing that goes through my head is,

"Lord Jesus Christ, Son of God, have mercy on me a sinner." I sit up in the bed, take a breath, and say the prayer again. Then I put on my glasses and feel my way over to the bathroom. I brush my teeth, take a shower, and then dry my hair, all the while trying to work the prayer down into my heart. If a worry or a fear or a thought of resentment pops up, I pause and turn my heart to Christ Jesus and say, "I can't handle this; please take care of it for me."

I then get dressed (an easy thing to do when all your clothes are black) and go into the kitchen. I am met there by Shelly, our geriatric dog. I let her out into the back yard. While she is outside, I change her water and put food in her bowl. I get out two glasses and fill them with juice—orange for Cynthia, apple for me. When Shelly is ready to come back in, she barks; I let her in and give her one-half of a dog biscuit. She heads for her food; I pick up the orange juice and head for the bedroom.

At this point, I'm still doing the prayer, but by now it's usually flowing more freely. I guess my heart has to switch modes of consciousness—or maybe just warm up—every morning. I put Cynthia's juice on the nightstand and wake her up if she's not already awake. We have had a fundamental rule for many years: No talking until everyone has had their juice. So I go on into the office and put on my cassock and turn on my phone. Sometimes I also quickly check my email, but, when Cynthia is up, I give her a hug, and we kiss, and, most mornings, we stand in front of the icon of the Mother of God that hangs in the hallway and say our prayers. By 5:40, though, I'm in the car and pulling out of the garage.

Which always makes me feel just a bit like Batman. We have automatic garage door openers, and, even though it's been four years, I'm still getting used to them. It's not like the gadget represents some sort of Bruce Wayne level of opulence (all the houses in our subdivision are equipped with them); it's just the sense of pulling out of a cave and the power of not having to get out of the car to open or close the door.

At any rate, I back down the driveway and out into the street; I make the sign of the cross, put the car in gear, and then I begin to recite the Breastplate of Patrick:

I arise today through a mighty strength,
The invocation of the Trinity.
Through belief in the Threeness,
Through confession of the Oneness,

Of the Creator of Creation.
I arise today through the strength of Christ's birth with His
    baptism,
Through the strength of His crucifixion and burial,
Through the strength of His resurrection and ascension,
Through the strength of His descent for the judgment of Doom.
I arise today through the strength of the love of cherubim,
Through obedience of angels,
Through service of archangels,
Through hope of resurrection to meet with reward.
Through prayers of patriarchs,
Through the predictions of prophets,
Through the preaching of apostles,
Through the blood of martyrs,
Through the innocence of holy virgins,
Through the deeds of righteous men.

By now, I'm turning left from Fence Post Pass on to Paso Fino. The houses are all dark, and no one is stirring. I drive past parked cars, and, on Wednesday mornings, past the green trash cans that everyone brings to the curb. This street also has a few cats that lurk under the streetlights.

I arise today through the strength of heaven:
Light of sun, radiance of moon,
Splendor of fire, swiftness of wind,
Speed of lightning, depth of sea,
Stability of earth, firmness of rock.
I arise today through God's strength to uphold me,
God's wisdom to guide me,
God's way to lie before me,
God's host to encompass me,
God's shield to protect me,
God's hand to save me,
From snares of devils,
From temptations of vices,
From everyone who shall wish me ill,
Afar and near, alone and in multitude.

I'm now turning right onto Blue Ridge Parkway. I cross a small bridge and drive through a neighborhood that's just a bit older than ours. Along this street, there are usually two or three cars running, as folks get ready to head out for the day.

I summon today all these powers,
Between me and those evils,
Against every cruel and merciless power
That may oppose my body and soul.
Against incantations of false prophets,
Against black laws of pagandom,
Against false laws of heretics,
Against craft of idolatry,
Against spells of witches and smiths and wizards,
Against every knowledge that corrupts man's body and soul.
Christ to shield me today
Against poison, against burning,
Against drowning, against wounding,
So that there may come to me an abundance of reward.
Christ with me, Christ before me, Christ behind me,
Christ in me, Christ beneath me, Christ above me,
Christ on my right, Christ on my left,
Christ in the heart of every man who thinks of me,
Christ in the mouth of every man who speaks of me,
Christ in every eye that sees me,
Christ in every ear that hears me.

I arise today through a mighty strength,
The invocation of the Trinity,
Through belief in the Threeness,
Through confession of the Oneness,
Of the Creator of Creation.

At this point, I'm crossing the railroad tracks that cut across East Park. I pull up at the stop sign on Old Highway 183, then I drive past the Sonic and Cedar Park Tire and Battery, to the intersection for Highway 183. I wait for three to five minutes for the light to change, and while I'm sitting there, I sing the troparion for St. Aidan:

O holy bishop Aidan,
Apostle of the north and light of the Celtic Church,
Glorious in humility, noble in poverty,
Zealous monk and loving missionary:
Intercede for us sinners,
that Christ our God may have mercy on our souls.

When the light changes, I move through the intersection, past the Cedar Park Cemetery and a place called Renegade Truck Parts and, later on, a small United Methodist church. On this part of the drive, there are fewer streetlights, more trees, and a lot of wildlife—sometimes a raccoon or two will gallop across the road; sometimes I will pass an alertly tensed group of deer; sometimes I will see a possum waddling down a driveway. On this section of the drive, I'm quiet since I'm almost at the temple.

By the time I get there, usually, Reader MT has already unlocked the door. I step through the tiny narthex and on into the nave. I say, "I will come into Thy house in the multitude of Thy mercy, and in Thy fear I will enter Thy holy temple"; then I make a metania and reverence the icon of St. Raphael on the left side of the door. I walk over in front of the holy doors and go through the service for entering the temple.

Beginning with the icon of Christ Jesus, I make three metanias before each image on the iconostasis, and I quietly recite the troparion for each one:

We reverence Thine immaculate icon, O Good One, and ask forgiveness of our transgression, O Christ our God. For of Thine own good will Thou wast pleased to ascend the cross in the flesh and deliver from bondage to the enemy those whom Thou hast fashioned. Wherefore, we cry aloud unto Thee: "Thou hast filled all things with joy, O our Savior, for Thou didst come to save the world!"

Forasmuch as Thou art a fountain of tenderness, O Theotokos, make us worthy of compassion. Look upon a sinful people, manifest thy power as ever, for hoping on thee, we cry aloud unto thee, "Rejoice!" as once did Gabriel, chief captain of the Bodiless Powers.

The memory of the just is praised, but thou art well pleased,
O Forerunner, with the testimony of the Lord. For thou wast
found worthy to baptize in the stream Him whom they foretold.
Wherefore, having mightily contended and suffered for the truth,
with joy thou hast preached also to those in Hades the good tidings
of God made manifest in the flesh, who taketh away the sins of the
world and granteth His great mercy.

O Prophet and Forerunner of Christ God's coming to us, all
we who with longing now extol thee are at a loss to honor thee
worthily, for thy mother's barrenness and thy father's long silence,
by thine all-renowned and hallowed birth were ended, and the
Incarnation of the Son of God is preached to all the world.

O Leaders of the heavenly host, Michael and Gabriel, unworthy
as we are, we implore you that by your prayers you encircle us
with the wings of the protection of your immaterial glory as we
fall down before you and fervently cry, "Release us from danger,
O marshals of the hosts on high."

I make three more metanias before the holy doors, and I enter the
sanctuary through the curtain on the left. I make three metanias before the
altar, saying the Jesus Prayer each time. After that, I kiss the Gospel book
and the altar itself.

I then light the two lamps on the altar, and I light a piece of charcoal for
the censer. I go out through the curtain on the right side of the iconostasis
and light the four hanging lamps. I enter the sanctuary again through the
left-hand curtain, then pick up my stole and bless it: "Blessed is our God,
who poureth out His grace upon His priests, as oil of myrrh upon the head,
which runneth down upon the beard, upon the beard of Aaron, which
runneth down to the fringe of his raiment."

Then I put some incense on the censer and bless it: "Blessed is our God,
always, now and ever, and unto ages of ages. Incense we offer unto Thee,
O Christ our God, as a savor of spiritual sweetness, which do Thou receive
upon Thy most heavenly altar, and send down upon us in return the grace

of Thine all-holy, good, and life-giving Spirit." I then take up the censer and stand in front of the altar. I offer this prayer: "Through the prayers of our holy fathers, O Lord Jesus Christ our God, grant me a holy presentation before Thy sacred altar and a worthy celebration of Thy Divine Service." I turn around and open the curtain. I turn back around to face the altar, make the sign of the cross, and then sing these words: "Blessed is our God, always, now and ever, and unto ages of ages."

That's how my life begins just about every single day of the year. But a few days ago, I wrote that if you focus on one spot, then eventually the Light begins to shine, and that is precisely what happens every single day during Orthros: "Morning, at the brown brink eastward, springs."[1] At first, the sky begins to shine like a distant wave, way off behind the houses on Blue Ridge Parkway. Then the light begins to flow up Park Street: it spills over the railroad tracks; it engulfs the Sonic and the Tire and Battery and Renegade Truck Parts, and the drivers on 183 pull down their visors and reach for their sunglasses. The morning fills up the cemetery; it rolls on past the United Methodist building, and it washes over the dark little dens of the raccoons and the deer and the possum. Then, just as I step in front of the icon of the Mother of God and cry, "The Theotokos and the Mother of the Light, let us honor and magnify in song!" the new day breaks in spectacular silence on the windows of the nave.

It's like that old Brazilian movie, *Black Orpheus*. Every morning, Orpheus takes his guitar and climbs up a ridge overlooking Rio de Janeiro, and he plays the sun up. At the end of the movie, after Orpheus has gone to the Underworld, one of the street kids he had befriended suddenly realizes that someone has to step in and take over Orpheus's job. So he grabs Orpheus's guitar, and, with the rest of the street kids, he races up to the spot that overlooks Rio and plays the sun up.

That's what I do every morning in Cedar Park. That's what thousands and thousands of other folks do in all the other Cedar Parks all around the world. Through the grace and mercy of Christ Jesus, we get to join with all the morning stars as they sing together and with all the angels as they shout for joy, and, right alongside them, we get to play this world into the light for one more bright and golden day.

And that is just one of the blessings of a simple and stable life.

---

1.   From "God's Grandeur" by G. M. Hopkins.

Wednesday, January 24
✣ *Xenia the Roman; Xenia of St. Petersburg*

Wouldn't you know it. This morning was one of those rare mornings when I'm not standing before the altar at 6 AM. Today was house-blessing day in Kerrville, so at 6 AM, I was sitting in the car at Dripping Springs. I drove out there early to miss the traffic, then I pulled into the parking lot of a little strip mall to read Orthros and the Hours and the Typika. By 7:20, I was on the road again to Kerrville.

It's always nice to drive out there and see JB and MB and PL. I blessed their homes; we visited together; PL and I did a little parish council business, and then they took me out for Chinese food (it was also JB's birthday). What's amazing about these folks is not only the distance they drive to services (two hours one way), but also the fact that they are some of the most positive and cheerful people in our community. If anyone has a reason to be grumpy or self-regarding, it is these folks; but they are happy to be part of the Church and grateful for even the limited connections they have with St. John's. Truly, God is wondrous in His saints!

While I was reading Orthros in Dripping Springs, a man pulled up and parked a few spaces away from me. He got out of his car and went into a realty office. He turned on all the lights in the office, started a coffeemaker, and then sat down at a computer. I included him in my prayers, and ever since then, I've been kind of glancing around at odd moments, hoping some anonymous angel is watching over me and including me in his prayers.

Saturday, January 27
✣ *The Transfer of the Relics of St. John Chrysostom*

I called Brendan yesterday evening to catch up. He's going to put on his sergeant's stripes in a couple of weeks. Tomorrow, he's going down to Lewisville to take the test for their police department. D, his girlfriend, says hi. His speech class is something of a pain, but his instructor is "an old guy who's pretty cool." I tell him I hope my students say the same about me. He's looking to get another car in April, and right now, it's between an Acura and a Nissan. He plans on coming by the weekend of February 11 when he goes down to San Antonio for his reserve duty. He asks about Cynthia and Katie, then I tell him that I love him, and he tells me that he loves me.

Man talk. I've never been especially good at it. But Brendan's patient with me, and I think we covered all the bases: vehicles, women, the work we do—and I'm thankful that he is always willing to talk about the love we have for each other.

Sunday, January 28
✠ *The Publican and the Pharisee*

Yesterday, Katie and I went down to the March for Life. Cynthia wanted to as well, but with her back, it was basically a choice between liturgy today or the march yesterday, and she chose liturgy. Close to thirty of us from the parish attended the event, and we walked down Sixth Street and up Congress Avenue behind our parish banner, singing "Holy God," the Polyeleos, "The Angel Cried," "Blessed be the Name of the Lord," and "Christ is Risen"—in several languages.

It seemed like there were a few more marchers than last year, and the whole thing also seemed a bit more raucous. But here's the weird part: There were far more people marching than observing the event. It was that same way last year, but there were news stories on all the local channels. This year, I only saw one short story, since most of the coverage went to a much larger anti-war demonstration later in the day.

So what's the point? Why participate in something that has so little discernible impact? The immediate impact on our local community may have been negligible, but the notes of our hymns are still echoing through the noetic realms, and the forces of darkness are still cowering beneath that bombardment.

I thought about that again this morning when we made GG a catechumen. The exorcism prayers in that service are filled with a lot of taunting language ("Fear God! Know the vainness of thy might which had no power even over pigs!"). We can be that bold, we can talk that kind of cosmic smack, because we know whom we serve, and we know that His victory is certain. It doesn't matter how blind the referees are; it doesn't matter how dirty the other side plays; it doesn't matter how many injuries we sustain; it doesn't matter how lopsided the score gets; it doesn't matter how many overtimes we have to endure. Christ Jesus is going to win; we are going to prevail.

Monday, January 29
✚ The Transfer of the Relics of St. Ignatius

Tonight I finished up the house blessings. I got to forty-two homes out of fifty-three: Not bad, considering the ice storm and all the different schedules that have to mesh in order to make that happen. At least four more families have told me they want to try to get their homes blessed after Pascha, so hopefully, we'll pick up those folks in April.

But it is good to be done for now. My right shoulder had been hurting from all the applications of holy water. I wonder if the archdiocese does Worker's Comp for liturgically related injuries.

Tuesday, January 30
✚ The Three Hierarchs

I'm sitting in the brand-spanking-new adjunct faculty workroom at the community college. Classes got bumped a week due to the ice storm, but all the sections met last week, and today, I'm going to hand back the first round of papers.

That's always an interesting way to meet people. The first assignment is to relate a personal experience; I encourage the students to be as personal as they can, since that typically means better writing. And they typically are quite willing to get very personal: This time, several wrote about family situations or sexual encounters or run-ins with the law. It's never easy to put red ink all over that kind of writing—and I tell the students that up front—but I'm glad they are at least willing to risk being real.

While they were writing last week, I noticed that one older student seemed to be having a hard go of it. He kept wadding up pieces of paper and sighing loudly. At the end of the class, he came up to me and said, "This was a really frustrating experience for me."

"I'm sorry to hear that."

"I wanted to write about why I became an atheist, but I figured that wouldn't go over too well."

"Why did you figure that?"

"Well . . . you're a religious man."

"Yes, I am . . . but I'm teaching writing."

"Oh . . . I'm sorry."

"For what?"

"That I made a mistake."

"If you want to call it that, but I'm glad we got it cleared up."

"Me too."

FEBRUARY

Thursday, February 1
✠ *Forefeast of the Presentation*

Tonight I spent some time with a young man who's been visiting the parish. He's been on a long journey, and the road has not been a kind one: divorce, loneliness, boredom, substance abuse, material prosperity in a social vacuum, intellectual curiosity in a spiritual void. As I sat there and listened to him, as I heard the pain in his voice, as I felt the longing in his heart, I realized that out there in the world—right out there, all over Austin—are hundreds of thousands of people just like him.

I often forget that Hades is not just a spiritual reality that exists in the next life; it intrudes upon this life as well. The darkness that weighs so heavily upon this man is a darkness that lies thick and fast all across Central Texas.

But I just listened as the man talked. Then, since we were running out of time, I told him that he was more than welcome in our community, and I briefly went over what the process of becoming a catechumen looks like. He was already aware of that information since he has been spending a good deal of time with Reader MT. But he said he appreciated the opportunity to speak with me, and he said that it meant a lot to know that he is welcome in the parish.

I invited him to stay for Great Vespers, and he said that he was already planning on it. In a way, the entire service was for him, because, apart from the chanters and Fr. Deacon BL and myself, only one or two others were present. At any rate, the service was extraordinarily beautiful, and, towards the end of "O Lord, I Have Cried," the man got to hear this heartbreaking sticheron:

Him that rideth in the chariots of the cherubim, and is praised
with songs of the seraphim, the Theotokos carried in her arms,

incarnate of her who knew no spouse. And she delivered Him who gave the law, fulfilling the order of the law, into the hands of the old priest, who, having carried Life, sought deliverance from life, saying, "Now lettest Thou me depart, O Master, that I may tell Adam that I beheld as a babe the immutable God, who is before eternity, and the Savior of the world."

In that hymn, Symeon the Elder says that he's going down to Hades to tell everyone there that it won't be too much longer. I picture him whispering into the night, "Hold on. He's coming."

I'm praying that the young man heard that whisper and that some light has begun to shine in his darkness; I'm praying that faint and fading light will soon become an entire horizon of hope. And even if that horizon is razor-thin and far off, even if he loses sight of it from time to time, I'll be praying that it will soon arc out across all of his Hadean isolation, and that it will become so bright that he will barely be able to look upon it.

Friday, February 2
✜ *The Feast of the Presentation*

"Why is it that on a feast day the whole of nature mysteriously smiles?"

That's one of my favorite lines from the "Glory to God for All Things" Akathist, and it certainly describes what today has been like. When I pulled into the parking lot this morning, a rich, full moon hung in a sky that was clear and shining. Orthros and liturgy were just as rich and clear; in fact, the services worked alongside and within the newly forming day the way melody and harmony create a new song, so that what we did this morning we did in union with this entire cosmos: the now-faded moon, and the sunlight streaming through the windows of the nave, and the water dripping off the low eaves of our little back porch sanctuary, and the spider working silently in the corner just above the table of the proskomidia, all of them were praying with us, all of them were falling down with us at the moment of epiclesis, because we are all of us together the new creation, and we presented to Christ Jesus this glorious hymn, just as He was presented to His Father in the temple at Jerusalem, and just as He forever presents Himself before His Father's throne in the Kingdom.

Saturday, February 3
✠ *Symeon the Elder and Anna the Prophetess*

The blessings of the feast continue to transform all kinds of things. I wrote my homily on Monday, and I wasn't especially happy with it, but after yesterday's liturgy, when I went home and began to work on it in preparation for Sunday, it didn't seem quite as bad as I remembered.

Today I went happily with Cynthia as she got a haircut and did some shopping. I took a book with me, but what made me so relaxed and easy-going and able to spend most of the day hanging around the mall and the hairstylist's was the fact that my heart was still full with all the blessings of the feast. It had nothing to do with any patience or kindness on my part. It was all due to the grace I received in yesterday's services.

And that grace even had a saving and transforming impact on my thoughts. At one point during the day, the idea came to me that I was a great guy for running around with Cynthia and waiting for her, but then I was immediately reminded of all the many, many years she has been running around with me through moves and career changes, and all the many, many ways she had to wait on me through graduate school and seminary and long hours of work.

Sunday, February 4
✠ *The Sunday of the Prodigal*

On Tuesday morning, Cynthia and I will both be going out of town. She'll be going to a conference on parenting in Denton; I'll be going to the Clergy Brotherhood Retreat in Wichita, Kansas. So we had a lot to do tonight. But after we had at least made a start on everything, we sat down and watched a little TV. And, as a special treat, we got to see the last few minutes of *Cinema Paradiso*.

Some film sequences I never tire of watching: Humphrey Bogart and Claude Rains walking down the rain-slick runway; Alan Ladd facing down Jack Palance in the saloon; Omar Sharif and Julie Christie packing up the hospital as the petals fall from the vase of yellow flowers; John Belushi and Dan Ackroyd sitting in the car in the tunnel ("We're sixty-five miles from

Chicago. We've got a full tank of gas, half a pack of cigarettes; it's dark, and we're wearing sunglasses"); John Wayne walking away from that open door after he's brought Natalie Wood safely home; Gwyneth Paltrow striding up that long stretch of beach as Joseph Fiennes picks up the quill and begins his next play; Tom Hanks standing in the middle of that lonely intersection out in West Texas.

The final scene in *Cinema Paradiso* will always be on that list. I'm not sure what all those other sequences say about me, but I know why I find the closing moments of *Cinema Paradiso* to be so meaningful: When the main character is watching all those recovered clips, as all those faded embraces and grainy kisses flash in front of him, it gives me hope that in the Kingdom, all the joyous fragments of our lives—even those moments that fear or forgetfulness or oppression have cut away—all those fragments will be spliced together in our hearts, and they will run endlessly and forever.

Tuesday, February 6
✠ *Barsanuphius and John*

It's 10:15 PM, and the day started at 4:30 AM.

This morning, after I got ready, Cynthia and I said our prayers, and then I left to go pick up Fr. Deacon BL and Fr. DB. By 6:15, we were on the road to Wichita.

The trip was pleasant and uneventful. It was good to be in the kind of country that has some real and visible distance to it, where you can look ahead almost into tomorrow. Also, it was good to see that the dirt in Oklahoma is still as red as ever and that Kansas still has hawks perched in just about every other tree.

We arrived at the retreat center about 3:45 PM. The speaker this year is Fr. Zacharias, a monk from the Monastery of St. John in Essex, England. Fr. Zacharias spoke at our retreat six years ago; I attended that retreat, and I have listened to the tapes of the talks many times since then, so I've been looking forward to this retreat. Fr. Zacharias began his first talk at 8 PM. The whole thing is being recorded, which is great, but tonight he had helpful things to say about how hard it is to combine intellectual activity and prayer of the heart. He also said that we constantly fall back from illumination, and that if we are unable to consistently humble ourselves, then we can always offer Christ Jesus glory and honor.

We did Small Compline at 9:30, and, as always, it was deeply moving. But I will write about that later. Now I need to get to bed.

Wednesday, February 7
✠ *Parthenius, Bishop of Lampsacus*

It's 9 AM. I'm sitting in the auditorium of the retreat center. All around the walls are large and badly done acrylic paintings of various saints. The series begins with the early fathers and includes most of the major Western saints. There is a stage in front of the auditorium, and over the stage, a large wooden crucifix. In the back of the auditorium are the book tables (I've picked out two books: one by Philip Sherrard and one on the Septuagint Old Testament).

Fr. Zacharias is about to speak on "The Awakening of the Heart through Mindfulness of Death." Now he is beginning his talk with some comments about the life of the heart and how important that life is—he is using the example of Job and his three friends, who sat quietly with each other for seven days before they ever spoke. Fr. Zacharias says that, according to Elder Sophrony, they "were taking the measure of their hearts." I'm going to stop writing now and just listen for a while.

Just a few things Fr. Zacharias mentioned in his talk:

❖ Elder Sophrony once said, "It is impossible to live as a Christian; it is only possible to die as a Christian."
❖ Quantity in prayer generally leads to quality in prayer.
❖ When you cannot pray, reproach yourself. Then offer your inability to pray as prayer.

But just as valuable as listening to Fr. Zacharias is being with the brothers for prayer. Last night was typical. We have a temporary chapel set up in one of the meeting rooms. There are a couple of candles on tall stands, an analogion with an icon of the Mother of God, and this year, a low table with a small icon of St. Silouan and a wooden box that contains a relic of the saint. The room is crowded with guys in black. It's almost completely silent except for the voice of the reader. After the psalms and prayers, we always sing hymns to the Mother of God: "Rejoice O Virgin" and "Awed by the Beauty." Bishop Basil leads the hymns, and the brothers sing them in a way that is very tender. But the whole scene is touching: a roomful of guys offering deep and reverent adoration to the woman who is their spiritual mother.

Thursday, February 8
✠ *Theodore the General*

Yesterday was filled with all kinds of extraordinary blessings. I left the retreat center and went to have lunch with my older sister, Rosemary, and her husband, Joe. They got married the same year Cynthia and I did. Right after that, Joe went to work for a company where he stayed for just about twenty years. But a few years ago the company was sold, he found himself out of work, and ever since then, he and Rosemary and their two kids have been chasing jobs around the country.

They are now in their third city, but, thank God, it's Wichita, Kansas, so I will be able to see them at least once a year. However, in addition to all the moving around, this past year Joe's father died, and then on top of that, Joe had to have an appendectomy.

Rosemary and Joe both looked worn out. They remain optimistic about the future and are looking forward to starting over in Wichita. But just being with them actually brought home how much pain they have had to endure. After lunch, Joe had to go to work, so I took Rosemary back to their apartment (the house they were living in before they moved to Wichita hasn't sold yet, so there's another source of stress). We visited just a bit more, and then I had to get back to the retreat. But I'm thankful that I got to share in their heartaches, even in such a superficial way. I'm going to carefully keep that pain in my heart and offer it up whenever I pray for them.

Last night, I was able to visit with my spiritual father, Fr. TM. I talked about what's going on in my life; he asked me some questions; I asked him for a blessing to do some special fasting; he heard my confession.

Two different encounters; two different visits, but both were the source of all kinds of blessings. Getting together with Rosemary and Joe wasn't a family obligation; they allowed me to share in something precious: their weariness and sorrow. Meeting with Fr. TM wasn't an ecclesiastical obligation: he allowed me to unpack my heart in his presence, and then he stood with me and prayed for me as I offered it all up to our Lord and Master.

At the end of Bernarnos's novel, *Diary of a Country Priest*, the main character—a priest—is dying. His last words are, "Grace is everywhere." The more I write in this journal, the more I think back over everything that happens in my life, the more I realize just how true that is.

Friday, February 9
✠ *The Leavetaking of the Presentation*

I thought I would try to describe Fr. Zacharias, the monk who has been speaking at the retreat. Fr. Zacharias is from Cyprus, but for most of his life, he has been at the monastery in England. He is fairly short; he wears several layers of black clothing, but each layer is faded to a slightly different tint; on his head is a small, round hat; from time to time, a silver cross and chain slips out from underneath the top layer of his clothing.

At first glance, his face appears to be obscured by his long, charcoal-grey beard and hair. His ears and his nose jut out prominently, and he has large, thick glasses, but you have to get up close to actually see his eyes or his mouth. He has a gentle voice; in fact, at times, his speech has an almost singsong quality.

But it's his eyes that are the most remarkable. After one of the sessions, I went up to Fr. Zacharias to ask him a question. He gave me a helpful response, but the way he looked at me was so open and accepting, and his eyes were so—well, they sparkled—that I actually had trouble looking directly at him. Thinking about it afterwards, I realized that he was so immediately available—without any of the usual warm-up through small talk or establishing some sort of common ground or identifying mutual acquaintances—that I was simply caught off guard. He had no barriers; he didn't hold me at arm's length; he wasn't sizing me up. I imagine he could see right through me, but, whatever it was he saw, it clearly didn't matter one bit.

That was startling; it made me feel grateful and joyful and unworthy all at the same time. But then, I suppose that sort of thing happens all the time when you hang out with saints.

Saturday, February 10
✣ *Haralampos, Hieromartyr*

Speaking of hanging out with saints, every year the Clergy Brotherhood Retreat ends with a Divine Liturgy. We serve the liturgy in the chapel of the cathedral. After the service is over, we have a final meeting, then everyone heads for home. But every year, before I leave, I always go into the cathedral itself in order to reverence the altar where I was ordained.

Just entering the building is a pretty overwhelming experience, but when no one else is around, it's even more profound. I walk up the long center aisle, and the soaring ceiling makes me feel really small. By the time I get to the dome, I've got my head cranked all the way back like a little kid. I make a metania in front of the iconostasis and walk around the edge of the massive, marble solea. I go into the sanctuary, and it is all shiny, smooth surfaces that reflect the gleaming metal of the candlesticks and the tabernacle and the fans. I make a prostration before the holy table, and then I kiss it. On the way back down the center aisle, I almost tiptoe; I just don't want to disturb the deep quiet that fills the whole building.

Of course, this whole time, the saints in the icons have been watching me. The figures in the New Testament scenes in the transepts, the prophets in the dome, the apostles in the sanctuary, the Mother of God in the apse, they are like stars come close to the earth. In their icons, the colors blaze and swirl in a stillness that stretches all the way into eternity. And as I walk back down the aisle, I can hear their great and gentle voices whispering in my heart: "See you next time. Have a good year. We're praying for you. Be a good priest."

Sunday, February 11
✣ *Sunday of the Last Judgment*

I've been at three liturgies in the last three days.

Friday I was at liturgy with the Clergy Brotherhood, Fr. Zacharias, and Bishop Basil. It's always a time of powerful blessing, and, at the end of the liturgy, we do a memorial for the departed priests and deacons and their wives.

Saturday was the liturgy for the first Souls' Saturdays. I love doing those services, but we didn't do it very well yesterday. We hardly ever do the first Souls' Saturday well because of all the variations Great Lent brings. But a lot of people were there, and we will have it down by next Saturday.

Today's liturgy was actually the best of all: everyone in the altar was focused and on task; the choir was singing well, and the nave was packed out with folks who were singing—and praying—for all they were worth.

Tonight, though, was almost a fourth liturgy. Katie was here all weekend, and Brendan came back through after his reserve duty. Cynthia cooked all afternoon, and then we had supper together and just had a good time being a family. Katie is now on the road back to San Antonio; Brendan is in the computer room doing some stuff for school; I just finished my prayers, and now I'm going to watch some TV with Cynthia.

I'm not sure I ever knew it was possible to be this happy.

Monday, February 12
✠ *Meletius, Bishop of Antioch*

This is a good time of year to be happy. This morning at Orthros we chanted this troparion:

> Today is the joyful forefeast of the Fast. Therefore, brethren, together
> let us run the race with confident hope and with great eagerness.

Great Lent starts in exactly one week, and I'm looking forward to it. It's a hard season, and it's inconvenient, and it requires a lot of effort, but then spring is the same way: it's wet and muddy and there's all that wind and threatening weather. But then those light green shoots begin to emerge from the earth, and all those fragile blossoms start to curl out from the branches, and one day the whole world just explodes with color and sunshine and music.

I'm praying that over the next seven weeks, all kinds of good things will begin to emerge from the wet and muddy parts of my life; I'm praying that the storms of worry and fear that often sweep through my heart will cause all sorts of new blessings to bloom; I'm praying that on the Great Day of Pascha, my soul will be bursting with hope and life and joy.

Tuesday, February 13
✛ *Martinian of Palestine*

On Sunday we had the annual parish meeting. During the meeting, several people said nice things about me. Later that day, a number of people complimented me on the homily and this journal. The same thing happened a couple of times yesterday.

But yesterday morning, the chair of the department I work in at the community college called and took me to task for not following a particular procedure. I wasn't even aware of the procedure, but the implication throughout the conversation was that I was trying to get away with something. I told the department chair that I would certainly follow the procedure from now on, and he appeared OK with that.

Now, spiritually speaking, my interaction with the department chair was far more valuable than all those nice compliments I received. But instead of embracing the opportunity for humility, instead of seeing the rebuke as a way of participating ever so slightly in the suffering of Christ Jesus, I sulked off and on throughout the morning and even whined a bit to Cynthia.

I firmly believe that nothing I encounter has escaped the loving attention of Christ Jesus. That means everything that happens to me and around me can be spiritually profitable. I hope that one day I will be able to act on that insight. I hope that one day I will be the kind of priest I'm supposed to be.

Wednesday, February 14
✛ *Valentinus, Hieromartyr*

It's about 9 PM. Today was St. Valentine's Day, and it's not something that Cynthia and I are big on, but we did get some carry-out Italian food, and I did pick up a couple of movies. We had a nice dinner, then we sat down to watch one of the movies and promptly fell asleep. I woke up fairly quickly, but Cynthia was pretty well out of it, so I helped her to bed, and now I'm sitting here writing about the woman I love.

She likes gadgets. She loves to try different kinds of food—actually, she loves to try just about anything new. She can't stand crowds, politicians, or cigarette smoke. She is passionate about children's issues. Honesty is extremely important to her. She can identify all the actors and actresses who ever appeared on *That Girl, Bonanza,* and *A Family Affair.* It's important to her to be organized. She enjoys how-to books. She prefers lemon in her water and lime in her Diet Coke. She is an expert on flan, cheesecake, and guacamole. She plays the piano beautifully, but never when anyone is around. She likes going to bed at night, but she doesn't like getting up in the morning. She frequently gets lost. She has the kind of skin poets write about. She's a really good mom. Her eyes are deep brown, and her smile always—I mean, always—leaves me with my mouth hanging open.

Whenever I get disappointed, whenever something doesn't go my way, whenever I fail, I always remember that the number one, all-time best thing in my life has already actually happened: Cynthia said she would marry me. And that's not some sort of second-best consolation prize. That's the way things really are. There's simply nothing this world has to offer that I haven't found in her heart; there's nothing this life can show me that I haven't seen in her eyes; there's no experience this side of heaven that I haven't known in her love.

Thursday, February 15
✠ *Onesimus the Apostle*

I'm a liturgical metronome.

When several people are chanting at weekday Orthros, I let everyone else do the troparia during the canon, and I just intone the refrain. That means I get to say, "Glory to Thee, O God, glory to Thee," or "Have mercy on me, O God, have mercy on me," or some variation of all that 112 times during the service.

It takes me back to my high school days when I was a drummer in the marching band. I was never particularly good at it—in fact, I was often spectacularly bad—but drummers do get to make a lot of noise, and if you're a drummer, people just assume that you're cool, even if you aren't.

Anyway, it was good training, because now I can at least keep a beat. And the refrains are themselves prayer; each and every one of them is just a basic and fundamental cry for mercy. So what I become at Orthros is what a priest is really supposed to be: the pulse of the parish, the heartbeat of the community, the one who keeps us in rhythm with the mercy that runs in deep and rich veins throughout the world.

Friday, February 16
✠ *Pamphilus and His Companions, Martyrs*

On Wednesday I got an email from an old friend named MW. He's a retired United Methodist pastor—in fact, he was my pastor when I was in high school. MW and his wife were coming to Austin for a function they attend every year, and he asked about getting together. We visited at the church this afternoon; I showed him around the facility, and then we talked for an hour or so.

Since he retired, MW has started collecting fountain pens. Apparently there are clubs and conventions and catalogs—who knew? After talking a while about his interest in pens, MW asked me if I had a hobby. And when I said no, he replied, "That's a recipe for burnout."

Saturday, February 17
✠ *Theodore the Recruit, Martyr*

Speaking of burnout, last week, JB sent me an email about a study the Church of England concluded late last year. It seems they have identified a new complex: Irritable Clergy Syndrome. According to the authors of the study, ICS is brought on by "angry congregants" and the Church of England's "feudal system of hierarchy."

There are all sorts of possibilities here. I see books and seminars and Twelve Step programs and film series and support groups:

"Hi. I'm Patriarch Jerome, and I . . . I have ICS."

"Hi, Patriarch Jerome!"

Not only that, but ICS could be a get-out-of-jail-free card in all sorts of situations:

"Fr. Amos, help me understand: Exactly why did you strangle that parishioner during last month's parish council meeting?"

"It's not my fault, Your Grace . . . I . . . I . . . have ICS."

"Oh, well, in that case—why didn't you just say so?"

I mean, this could be the best thing to hit the Church since electric lampadas.

Sunday, February 18
✠ *The Sunday of Forgiveness*

It's been a long weekend of services. Saturday morning we did the second Souls' Saturday liturgy; it was solemn and tender, just the right tone for commemorating the departed. Great Vespers on Saturday evening was well-attended. It was a rich and powerful service, and I'd like to think that all those people showed up because I placed such an emphasis on attendance at Saturday Vespers in my annual report. However, we had a pre-Lenten wine and cheese party after the service, so I think that probably also had a lot to do with the spike in attendance.

Unfortunately, the surge didn't carry through to Sunday morning. Lots of people had told me they were going to be out of town this weekend, but I don't think I realized quite how many were going to be gone until I turned around for the Gospel reading and saw the smallish turnout. Still, it gave the liturgy an empty and contemplative quality, and that was actually a good reminder. As Martin Thornton used to say, "a large congregation is whopping good fun," but there are more important indicators of the spiritual health of a community.

Like Forgiveness Vespers. Many of the people who were traveling made a special effort to get back just for the service, and, as a result, I counted at least seventy people in the nave. And it was a magnificent experience. I always take that opportunity to ask the entire community to forgive my sins. Bishop Basil started doing that at our Clergy Brotherhood Retreat about six years ago; I decided that if my father in Christ needed to do that, then so did I. Here's what I said to my parishioners this evening:

> Brothers and sisters, I want to ask your forgiveness for my harsh-
> ness, my stubbornness, my impatience, and my unwillingness
> to listen. Please forgive me for the times I have pushed you too

hard, and for the times when I have not pushed hard enough.
Please forgive my lack of compassion and my failure to bear your
burdens. You are a good parish, and you deserve a good priest. The
Father, Son, and Holy Spirit are faithful, though, and one day you
will have the kind of priest you deserve.

We then exchanged words of forgiveness. To me, what makes the
experience so profound are the young children. When I think about the
people who irritate me, the people who get on my nerves, what I invariably
end up doing is imaging them as the sum total of all their unpleasant qualities.
Thus, they are no longer people; they are bullies or liars or idiots. But when
I bow down and ask forgiveness of a four-year-old, when I look into those
eyes that are simultaneously trusting and cheerful and just a bit frightened,
then I remember what is actually going on within all those people who
exasperate and annoy me. Behind all those unpleasant qualities are the same
innocence and hope and timidity that are so front and center in all those
little kids. And I'm not talking psychobabble here; this isn't about getting
in touch with everyone's inner child. When I exchange words of forgiveness
with a four-year-old, then I am reminded why St. John the Evangelist calls
his parishioners his "little children"; when I bow down before a little kid, I
am reminded that all of the people who have been placed in my care are my
Lord and Master's "little ones." And He has some really harsh things to say
about the people who mess with His lambs.

Monday, February 19
✣ *Clean Monday*

You know Great Lent has started when everything starts breaking down.
We've taken my car in to get the brakes worked on. Fortunately, Cynthia is
off work today, so it wasn't a big deal.

Tuesday, February 20
✣ *Leo, Bishop of Catania*

I've been thinking about what my friend MW said to me about having a
hobby and avoiding burnout. I've also been thinking about Irritable Clergy

Syndrome. When I was in seminary, I worked on the staff of a large United Methodist congregation in Dallas. My office was across the hall from the choir director's office, and he had a big sign on the wall above his desk that said, *Church Work Is Not Pretty.*

And it's true. A quotation from *A Canticle for Leibowitz* sums it all up. In the final section of the book, the last abbot is talking to the monk who will lead the remnant of the order into space:

> Are you going to submit to the yoke, son? Or aren't you broken
> yet? You'll be asked to be the ass that He rides into Jerusalem, but
> it's a heavy load, and it'll break your back, because He's carrying
> the sins of the world.

On most days, that's what it feels like to be a priest. So I understand why clergymen turn to stamp-collecting and racquet ball and golf. I understand why they come up with things like ICS.

But I also know this: That's not what we have been called to. I have a piece of glass on the top of my desk, and under the glass are some photos and icon cards. There is also a quotation that I clipped from one of Bishop Basil's old clergy memos. I got the memo a few months before I was ordained. The quotation is taken from a brief speech St. Raphael Hawaweeny made when he was presented with a pectoral cross:

> It is true that I worked a lot and endured even more grief, but
> no matter how much I worked and how much grief I endured, I
> consider myself only to have done my duty as a priest and servant
> of God. Can we servants of God and spiritual pastors expect
> anything in the life except labor and grief?

So what becomes of burnout? When we moved into our current facility, I put two icons just inside the doors to the altar area. On one side is an icon of Christ Jesus bound, with a crown of thorns and a purple robe. On the other side is an icon of Christ Jesus lying in the tomb. Those icons express the eternal burnout, the divine *kenosis,* that consumes and transforms all human burnout. And after each and every service, I reverence one of those icons as I leave the altar. I draw the energy I need to be a priest from the fiery depths of my Savior's never-ending love.

Wednesday, February 21
✠ *Timothy of Symbola*

We've got the car back, and my wallet is smoking. But I'm thankful that I can get to where I need to go.

Of course, where I've been going this week is to services. We have three every day this week in the temple. I'm used to doing two each day, but every year, tacking on that third service always forces me to really stretch. Like at Great Compline last night and Monday night. I did not want to be there; absolutely nothing in me was attracted to what we were doing. The psalms and the chanting were like a drill gnawing away at the solid and sheer walls of my heart.

But that's actually when I know the services are doing me some good. It just takes that extra effort to get beyond the liturgical warm fuzzies and the expectation of visiting with friends after the service. Once all that has been cleared away, then the real work can begin. And even though it's frustrating and boring and even psychologically painful, it's real and genuine spiritual growth; it's not something I'm producing, and it's certainly not something I'm imagining, and good things will come of it.

Thursday, February 22
✠ *The Martyrs of Eugenios*

We did our first Presanctified Liturgy last night. As I was driving to church, the setting sun was turning the edge of the clouds purple. Then the altar cloths were purple, and my vestments were purple; the incense was purple, and the wine was purple. The thick red glass of the lamps reflected all that purple, and by the time the service was over, the palms of my hands were purple with carpet burns from all the prostrations.

Then I went home and sat down to a big bowl of corn soup. The soup was bright yellow, and in the round bowl, it looked like a golden halo glowing behind the head of some great saint.

Friday, February 23
✠ *Polycarp, Hieromartyr*

Yesterday afternoon, after I got home from the community college, there was a message on the machine from JD. His daughter, BD, had been taken to the hospital, so I drove down to south Austin to see them.

On the way to the hospital, and as I was driving back home, I practiced the first stasis of the Akathist hymn. It brought back memories of being a hospice chaplain and practicing the hymn as I made my rounds. I would drive across miles and miles of wide open roads, surrounded by horizons that stretched out in all directions, and many times, I would just roll down all the windows in the car and sing along as the wind roared around me:

An angel chieftain was sent from heaven, to say "Hail" to the Theotokos . . .

Sometimes I would stop at a roadside park or a cemetery, get out of the car, and sing through an entire stasis. I think if I drove down those same roads today, if I stopped in those same desolate and dirty parks or in those same lonely little cemeteries, I would still be able to hear the hymn. Something that beautiful simply has to be eternal.

Sunday, February 25
✠ *The Sunday of Orthodoxy*

I still find it unbelievable that I sing for a living. I'm not a very musical person, and many times during the liturgy I find myself thinking, "How in the world did I get here?"

Like during the dialogue at the beginning of the anaphora. Fr. Deacon BL has the first line, so he sets the pitch:

Let us stand aright. Let us stand with fear. Let us attend, that we may offer the holy oblation in peace.

Then the choir and the congregation respond:

A mercy of peace. A sacrifice of praise.

And at that point, I'm picking up the hand cross and listening for the pitch, and as I turn and face the congregation at the holy doors, I always feel like a musical trapeze artist who is swinging back and forth, building momentum for that supercolossal death-defying triple vocal somersault:

The grace of our Lord Jesus Christ and the love of God the Father and the communion of the Holy Spirit be with you all.

And from the other trapeze comes the response:

And with thy spirit.

By then, I've already placed the hand cross back on the altar. I turn back around, and facing the congregation with my hands raised, right there in front of the saints and all the heavenly powers, I let go of my trapeze, and I launch out into the void between the notes, stretching for that pitch that will land me safely on the other side of the interval:

Let us lift up our hearts.

Of course, sometimes I miss it altogether, and I end up bouncing around down in the net, dodging the notes that have come crashing down along with me. In fact, a lot of times, after I've already made my leap into musical space, I discover that the choir and the congregation are actually using a completely different trapeze down at the other end of the tent. Now that's a *really* special feeling: you're hurtling through the air, completely off key, and there's no one to catch you, so all you can do is hope that the crash isn't going to be too painfully embarrassing.

But then, sometimes my voice locks onto that pitch, and I connect with the choir and the congregation, and the music swings us together out and up and over this world, hurling us into the realms of the Spirit, and the liturgy becomes a genuine ascension. But those moments of ascension are not a straight-line rocket launch into the Kingdom; they are more like a dazzlingly chaotic procession in which we wheel and race and tumble and roll, flying with the angels and filling our hearts' heaven with brilliant trains of praise and spectacular trails of glory.

Monday, February 26
✠ *Porphyrios, Bishop of Gaza*

Not too long ago, someone who has been reading these entries on the parish website asked me if I keep two sets of journals—one in which I describe all the nice stuff that happens and one in which I gripe and complain about all the bad stuff.

But I have only one journal, and when I started writing in it, I made the decision that I wasn't going to focus on unpleasant things. That doesn't mean that there isn't a whole lot of ugliness and pain in my life—you can't be a priest and not deal with sin and suffering on a daily basis. But I've chosen not to concentrate on that sort of thing.

Part of my decision is based on the fact that there are a great many confidences I have to keep. People tell me things that I don't relate to anyone else—not even to Cynthia. So even though I spend a significant part of each and every week dealing with family crises and marital conflicts and parish discord, the vast majority of those things will never make it into this journal.

But that doesn't mean that I'm editing reality and somehow presenting a version of my life that is airbrushed and retouched beyond all recognition. What I'm attempting to do is what St. Paul encourages all Christians to do in his letter to the Philippians:

> Brethren, whatever is true, whatever is honorable, whatever is just, whatever is pure, whatever is lovely, whatever is gracious, if there is any excellence, if there is anything worthy of praise, think about these things.

Certainly no one could ever accuse St. Paul of looking at the world through rose-colored glasses. But what I think the apostle is doing is urging us to focus on those things that will make it into eternity—and sin and suffering will not be present in the Kingdom. In this world, sin has a certain salacious appeal; suffering can provide us with drama and inspiration. But they are both going to burn up in the atmosphere of heaven.

In fact, I think church history will look very different when we are able to view it from the perspective of the Kingdom. In this life, we see the story of the Church as one of clashes and conflicts; it's often just an account of controversies and heresies and the personalities that fueled them. But when we finally see the history of the Church from the context of heaven, I don't think Arius is even going to be visible; the iconoclasts will have disappeared—as will all the other movements, reformations, schisms, and denominations. And as far as our petty parish politics are concerned, it will be as if they never even existed. What we will then be able to see is the life of the Church in the daily work of the Spirit, a work that takes place primarily in the human heart. And that is what I'm doing my best to write about in this journal. I'm simply trying to track the things that are eternal—grace, hope, joy, and love.

Tuesday, February 27
✠ *Repose of St. Raphael Hawaweeny*

Last night at Vespers we sang stichera for St. Raphael, and this morning at Orthros we chanted his canon. I've felt a particular connection to St. Raphael for a long time; I read through his Akathist at Small Compline two or three times a month.

Since St. Raphael is the good shepherd of the lost sheep in America, we have made him the patron of our evangelism program. We've going to have two outreach programs this year, one in April and one in October. We're going to try to introduce people to Holy Orthodoxy, and as a community, we've put together a list of over ninety people we would like to see at those events. We keep the list in the nave; it's in a binder that has St. Raphael's icon on the cover. I've been encouraging people to pray through the list when they come to services, and I've actually seen a few people doing that.

Last Sunday I preached on evangelism, and today I've been working on another homily about evangelism. I worry sometimes about wearing people out, but then I remember that in order for us to pull off something like these outreach events, everyone has to hear about it at least eight different times—at least that's what the experts say. But whatever—it's St. Raphael's day, so there's not a better time to be writing about outreach.

Wednesday, February 28
✠ *Basil the Confessor*

I finished my homily yesterday. I don't think it's as good as the one last week, but maybe it will get better between now and when I work on it again on Friday.

Honestly, though, I sometimes wonder why I continue to push the subject of outreach. Few priests even talk about it, except some of the guys who used to be part of the Evangelical Orthodox. When that group was received into our archdiocese, there was a whole lot of energy surrounding the topic of evangelism, but now that seems to have faded. To be sure, Fr. MK, our diocesan missioner, spends all his time doing evangelism, but practically speaking, that translates into working with new missions. Once a community is fairly well established, outreach seems to become less of a priority.

Of course, when I was a United Methodist pastor, there was constant talk about growth and numbers and the techniques and technology that can produce more growth and bigger numbers. I certainly don't want to go back to that kind of insanity. But neither do I simply want to fall back into the approach that most Orthodox communities use: "Hey, when folks visit, we invite them to coffee hour."

It does get a bit lonely at times. But then I think about that Syrian priest who traveled all over this country on trains and in wagons and by horseback and on foot, just so the Church could get started. Now that must have been lonely. So I know that St. Raphael understands. I know that he's praying for me and for my community and for our efforts to help the Church grow and flourish.

And that's enough.

MARCH

Thursday, March 1
✠ *Evdokia, Martyr*

Last night we did our best Presanctified Liturgy so far. There was a great deal of quiet expectancy, and the music was beautiful.

I've always wondered why the priest puts the aer over his head when he's processing with the diskos and chalice. I've never seen anything written about it, so I just assumed it was a combination of reverence and logistics (two hands; three items; put one of them on your head). But this year at the Clergy Brotherhood Retreat, I heard someone draw a comparison between the entrance during the Presanctified and the funeral service for a priest: The priest puts the aer over his head at the entrance, and the aer is placed over his head when he's lying in his coffin. And that idea has given me a whole lot to think about.

The only men who are worthy to bear the precious body and life-giving blood into the Kingdom are those who have already died, those in whom self-interest and self-justification have ceased to exist. These are the men whose lives "are hidden with Christ in God"; what they carry on the diskos is their very identity, the pulsating center of all life, but they themselves are empty, their hearts are silent and still.

During Great Lent, we are reading passages from St. Isaac of Syria at Orthros. He understood this whole dynamic really well:

> Humility collects the soul into singleness by silence—and makes
> it concentrate within itself . . . a truly humble man only wishes to
> plunge away from himself into himself, to become nothing, as if not
> existing, not yet come into being. And while such a man is hidden,
> enclosed within himself . . . he remains wholly with the Lord.

That's what I want to be—wholly with the Lord. I'm a long way from that, but I'm hoping that, by the time they put the aer over my head when I'm lying in my casket, I will already be alive in Christ Jesus, alive in that empty, hidden, silent way.

Friday, March 2
✤ *Theodotus, Hieromartyr*

This afternoon, I'm going to get started on *The Ladder of Divine Ascent*. I always read through it during Great Lent, but I haven't been able to get around to it until today.

Actually, I don't even own a copy of the book. What I have is a photocopy of the translation Bishop Kallistos Ware did for the Classics of Western Spirituality series. It's several hundred unbound pages that I keep in a binder (I think the binder originally came from one of those United Methodist workshops I used to have to attend). When I first discovered the *Ladder*, it was out of print. So I checked it out from the seminary library and stood over a copy machine for the better part of two hours, feeding it nickels and dimes and quarters.

The *Ladder* is back in print now in several editions, but I've never replaced my old loose-leaf copy. It's got too much underlining and too many notes, and every year when I open it up, I find that wonderfully distinctive voice: gruff, bracing, ironic, lyrical. Great Lent wouldn't be Great Lent without St. John. In his poem, "The Bee," James Dickey talks to his son about old football coaches:

> Dead coaches live in the air, son live
> In the ear
> Like fathers, and *urge* and *urge*. They want you better
> Than you are. When needed, they rise they scream
> When something must be saved.

That's the way it is with St. John and me—only he isn't dead. At least, not in the way the world understands that word. He's alive, and every spring he gets in my face:

"Wilcoxson! Have you forgotten everything since last year? Drop and give me twenty—that is, if you can still do a prostration! The priesthood isn't what it used to be, that's for sure!"

Sunday, March 4
✠ *Gregory Palamas*

Mrs. O died yesterday afternoon.

I had been to see her on Thursday; she wasn't responsive, so I just sat by her bed for a while and prayed. But yesterday, VP called about two PM and said the nurses had told her Mrs. O was starting to decline. I told VP that I would go on up to the hospital, but twenty minutes later, as I was walking out the door, VP called back and said that she had died.

When I arrived at the hospital, Mrs. O's body was still in the room. It was a semi-private room, but a plastic curtain had been drawn around Mrs. O's bed. The nurses had dressed her in a fresh gown and brushed her hair. The expression on her face was one of deep calm. Mr. O was sitting in a chair beside the bed. He had been there when she died.

Mr. O and I spoke briefly, then I stepped back through the curtain to find a chair. In the next bed, a middle-aged woman was reading a copy of *Texas Monthly*. When I asked if I could use one of the chairs by her bed, she said, "Certainly." I carried the chair in through the curtain and sat next to Mr. O. He told me how she had died—"She just took a breath and swallowed and was gone. It was very peaceful. No pain at all"—and then we just sat there together.

After a short time, VP arrived. A few minutes later, her husband and son came in. We did the first memorial service together, and then I excused myself. As I left the room, I noticed that the woman in the next bed was still reading her magazine. It reminded me of those lines from "Musée des Beaux Arts":

About suffering they were never wrong,
The Old Masters; how well they understood
Its human position; how it takes place
While someone else is eating or opening a window or just
Walking dully along.

That's certainly true of the world, but things shouldn't work that way in the Church. So as I drove home, I called Reader MT and asked if there was anyone at the temple who could begin reading the Psalter and saying the memorial prayers. They were having a chanters' workshop, but by the time I got there around 3:30, RT and Reader PW had walked out to the bench that sits under the trees, and they had worked their way through three kathisma. I took over at that point and read another four kathisma. When it came time for Orthodox Instruction, Reader MT took over and read up through the tenth kathisma.

This morning, at the end of the liturgy, we did the second memorial service for Mrs. O; her funeral will be Wednesday morning.

Monday, March 5
✤ *Conon, Martyr*

Great Lent doesn't leave much time for journal writing. Orthros is about thirty minutes longer, and the hours are also about thirty to forty-five minutes longer. So today, I've already spent three hours in the services—after we finish Vespers and Great Compline, and after I read the Midnight Office at home, the total will be close to six hours. Still, that's what keeps me alive.

Tuesday, March 6
✤ *The Martyrs of Amoria*

It's 11 PM. I just finished the final kathisma and the last memorial prayer for Mrs. O. Earlier this evening, Cynthia and Shamassy JL and I drove over to Georgetown for the third memorial service.

Mrs. O's body was dressed in a pretty dress—I think it was violet; there were also some nice flower arrangements. But the funeral home chapel was so oppressively impersonal that it was difficult to pray. The room was clean and color-coordinated, but it was basically a big box, aesthetically vacuous and acoustically dead. As a result, everyone at the service seemed a bit disoriented.

I'm glad the funeral service itself will be at the temple.

Wednesday, March 7
✠ *The Hieromartyrs of Cherson*

It's 8:30 AM. I'm sitting in the altar waiting for the people from the funeral home to arrive. Reader MT had a death in his family this week, so he is out of town. There is no one else in the building.

I did Orthros by myself, and then the Hours and the Typika. Now I'm just sitting here, writing in this journal, listening to the birds in the tree right outside the window, and watching the soft morning light that is slanting across the floor.

I pray that Mrs. O is in a place that is just as beautiful and just as still and even closer to the Most Holy Trinity.

Thursday, March 8
✠ *Theophylact the Confessor*

Mors stupebit.

Today that line from Verdi's *Requiem* kept sounding in my head and heart. It means, "Death shall be amazed." And I'm sure Death is stupefied after today's events. Mrs. O's casket came close to filling up half of the nave, but I'm still glad that we had the service in the temple because everyone was able to group themselves around the casket, and it was just like it was supposed to be—like Mrs. O was joining us for one last service.

Mors stupebit.

About half of the folks who came to the service were not Orthodox, but they stood patiently and respectfully throughout the entire hour. The chanters did a fine job, and when it came time for the last kiss, the folks who came forward did so with tender dignity. Afterwards, a number of the people who weren't Orthodox made a point of telling me how beautiful it all was.

Mors stupebit.

The graveside service was at the Liberty Hill Cemetery. Fr. Deacon BL and I rode with the funeral director in the front car. It took about thirty minutes to get there; we drove through farmland that is rapidly becoming subdivisions. When we arrived, I was surprised to see how many people had been in the procession. The day was clear and bright, but the wind was blowing, and Mrs. O's grave was right next to the highway, so when we did the final memorial service, the sound was almost immediately swept away. But we sang on, and by the time we got to the last round of "Memory Eternal," I think everyone there was singing with us.

Mors stupebit.

Lots of people worked hard to bring dishes for the mercy meal, and when we arrived back at the temple, the tables were all set up, and the food was all laid out. The meal that followed was a happy one with folks standing around talking, and kids running into the building and then back out into the sunshine.

Mors stupebit.

Later that day, I was driving back to church for the Presanctified Liturgy. The sun was just beginning to slip behind the trees as I drove past the Cedar Park Cemetery. I thought about that other cemetery out along that other highway, and I thought about Mrs. O, and how she is now in the presence of our Lord and Master, where the light never wanes and where no darkness ever falls.

Mors stupebit.

Friday, March 9
✠ *Forty Holy Martyrs*

Yesterday was Katie's birthday. We called her at 5:30 AM and sang "Happy Birthday" to her voice mail; she didn't pick up.

Today is a lot like the day she was born. We used a midwife and did the whole thing at home. Cynthia went into labor about 4 AM, and about two hours later, Katie arrived. Brendan woke up about 7 AM. He was three at the time. He and I fixed some breakfast, then we went out and sat on the steps of that little duplex we lived in.

There were flowering trees in that neighborhood, and there are a few of those trees in the subdivision where we now live. I remember looking at those trees and thinking that they looked like explosions of color—bursts of white and yellow and wine red and violet—and how they were just like the joy that was quietly exploding over and over again all through my heart.

Saturday, March 10
✠ *Codratus, Martyr*

Several times at Orthros this past week, we used this hymn as the irmos for the sixth ode of the canon:

Grant me a garment of light, O Thou who coverest Thyself with light as with a garment.

For some reason, that image of a garment of light kept coming back to me all week long. I found myself wondering what it would be like to be clothed in light. And last night, I think I found out.

We were doing Small Compline with the Akathist to the Mother of God. When it came time to do the hymn itself, I stepped in front of the icon of the Theotokos, made a metania, and then started to sing the third stasis of the hymn.

Right away, I noticed that my voice was clear and that I was hitting all the notes with little effort. I wasn't even breathing hard at the end of the first stanza. And then, as I was censing the icon, I was suddenly enveloped by happiness. I was embraced by joy.

But it wasn't a feeling. It was exterior to me. And by the time I started the second stanza, I understood what was happening: When the priest sings the Akathist, he takes on the role of the Archangel Gabriel, and he calls out to the Mother of God the way the holy archangel did. The greeting that Gabriel used is sometimes translated "Hail," sometimes "Rejoice," but last night during the service, as I sang that greeting over and over again, I discovered that they are one and the same thing. Because the joy that enfolded me was the presence of one of the bodiless powers, standing there with me and saluting the Mother of God.

But that happiness was also bright; it was radiant, and it rested on me like a garment of light. Perhaps it was just the reflection of the great creature standing there with me, but for the last two or three lines of that stanza, it was as if I was part of a sunrise, out along the glowing curve of this world, and my voice was ringing out with many, many other voices, voices that were much more beautiful and much more ancient, and we were all singing the praises of the Queen of the Heavens.

By the third stanza, my voice wasn't nearly as clear. I was also out of breath, but it wasn't from singing—it was from excitement. When I got to the alleluia at the end of the stasis, I could barely hit the notes. But I can still feel that joy, and it gives me hope—hope that one day I will be able to actually wear one of those garments of light.

Sunday, March 11
✣ *Adoration of the Cross*

It's been a nice weekend. Yesterday we drove down to see Katie. We went to her favorite Mexican restaurant for a birthday lunch; we sat outside and watched the birds and the falling leaves and a wedding party. On the way home, we stopped in San Marcos, and Cynthia looked for shoes.

There weren't many people at Great Vespers, but for some reason, there were lots of confessions. This morning we had another crowded liturgy, and the service for the Adoration of the Cross was exhilarating. We then had a parish council meeting; we had a lot of stuff to cover, but we were done a bit before 3 PM.

Even daylight savings time hasn't been too big a deal—I just went to bed an hour earlier last night. However, someone forgot to notify the deer about the time change. This morning I got to church about 6:30, and it was still dark. I walked out among the trees and went through my homily. By 7, I was headed towards the building, but the light was just barely beginning to show through the clouds. I was about halfway across the parking lot when I heard a deer snort. I couldn't tell exactly where the noise was coming from, but I did have the good sense to stop. That's when I heard the hoofs skittering across the asphalt just a few feet away. I saw/heard at least three as they plunged into the scrub cedar on the west side of the parking lot, but I know there were more than that.

And I heard still more snorting as I walked on into the building. They were probably warning all the other deer, letting them know that some idiot human had gotten up real early and was wandering around the parking lot.

Tuesday, March 13
✠ *Nicephorus, Patriarch of Constantinople*

Yesterday the belt on my car engine came apart. Thank God, I was able to get it to a mechanic, and it should be ready today, but the Great Lent Machine Meltdown continues apace.

Wednesday, March 14
✠ *Benedict of Nursia*

Today we purchased our plane tickets for our trip to England and Scotland. It's going to be a pilgrimage to some of the most holy places in the British Isles. We'll fly into London, then go to the Monastery of St. John in Essex. We will then travel to Durham and Lindisfarne and Iona, and we will fly back home out of Edinburgh. Most of the travel while we are in England and Scotland will be by train, with a few buses and some ferries.

We've been working toward this for close to a decade, and both Cynthia and I are getting really excited. But as I was driving back from the travel agent, the thought occurred to me: Why am I not as excited about going to heaven? I've been working on that trip even longer and harder than this trip to the British Isles, so why am I not looking forward to it even more?

I'll have to think about that one.

Thursday, March 15
✠ *Aristobolus, Enlightener of Britain*

Here's another thing I'll have to think about: Why don't we have holy places here in the United States? In the British Isles, in Europe, in the Middle East, in Russia, there are wells and groves of trees and caves and mountains and monasteries and churches that people visit—and they visit all those places because they are associated with saints. But here in America that concept hasn't yet taken root.

There's St. Herman's island and St. John Maximovitch's cathedral. St. Raphael is buried at Antiochian Village. Those men are all great saints, but people aren't as drawn to those places as they are to the ancient pilgrimage sites. Maybe it just takes hundreds and hundreds of years of piety and prayers and patience—oh, and miracles, too. A holy place must have miracles.

I wonder if the whole idea will even work in this country. But it will have to work; otherwise, Orthodoxy itself doesn't stand a chance. If we actually believe in the Incarnation and the sanctification of this entire creation, then it follows that there simply must be holy people, and those holy people will invariably sanctify the places in which they live.

So one thousand years from now, will people be coming to Cedar Park to visit the Church of St. John? Will they bring picnic lunches and spend the day out under the trees? Will they light candles and pray to the saints that our community has produced?

Maybe the first step to making sure that happens is believing that it needs to happen.

Saturday, March 17
✤ *Patrick, Enlightener of Ireland*

Yesterday afternoon, Brendan came through on his way to his reserve duty in San Antonio, and Cynthia and I took him to lunch. He talked about the car he's going to buy later this month and the new class he's starting; he also told us about some recent arrests he's made (his active duty assignment is with a unit of military policemen). I still have a hard time picturing him with a gun and a badge, but it's interesting to hear him talk about it.

This morning Cynthia and I went down to St. Elias. Fr. MK is doing a retreat for them this weekend. We got to visit with him for just a bit, and then we sat in on one of the sessions. At the break, Cynthia made her confession with Fr. MK. Then we had to go back home, since she has a training seminar coming up on Tuesday, and she still has some work to do on it.

It was good to see Fr. MK and to catch up on how Khouria AK and the rest of his family are doing. It was even better to sit next to Cynthia in church. We haven't done that in I don't know how long. Just sitting together in the presence of the Most Holy Trinity . . . a wonderful way to spend the morning.

Sunday, March 18
✠ *John Climacus*

"If you keep on piling up wood, it will one day catch fire."

I read that back in seminary in a book about sermon preparation. I think Goethe is the source. At any rate, it's true, because today the spark of insight and inspiration ignited some thoughts that I have kept stored up for a long time, and that fire is still blazing brightly.

The point of combustion was a document I was reading to my church school class—I always teach the middle school and high school kids. The document is an old photocopy of *The Martyrdom of Saints Perpetua and Felicitas*. It was originally a handout in a seminary class, but the story was so compelling I just hung onto it all these years. And since we are reading accounts of the martyrs in church school, I got up in the closet and dug the photocopy out of a box and shared it with the young people in my class.

The *Martyrdom* contains fragments of St. Perpetua's journal, and it also includes an account of a vision that was granted to one of her fellow martyrs, a man named Saturus. In Saturus's vision, the martyrs come to a place of light. They hear angels chanting the Thrice-Holy Hymn, and then they are brought before a group of elders. The martyrs exchange the kiss of peace with the elders, and then the elders say to them, "*Ite et ludite.*" "Go and play."

Several of the young people in the class commented on how cool that sounds. I couldn't agree more, but that command, "Go and play," immediately reminded me of a parish life conference I attended when I was a deacon. It was the last day of the conference, and I was assigned to escort Bishop Basil from his hotel room to the hierarchical liturgy down in the hotel ballroom. He and I were waiting for the elevator, and I was casting around for something to say, so I commented that he must be tired after a week's worth of activities. He turned to me and smiled; then he got that twinkle in his eye, and he said, "But that will all vanish once we get downstairs and the liturgy starts, because the liturgy is the playground of the Holy Spirit."

The playground of the Holy Spirit. That's the flash of memory that was ignited when I read what the elders said to the martyrs: "Go and play." And then that recollection of the liturgy as the Holy Spirit's playground caused another memory to burst into the fire of insight. It was something my mother wrote in a letter a couple of years ago; she was comparing her experience in a Western Rite service to our liturgy at St. John's, and she referred to "the sheer broadside of the Byzantine Rite." That observation has stayed with me, not only because it is especially apt, but also because it reminded me of one of the games I used to play when I was a child—pirates!

Of course, one of the great things about playing pirates was the fact that you could dress up—eye patches, sashes, big hats with feathers, oversized boots—or you could dress down—just take off your shirt and shoes, roll up your pants, and tie a bandanna around your head. The best locations for buccaneering were the homes of my grandparents; they had big porches with wooden floors, and you could stride across those and easily imagine yourself on the deck of a sleek and fast-moving ship. So each summer there would be weeks where I would look like a walking Howard Pyle painting, and my grandparents' porches would look like the sets of an Errol Flynn movie.

And sometimes, on Sunday morning, I still feel like the "Pirate Don Dirk of Dowdee":

> His coat was handsome and cut with a slash
> And often as ever he twirled his mustache
> Deep down in the ocean the mermaids went splash
> Because of Don Dirk of Dowdee.

It used to confuse me when all those old memories would spill into my heart. After all, I'm a priest. I'm serving the Divine Liturgy. So why do I feel like I should be shouting, "Avast!"?

But the fuse fire of insight that began with the elders' command to the martyrs and ran through Bishop Basil's comment and then my mother's observation has put all that in a new and joyous light. Because it's not so much about being a pirate—it's about the fact that the liturgy is the playground of the Holy Spirit. But all the good fun I've ever had in this life is also reflected in the liturgy. So when I hear that first liturgical broadside on Sunday morning, it's not at all surprising that I reach for the cutlass that swings at my thigh, and it's not at all strange that I feel for the zigzaggy scar at the end of my eye. Because those were some of the best times I've ever had, and that is the way we will be playing for all eternity.

A great and holy elder will give us a solemn command: "Go and play." And then, liturgically speaking, it will be like all those summers I spent as a front porch pirate. The door will bang behind us, and we will run out into the sunlight, and all our friends will be there, and school will be out, and time will be forgotten, and no one—no one—will ever call us back inside.

Monday, March 19
✠ *Chrysanthus and Daria, Martyrs*

Speaking of holy play, a couple of weeks ago, BG gave me a small painting. It's a portrait of me. I'm dressed in my cassock, and I'm doing a cartwheel. BG said that he had overheard me talking to one of the young girls about doing cartwheels: Not too long ago, after a service, when just about everyone was at coffee hour, this girl was doing cartwheels in the nave. One of the women in our community told her she shouldn't do that, but later, I pulled the girl aside and told her that I just do the cartwheels in my heart. I told her that's what it's like when I'm serving at the altar.

Tuesday, March 20
✠ *Cuthbert, Bishop of Lindisfarne*

This morning on the way home from Orthros, I was sitting in a long line of cars, waiting for the light at the 183 intersection. The young woman in the car ahead of me wasn't paying attention to what was going on—in fact, her head wasn't visible. She was busy with something down on the floorboard of her car.

When the light changed and the cars began to move, I knew there was no way we would make it through the intersection; the line was just too long. But the woman hadn't noticed that the cars in front of her had even moved. I thought briefly about getting out of the car and tapping on her window, but then I figured that would really startle her. So I just honked my horn as lightly as I could. She sat up in her seat, the car lunged forward, and she sped up to the intersection.

But the next time the light changed, the same thing happened. I don't know what was going on, but she was absorbed in what she was doing down there on the floorboard, and this time, we were at the front of the line. I waited a few seconds after the light changed, then I touched the horn again. Just like before, she sat up, and the car raced through the intersection. Only this time, she also looked in her rearview mirror and flipped me off.

I suppose it was a typical morning in traffic. But I've felt bad about it all day long. I wasn't in a hurry; I wasn't angry; I was just trying to get her attention. But there's no way she could have known all that. So I was most likely the beginning of her bad day.

Not only that, I caused her to sin. The only reaction I had to her gesture was one of regret. Right then, I knew I should have just let her go ahead and do whatever it was she was doing.

So all day, I've been praying for her—and for my own stupidity and my uncaring heart.

Lord, have mercy.

Saturday, March 24
✠ *Forefeast of the Annunciation*

This day had a painful beginning and a beautiful ending.

This morning Cynthia and I drove to Burleson to visit her mom. Visiting with Mrs. E is never easy. She is almost completely deaf, and she has little interest in anything or anyone beyond the walls of the room in her assisted living facility. That makes talking to her really laborious. Of course, that's not a big deal; if anything, it's an opportunity to be patient and kind and helpful. The hard part comes when Mrs. E talks, because, sadly, just about everything she says is callous or critical or just downright cruel.

For example, this morning, Cynthia asked Mrs. E if she ever received the Christmas present we had sent her. Cynthia had worked hard to come up with an appropriate gift, and she finally found something that she thought her mother would enjoy. She ordered it online and had it delivered to her mom's address. But since Mrs. E had never mentioned it, we weren't even sure if she had even received it. In retrospect, it would have been better if we had not brought it up, but we did, and this is what she said:

"Oh . . . that thing? Yeah, I got it, but I didn't know what it in the world it was. I asked S what she thought it was, and she said she didn't know either, but she said she thought she could use it, so I just gave it to her."

S is the long-time friend of one of Cynthia's half-sisters.

The response stunned both Cynthia and me. For a minute or two we just sat there in silence. We then forged ahead with more small talk; we managed to make it through an entire hour, but we didn't have the stamina for more than that.

As we drove away, Cynthia cried, and I held her hand. Later, we stopped and got something to eat, and we talked about how hard it is to love people who work so hard at being unlovable. Because it's not the issue of forgiveness; that's a given. It's not even the issue of compassion; we both know that Mrs. E has had a tough life. It's the prospect of having to subject ourselves directly to that toxicity every couple of months. That's the hard part.

But talking about it helped. So did the chips and the salsa we shared at lunch. And so did the drive home under a blue sky filled with bright, white clouds, through banks of bluebonnets and past hillsides covered with Indian paintbrush.

We got home just in time for Great Vespers. There were also lots of flowers in the nave, and the Annunciation hymns were glorious, and at some point in the service I realized that even if Mrs. E is never going to be the kind of mother she should be, there is another woman, a woman whose motherhood transcends mere biology; a woman whose compassion is even more healing than chips and salsa; a woman whose love fills this world with hope the way the sky gets filled with clouds, the way a field is filled up with the flowers of spring:

> Rejoice with Jerusalem,
> and be glad for her,
> all you who love her;
> rejoice with her in joy,
> all you who mourn over her,
> that you may suck and be satisfied
> from her consoling breasts;
> and you shall suck;
> you shall be carried on her hip,
> and dandled upon her knees.
> As one whom his mother comforts,
> so I will comfort you;

You shall be comforted
in Jerusalem. (Isaiah 66:10ff)

Sunday, March 25
✠ *The Feast of the Annunciation*

This morning I was going through my sermon out under the trees, and I noticed that all the leaves had come out during the night. It was as if the trees decided to adorn themselves in honor of the Mother of God. And the sun rose into a sky that was Theotokos blue, and the stars stayed out late in order to join in the celebration, and we made our offering as well, with a joyful Orthros and a Divine Liturgy that was brighter than all the lights of heaven.

Tuesday, March 27
✠ *Matrona, Martyr*

Brendan sent us pictures of his new car—on our phones.

I don't think I'm cut out for this century.

But I'm happy about his car. He saved a whole lot of money and did a whole lot of research and waited until he could get just the one he wanted. I couldn't tell much about the car from the picture; it was way too tiny. But I could tell the car is sleek and black and nothing at all like his first automobile—a dull orange stereo on wheels that his friends dubbed "the Cheeto."

I will have to remember to bless it when he comes through town next month.

Thursday, March 29
✠ *Mark, Bishop of Arethusa*

Yesterday we served the final Wednesday night Presanctified Liturgy.

This year there was something spiritually apprehensive about being left alone in the altar with the consecrated Lamb. During the reading of the kathisma, Fr. Deacon BL and I prepare the Lamb for the transfer to the proskomidia table. But in between the stases, Fr. Deacon BL has to go out into the nave and intone the little litany, so I am by myself in the altar before the Very Presence.

Each time Fr. Deacon BL left, I felt like I did whenever I've gone to get an X-ray. The technician gets you all set up and arranged, but then that person steps out of the room before the radiation is released. So you end up all alone with this power that permeates your very body.

But in the altar I'm standing before a power that also searches my soul. Like it says in the post-communion prayers:

> Thou who art a fire consuming the unworthy: Consume me not,
> O my Creator, but pass through all my body parts, into all my
> joints, my reins, my heart. Burn Thou the thorns of all my
> transgressions. Cleanse my soul, and hallow Thou my thoughts.
> Make firm my knees and my bones likewise. Enlighten as one my
> five senses. Establish me wholly in Thy fear.

I can hear the people singing through the curtain, but it seems far away because this light radiates from the diskos, a light that creates all kinds of distance between me and my thoughts, a light that shows up the vast difference between the person I am and the person I should be, a light that breaks my heart and turns the shattered pieces into glowing coals of hope, a light that is greater than the sun.

Then a voice rings out from way back on the other side of the light, and it's mine doing the exclamation for the litany, and Fr. Deacon BL comes into the altar, and we bow and turn to the business at hand.

But it's not as if the light goes away. The glory of the Most Holy Trinity is always shining on us and on this world. It's just like William Blake said—we have "to learn to bear the beams of love." I'm thankful for the practice—for the radiation treatments—I got during this Fast.

Friday, March 30
✠ *John Climacus*

Today at the Sixth Hour we finished the Book of the Prophet Isaiah. It's read through every year during Great Lent, but today this passage caught my eye:

I am coming to gather all nations and tongues, and they shall come
and see My glory . . . and they shall bring all your brethren from all
the nations as an offering to the Lord . . . just as the Israelites bring a
cereal offering, in a clean vessel to the house of the Lord. And some
of them also I will take for priests . . . says the Lord.

That's me. I'm one of the priests the prophet is talking about. I'm a
fulfillment of what the Most Holy Trinity promised to the people of Israel
way back in the Old Testament. Right here in Cedar Park, Texas.
Darn.

Saturday, March 31
✠ *Lazarus Saturday*

Last night before bed, I read Small Compline and the Canon for Lazarus
Saturday. I like this troparion:

The palaces of hell were shaken, when in its depths Lazarus once
more began to breathe, straightway restored to life by the sound of
Thy voice.

I'm picturing a dark city that stretches out across an endless plain. There
are massive towers and high walls and great halls, and these palaces are
filled with cries and clamor as the mighty demons go about the grim and
relentless business of hell. But it all comes to a sudden stop—silence falls
across the vast metropolis—when an unattended corpse in some back alley
corner takes a sudden, sharp, and short breath.

The demons look at one another. Fear has seized their hearts. Not a
single one of them speaks, but they are all thinking the same thought:
He's coming.

APRIL

Yesterday after the liturgy, everyone worked hard to get things cleaned up for Holy Week. One major focus was the removal of a large tree limb that was jammed up against the back porch. KS, one of our long-time members, was in charge of the effort: he was wielding the chain saw, and he had his son, SS, posted up on the roof so that the limb wouldn't hit the building. As further insurance, he tied ropes around the branch and recruited five people to pull on the ropes so that the limb would fall away from the roof.

When I was watching the operation, there was lots of discussion about exactly where the limb would fall. Two of the people manning the ropes were actually engineers, and they had concerns about KS's safety. Others were worried about SS being up on the roof. Still others were worried about the roof. But they all finally decided to continue with KS's plan.

After several long breaks caused by chainsaw malfunction, the limb was finally brought down. And, despite all expectation and planning, it landed squarely on the roof. No one was hurt, and the building suffered no damage. But everyone involved with the operation expressed not only relief, but also a certain amount of disbelief and dismay—the ropes appeared to be positioned correctly, KS had made all the right cuts in all the appropriate places, SS was pushing on the branch as hard as he knew how, and the limb still fell right on the roof.

There's an expression some of the Arab priests I know often use: "What can you do?" To be used correctly, the expression has to be accompanied by a slight shrug and a wave of the hand. But it's a good way to blow off steam when things happen that are just beyond our control. And a whole lot of life works that way: You have a good plan; you've got all your help lined up;

you take all the right steps and all the necessary precautions, and thud—the thing goes ahead and falls flat on the roof. What can you do?

Actually, I've been hearing a lot of those thuds lately.

For the past several years, the parish has been raising money to send high school seniors on mission trips. We've generated several thousand dollars, and this year we had two good young people who were qualified to go. So they filled out the applications, and I wrote letters, and they were both accepted. But in the last two weeks, I've learned that one will not be able to go due to an unexpected college commitment, and the other probably won't be able to participate, either. What can you do?

Several of our catechumens and a few of our long-time visitors appear to be having second thoughts. Of course, that's why it takes several months to become a catechumen, and that's why it takes close to a year to be received into the Church. It gives folks the time they need to sort through all their thoughts and feelings and expectations. And every once in a while, people do just drop out and disappear altogether. But it's always sad to see them lose interest—especially when they were so excited and enthusiastic to begin with. What can you do?

Then there are all those people who have all those ongoing struggles: the folks who aren't sure they can actually stay married; the people who have horrible jobs; the folks who just don't know what to do with their kids; the people who drink too much or eat too much or look at internet porn. And a lot of times I just end up standing there with them, and in what seems like slow motion, we watch those big old branches fall right down on their lives over and over and over again. What can you do?

That expression is a good one for blowing off steam, but it's not the final answer. Whenever my own plans and projects start collapsing around me, when the dull thud of disappointment begins to echo back and forth in my life and in the lives of those I care about, I eventually end up thinking about the first Paschal homily I ever heard.

Of course, priests don't typically preach at Pascha, but this particular priest was 87 and a bit eccentric, and so he insisted on delivering a sermon. But I'm glad he did. He spoke about a Paschal service he participated in at a refugee camp just after World War II. Most of the refugees were Romanian, and since Romania had been an ally of Nazi Germany, the camp was being guarded by American soldiers. The priest said that he had vestments, but the altar was a wooden table, the diskos was a metal plate, and the chalice was a small bucket. The chanters had to do everything from memory.

They sang "Christ is Risen" all through the night. Before they were done, even the guards were singing along with them. The priest closed his homily with these words: "Keep singing. No matter what happens, keep singing. Eventually, everyone else will start singing, too."

And that's what I always do. I keep singing. I go to the services, and I sing about hope and trust and faith and the mercies of our great God and Savior, Jesus Christ.

And that's really what Holy Week is all about. Branches may be crashing all around us, but this morning, we picked up those branches, and we waved them in the air, and we served a Palm Sunday liturgy that was breathtaking. Our plans and predictions may end up being precisely wrongheaded, but later in the week, we're going to go ahead and nail all those plans and predictions to the cross, so this morning, we just marched through the sunlight and up and down the parking lot. It's only a matter of time before we hear the next thud, but this morning, we went ahead and did what we could do: We made BN a catechumen—and he was focused and intent, and his eyes were bright, and, when we sang all together, he sang right along with us.

Monday, April 2
✠ *Great and Holy Monday*

Holy Week has started well.

The trees are full of glowing leaves. The grass in the field out behind the fence is "long and lovely and lush." This morning a possum was waddling across the parking lot, and two deer poked their heads out from among the cedar trees.

And the services have been well attended. Last night at the first Bridegroom Orthros, this morning at the Presanctified Liturgy, and then tonight again at the Bridegroom Orthros, there have been a whole lot of people. I know many of them are making a special effort to be part of this special time.

Not only have the services been well-attended, they have also been done well. The chanting has been exceptional, and folks have been quiet and attentive.

Things haven't always been that way. The first time I did Holy Week here at St. John's, there was a great deal of anxiety and confusion—and even some outright conflict—among the chanters. Children were constantly disrupting the services. Teenagers wandered in and out of the nave; a few would even lie down and go to sleep in the narthex. Many of the people had a tremendous concern for liturgical procedure, but little concern for basic reverence.

But the people of St. John's really didn't want to be that way. And they have worked very hard in order to bring about change. It's taken several years, but the change has been evident this week in the services: there is dignity; there is peace; there is order and reverence.

Tuesday, April 3
✣ *Great and Holy Tuesday*

A great deal of mythology surrounds Holy Week.

People often talk as if this week placed extraordinary demands on the priest. Folks frequently come up to me and say, "Are you holding up all right? Are you going to be able to make it?"

It's not that I don't appreciate the attention, but I don't want people to get the impression that what I'm doing is somehow heroic. Because the truth is, I don't do any more services during Holy Week than I do any other week of the year. Now it's true that we do not typically have a service on Saturday morning or Sunday night, and the scheduling of the services is different. But the number of services I end up doing is roughly the same: I do two each and every weekday of the year, and I do two each and every day of Holy Week. (Reader MT actually participates in three services every weekday of the year, since he is responsible for Small Compline every night at 9 PM; so for him, Holy Week actually represents something of a break!)

People also often talk as if the Holy Week services were especially complex. But that isn't true, either. The services are different, since they have many unique features. But just about all of them follow the basic outline of the standard services of Vespers and Orthros. So it's not as if you need all sorts of arcane knowledge in order to do the Holy Week services well. You just need to have done the regular services throughout the year.

To be sure, Holy Week is a very busy week. There are all those confessions and all those questions about flowers and eggs and candles. So, like it says in the aposticha verses for several of the services, you really gotta have that "fatigue-loving purpose." But there's nothing heroic about the schedule; there's nothing mysterious about the services. If anything, getting through Holy Week boils down to staying in shape liturgically throughout the rest of the year. I'm just thankful I'm part of a community that understands just how critical that is.

Wednesday, April 4
✣ *Great and Holy Wednesday*

I'm sitting on the bench out back, under the trees. It's a little after five in the afternoon. There's a good deal of wind and some clouds gathering off to the north, but the sun is also shining, and it's rich and golden and warm.

I'm looking through the Unction Service in preparation for tonight. I love this service. What I especially love about it is the overwhelming emphasis it places on the love of the Most Holy Trinity. Over and over again, through the Epistle readings and the Gospel readings and the prayers, the message is that the Father, Son, and Holy Spirit really do love us. They are not angry with us; They are not disappointed with us; They are not frustrated with us.

I just wish more people understood that.

Thursday, April 5
✣ *Great and Holy Thursday*

I love listening to the Scriptures in the services. Reading the Bible alone is great, but when the passages are read in the services, it's like taking a beautiful gemstone and placing it in an equally beautiful setting: the setting only enhances the stone, displaying its depth and drawing out its features.

Like this morning at the Vesperal Liturgy: We heard about Moses hiding in the cleft rock as the glory of the Lord passed by; we heard about the Lord confronting Job from out of the whirlwind; then we heard about the same Lord washing the feet of His friends, one of whom was about to betray Him.

Friday, April 6
✠ *Great and Holy Friday*

Last night we did the service of the Twelve Passion Gospels. The procession with the cross during that service is one of my favorite moments in the whole week.

The cross we have isn't huge, but our small space makes it seem bigger and bulkier than it actually is. That means I'm always concerned about hitting a ceiling fan with one end or whacking a parishioner with the other. And although I know the hymn for the procession, I still feel like I have to carry a copy of the music with me, so that means I don't have any free hands. Then, on top of everything else, the third bar of the cross is positioned awkwardly, so it's hard to rest the main cross bar on my shoulder.

But even with all that going on, the procession is always a profound experience.

Last night, I had made it through the nave without hitting anyone or anything, and I was standing in front of the holy doors finishing the hymn. I had my right hand under the main cross bar, and the weight of the cross itself was distributed across my shoulder and my back, so I thought, "Ok, this will work until I finish the hymn. I'll just keep it balanced this way."

I sang a few more lines of the hymn, but then I suddenly realized that I was holding the piece of music with both hands. It simultaneously occurred to me that the cross wasn't resting on me; I was resting on it. In fact, I was leaning on it—it was actually holding me up. I'm not sure about the physics behind all that; I must have ended the procession with the cross at an even better angle than I had realized. But the spiritual application was absolutely clear: Many times I refuse to treat problems and hardships (and even inconveniences) as crosses because I'm somehow convinced that I can solve things all on my own. During Great Lent, we were reading St. Isaac of Syria at Orthros, and here's what he has to say about this way of looking at things:

This knowledge does not ascribe control of the world to God's Providence; on the contrary, all that is good in man, all that saves him from harm, all that naturally protects him from difficulties and the many adversities which accompany our nature, both secretly and openly, all this appears to this knowledge to be a result of its own care and its own methods. Such is the opinion this blasphemous knowledge has of itself. It imagines that all things happen through its own providence . . . all the same it cannot exist without constant cares and without fears for the body, and is, therefore, prey to faint-heartedness, sorrow, despair and fears.

But the cross makes every burden light; it is the easiest of yokes. And it's not an additional, spiritual consideration that we factor in after every other avenue has been considered and every other approach has been tried—it is the one thing that will give us balance; it is the one thing that we can actually lean on.

As I finished the hymn, as I was being held up by the cross, I was praying that I would be able to remember that moment throughout the coming year.

Saturday, April 7
✠ *Great and Holy Saturday*

This morning I gave myself and the world an Easter present.

For the past six years, during my intercessions, I've been praying for a list of people who are my enemies. About thirty people were on the list.

I was once very close to some of these people; there were a few for whom I didn't even have names. But each of them had, in some way, hurt me, or they had hurt someone I love.

❖   When I was in high school, I was walking to church on Saturday morning. I forget why I was going to church on a Saturday—some sort of youth meeting, I think. But it was a quiet day, a beautiful day, and, as I was walking down the sidewalk, a car pulled up to the curb alongside of me. I didn't recognize the car, and I couldn't see the driver. So I stepped closer to the street and bent over to get a look at the person in the car.

It was a man I didn't recognize, and he was naked from the waist down. There was a pillow on the seat next to him, and the seat and the floorboard were strewn with porn magazines. I was so shocked, I just stood there. The man gestured to me, indicating that I should get in the car, but I didn't move. Another car had turned onto the street and was approaching from the other direction, so the man pulled away from the curb and quickly drove out of sight.

❖   When I was a United Methodist pastor, there was a woman in one of the congregations I served who had two sons. Both boys were in elementary school; the youngest boy talked to himself and to his mother during just about every single sermon. We had a small sanctuary; he had a loud voice; lots of people were annoyed; many of them wanted me to do something.

One Sunday after the service was over, I saw the woman up at the front of the sanctuary. Only a few people were still in that part of the facility, so I thought it would be a good time to talk to her. I walked up to her and explained the situation as diplomatically as I knew how, but I did tell her that her son was being disruptive and that people were complaining.

She said, "Thanks for your support," and then hit me on my left shoulder. I don't think she meant to hit me as hard as she did. I think it was supposed to be more of a sarcastic "Atta boy" kind of tap. But she was really angry, so she ended up just slugging me. Then she walked out of the sanctuary.

❖   After I left United Methodism, my hospice chaplain job just wasn't bringing in enough money. Our little Orthodox mission was too small to pay me a salary, so I started looking around for another job. The International House of Pancakes was hiring dishwashers, and that's how I had put myself through college, so I applied for the position. But since I spoke English, the manager put me on the front line as one of the cooks.

I was truly an awful cook. Then one night, I glanced up from my range, and out across the dining room, I saw a man looking at me. I think he had been standing there for a while, waiting for me to look up. He was about my age; he had once been a member of my United Methodist congregation. When my eyes met his, he sneered, laughed, and shook his head. Then he turned around and sat down in one of the booths.

Now it's not that I've been walking around grinding my teeth over these people. But I know that my encounters with them and the others on that list scarred my heart, and I want those scars healed. Because it's hard to love with a heart that's all scarred up. So it's not just about making me a better person; it's about making the world a better place.

So each day for the past six years, I have prayed through the list, and each day I have made a prostration at the end of that prayer. At each and every liturgy over the past six years, at the service of the proskomidia, I have read through the list just before I place a piece of bread on the diskos for myself:

O Lord, remember my unworthiness and forgive all my transgressions, both voluntary and involuntary.

I know that the forgiveness of my sins is forever linked with my willingness to forgive the people on that list. So I've done my best to forgive them and even to try to wish them well.

At the beginning of Great Lent, I spoke with Fr. TM, my spiritual father, and I asked him if it was time to wrap the whole project up. He agreed, and so all through the season, I've been getting ready to do what I did this morning: Before I went to church for the liturgy, I read through the Hours and the Typika, and then I took out the list and read over it one more time, making a prostration at each name. Then I tore up the list and threw it away.

And that was that. No emotion. No overwhelming sense of relief. Project completed. Job over.

But at the end of this morning's liturgy, the choir sang their festal version of "Blessed be the Name of the Lord." Reader DN, one of our chanters, calls it "the Hollywood version," and it really is over the top: it has all these parts and lots of opportunities for harmony, and, even though the whole thing is only three lines long, it sounds like a symphony, and everyone loves it—they just sing and sing and sing and sing.

And while they were singing, my eyes began to water, and I started to laugh. I thought to myself, "OK, this is it; I'm having a nervous breakdown," but then I realized that it was all that forgiveness finally working its way out and breaking through.

I stood up in front of the altar and turned around to give the final blessing. The floor of the nave was strewn with the leaves and flower petals that I had scattered during the great Resurrection Prokeimenon: "Arise, O

God! Judge Thou the earth! For Thou shalt inherit among all the nations!" But as I gave the blessing, it was as if the air of the nave was also filled with petals and leaves, as if some great high-priestly hand were strewing blessings upon us with regal abandon, blessings of hope and healing and mercy:

> My beloved has gone down
> to his garden,
> to the beds of spices . . .
> to look at the blossoms of the valley,
> to see whether the vines had budded,
> whether the pomegranates were in bloom.
>
> Then he showed me the river of the water of life . . .
> also, on either side of the river, the tree of life . . .
> and the leaves of the tree were for the healing of the nations.

The leaves and petals quiver in the air around me as I give the blessing for the end of the liturgy, and they float past the high school kid who's watching the car pull out of sight, and they drift past the pastor who's shaking his head and rubbing his arm, and they swirl around the cook who lowers his head and bites his lip and turns to his next order.

Sunday, April 8
✠ *Pascha*

All week long the weather has looked like something out of a Disney movie. It has been bright and sunny; the trees and flowers have been in full color. Just the sort of weather you would want for Holy Week.

But yesterday, a major cold front came through. The highs have been in the low 40s. We even had several rounds of sleet and snow.

That put a dent in the number of folks who were able to come to the service last night, but the end result was that the nave was barely full and not cram-packed as it is most years.

Also, we couldn't go outside for the procession, but we improvised and were able to do just about everything inside.

I'm sitting at our kitchen table now, and it's about 9 AM. In just a moment, I'm going to start writing my Pascha notes, but right now I'm just Paschasizing. All during Great Lent, Bishop Basil sent the clergy homilies by St. Theodore the Studite, and in one of those homilies, St. Theodore uses the word *Pascha* as a verb. And I think that's what I'm experiencing right now: the power of Pascha, the energy of Easter. So, as I'm sitting here, bubbling over with Paschalization, I'm going to write down a few images that have stayed with me from the Feast:

❖ Yesterday morning, we chrismated the E family. There are five of them, so there was a lot of anointing, washing, snipping, and blessing. I was reminded once again just how physical and intimate and hands-on and transforming the whole experience is. Being received into the Church isn't just a matter of a handshake and a smile and some pleasant words: you get oil on your feet, and water drips down onto your face, and you actually lose some of your hair, and there's candle wax all over the place. And then there are the words themselves, words that make us warriors invincible in every attack and victors even unto the end, sons and daughters of the Kingdom who are blessed to behold the good things of Jerusalem all the days of their lives.

❖ At the feast itself, I sat across from a young man the contents of whose Pascha basket consisted of beef jerky, a large bag of sour warheads, a chocolate bunny rabbit, and a half-gallon jug of milk. I hope he makes it to Agape Vespers this afternoon.

❖ Yesterday afternoon, my brother-in-law Joe called. He said that he and Rosemary, my older sister, "had a few questions about Orthodoxy," and that "they were thinking it might be fun to go to a service this weekend." We talked briefly about some basic questions (icons, Eastern Rite and Western Rite), and, since they now live in Wichita, I told them about the cathedral. They were surprised to learn that the Easter service began at 11 PM (they've been attending Baptist congregations for a number of years), but they also said they thought they "would give it a try." Shortly after that, Brendan called, wondering if I knew when the services would begin at Holy Cross in Wichita Falls.

There's more, but I'll leave that for the days ahead. Right now, I'm going to turn to my Pascha notes, which actually seems the perfect thing to do with all this leftover festal fervor—channel it into gratitude, and share that thankfulness with the people I love.

Tuesday, April 10
✠ *Bright Tuesday*

This is Brendan's twenty-eighth birthday. Later today, we're going to call and do our annoying parent thing and sing "Happy Birthday" to him over the phone.

He was born at Presbyterian Hospital in Dallas. I was with Cynthia in the delivery room, and then with her in the hospital room for two or three days after. I still remember when it was time to go home, and they brought Brendan to us in this bassinet on wheels. The nurse said, "Here you go!" Then she turned and walked out of the room. We weren't even sure how to get him out of the bassinet.

Given that start, I think he's done really well.

Wednesday, April 11
✠ *Bright Wednesday*

More Easterizing.

The first Paschal liturgy on Great and Holy Saturday includes all those Old Testament lessons. The second lesson comes from Isaiah 60, and this year I noticed for the first time all this stuff about camels:

A multitude of camels shall cover you,
the young camels of Midian and Ephan;
all those from Sheba shall come.
They shall bring gold and frankincense,
and shall proclaim the praise of the Lord.

There are also camels here in Cedar Park. Out on Highway 183, there's a used car dealership called Austintatious Autos. They have a large inflatable camel out in front of their facility all the time; I think that's supposed to symbolize that they can provide financing. Anyway, most weekends, they also have one or two real camels out on the lot. Folks stop and take pictures, and sometimes kids ride on them.

I've been able to watch the camels while sitting in weekend traffic, and they don't look as if they are at all mistreated. In fact, they seem to enjoy being the center of so much attention. But this past Saturday, when I heard that passage from the prophet Isaiah, I immediately thought about the camels at the used car dealership, and I realized that, even though they appear content and well-fed, that is not their destiny. They were created "to proclaim the praise of the Lord." Just like us, they were meant for greater things.

Thursday, April 12
✛ *Bright Thursday*

Yesterday, I got up really early and made a quick trip to Dallas. My mother's sister, Kathy, had flown in from Georgia for a few days, so I drove up to see her and my parents. Cynthia doesn't have any time off to spare, so she went ahead and worked.

On the way, I recited the Paschal Hours in the car:

In that we have beheld the resurrection of Christ, let us worship the holy Lord Jesus, the only sinless One. Thy cross do we adore, O Christ, Thy holy resurrection we praise and glorify.

That was fun—but since the Bright Week version of the Hours is so repetitive, I frequently lost my place ("Am I on the third or the fourth? Oh, well . . ."), which is actually very similar to the way the rest of my life works: flying through the darkness, not exactly sure where I am in my prayers, but forging ahead anyway.

When I got to my parents', we had breakfast and then went to the Arboretum. It was nice to wander around the gardens in the cool sunshine; it was a very Paschal thing to do. My younger sister Alice joined us—and it turns out that she and her two sons were chrismated at the Feast! I knew they were catechumens in my parents' parish, but I thought it would be Pentecost before they were received into the Church.

My brother Brigham came by at lunch. It was nice to be together with everyone. Kathy caught us up on all the news from Donalsonville, my mother's hometown; Pop filled us in on all the latest from Farmersville, his hometown. While we were eating, my older sister Rosemary called. She said that she and her husband Joe had attended Pascha at the cathedral; they weren't able to stay for the whole service, but she said they liked it and that a lot of people were friendly, and that they are thinking about going back.

I left shortly after lunch. I practiced some of the presentations I'll be doing for the Introduction to the Church event next week, and I was home by 5 PM. Cynthia and I collapsed on the couch, but later that evening, Brendan called and thanked us for the birthday greetings. He said that he had gone to our old parish in Wichita Falls for Pascha and that everyone there said to tell us "hi."

I love Pascha.

I love my family.

Monday, April 16
✛ *Faith, Hope, and Love, Martyrs*

This morning I got an email from JH. He and I served as United Methodist pastors. He left the denomination a few years after I did, and now he teaches at a community college in East Texas.

It was a brief note. He simply said that his wife, MH, has been diagnosed with breast cancer, and that she will begin six months of chemotherapy this week.

Tonight I called JH, and we talked a while. He said that MH will need to have surgery when the chemotherapy is over. The treatments will be done in Dallas, so they will also have lots of driving. JH and MH have two sons, and the oldest will be starting college this fall.

I told JH that we would be praying for them. After we hung up, I sat and thought about what it would be like if something similar happened to us. I didn't think about it for long. After a decade of hospice work, I know what it would be like. Without the brown eyes that look over at me every night from the other pillow, without the hand that reaches out for mine, my heart would . . . well, let's face it, it would stop. It would just quit. And I would cease to exist.

Tuesday, April 17
✜ Symeon, Hieromartyr

During Great Lent, as I was reading through the *Ladder of Divine Ascent,* I noticed this sentence towards the end of the book:

But all the loaves of heavenly bread do not have the same appearance.

St. John was talking about the wide variety in prayer rules and ascetic practices, but it got me thinking about the wide variety of prosphora loaves folks bring for the liturgy—and they definitely do not all have the same appearance.

Some of the loaves are pretty close to perfect. They are actually round, and the seal is clearly visible; the crust is nice and soft, and the bread tears easily, but it doesn't crumble.

The other extreme is freezer bread—what the deacon I served with in Wichita Falls used to call "moon rocks." Thankfully, most of the folks who bake prosphora bring several extra loaves. We put the additional bread in the freezer, and we use it on those Sundays when no one has signed up to make prosphora or when folks simply forget.

Sometimes a loaf will have been in the freezer for months, but we will put it in the microwave and nuke it until it actually smells like it's fresh out of the oven. But it doesn't handle that way: the crust comes off in large flakes, and the bread is tough and dry. Fr. Deacon BL and I also have to be careful at the altar because the freezer bread always produces a lot of crumbs.

But in between the perfect loaves and the moon rocks, our community produces an amazing variety of prosphora:

❖ Rather than making several separate loaves, one man in our parish just makes one large loaf. And I mean large: the circumference is about the size of a small bicycle tire, and the loaf stands about six inches tall. It probably weighs at least ten pounds, and you have to pick it up with both hands.

❖ One woman makes the traditional Middle Eastern flat loaves. They are almost as wide as the bicycle tire prosphora, but they are thin, and each has several seals.

❖ Still another woman always brings a large bag of tiny loaves—
sometimes as many as forty or fifty. Not too long ago, one of the
altar servers glanced at the bag full of little loaves and exclaimed,
"Wow. Baby bread." We use them for the antidoron at the end of
the liturgy.

And then there are those folks who—well, there's no other way to say it:
They just don't know how to cook. Sometimes the loaves they bring aren't
even bread yet. They're just misshapen lumps of still-damp dough. There's
no seal to speak of, and when we put particles of the bread into the chalice,
they sink straight down to the bottom like little ball bearings.

I have heard of priests who will only accept prosphora of a certain quality.
They feel it is not proper to offer substandard bread at the liturgy. And part
of me identifies with that. But then I think about the prayers I offer and how
substandard they are. In fact, just about all of them are half-baked. So I'm
sure that the angels shake their heads at times or just turn away and try not
to laugh. But the Father, Son, and Holy Spirit always receive my offerings, so
how can I refuse what someone else brings?

Wednesday, April 18
✚ *John, Disciple of St. Gregory of the Decapolis*

Writing about bread has also caused me to start thinking about bread
crumbs. At the end of the liturgy, as I'm folding up the antimension, I always
consume any of the crumbs that might have fallen on the cloth.

When I was first ordained, I thought this was just about one of the
strangest parts of the job—picking about the altar for tiny pieces of bread.
But now it's one of my absolute favorite things to do, because, as the priest, I
get to partake of all the extra grace that has been left lying around.

Of course, I certainly need it. In fact, ruffling through the folds of the
antimension always reminds me of what the Canaanite woman said to Christ
Jesus: "Even the dogs get to pick up the crumbs under the Master's table."
And that's what I do at the end of each and every liturgy—I snuffle around
on the altar and snap up all the leftover blessings.

I also try to take that same perspective with me into the week. I keep a
lookout for the manna that might have been missed. In each of the events

of every day, I try to keep my spiritual nose to the ground, searching for the crumbs and crusts of the bread that has come down from heaven, sniffing out the grace that might otherwise have been overlooked.

Thursday, April 19
✠ *Paphnutius, Hieromartyr*

I'm in Marble Falls. I'm sitting on the hood of our car in the parking lot of Central Texas College. There's a nice view from here: The parking lot is on the side of a hill. Below me is a field full of blue and yellow flowers. Beyond that is a thick forest of live oak and scrub cedar. Beyond that are the rolling ridges of the Hill Country.

Cynthia is inside doing a training seminar for what looks to be fifty or so child care workers. I'm sitting out here thinking about one of our former catechumens, a woman named CL. Yesterday, CL told me that, even though she has been a catechumen for two years, she is going to be confirmed in an Episcopalian parish because they will allow her to be a reader.

What she told me wasn't a surprise—and the way she told me was very gracious. Still, I was sad and disappointed. But I wasn't sure why I felt that way. It's not that the Episcopalians won, and we somehow lost. It's not even that CL has somehow let us down. I couldn't put it into words until I ran across some comments in a book by Archimandrite Vasileios called *Hymn of Entry*. We are using it in our Paschal book study, and the archimandrite states that the Church approaches other Christian groups "with the realization that [she] sees clearly and differently, and with all the pain that this brings with it."

So the sadness and disappointment I'm feeling—the sadness and disappointment our whole community will feel—are normal. It's the pain that comes from living with the truth. Because seeing clearly and maintaining that focus isn't easy. There is a price to be paid for that kind of faithfulness. It's a whole lot easier to just tell people what they want to hear; it's much more convenient to simply ignore those aspects of the Tradition that folks find objectionable. But there is also a price for making deals with reality.

And I know something about the cost of those deals. I made many of them as a United Methodist pastor; I just pray that being a reader in the Episcopal communion doesn't prove as costly for CL.

Friday, April 20
✠ *Theodore of the Hair Shirt*

Actually, I guess it's Saturday, since it's two AM.

Cynthia is in San Antonio. Katie will be graduating from nursing school soon, and she will be moving back in with us while she pays off her school loans. So Cynthia went down to help her wrap up some moving details.

But I woke up about twenty minutes ago and noticed that she wasn't in bed. A lot of times, when her neck or hands are hurting, she will just get up and watch TV for a while. I thought that's where she was, but when I went into the living room to check on her, I remembered she is spending the night with Katie. By then, I had already turned the light on, and Shelly, the dog, decided that it must be time to get up, so I had to let her out and then feed her.

We make quite a pair, Shelly and I.

Anyway, since I'm up, I figured I'd write for just a few minutes. Tonight—or, I guess, last night—we started the outreach event we've been working towards with our St. Raphael Project. I'd been praying that we would have forty new people at the event; we had six. Combined with the folks who invited those people, plus a few of the catechumens who showed up, there were close to twenty in the room. So the group was a nice size, and we actually had a good time. I think the visitors will even come back for tomorrow's—make that today's—presentations.

But why didn't we have more new people? I don't know. I do know that a lot of folks have been praying faithfully. I do know that many of our parishioners invited their friends and family members. But as I'm sitting here writing this, I keep flashing back on a line I read several weeks ago. It comes from a French author, Antoine de Saint-Exupery; I ran across it in a commentary I regularly read, and it has just stayed with me: "Prayer is fruitful to the extent that God does not answer it."

I'm still working my way through that insight, but I think it has to do with the fact that we focus our prayers too narrowly. We look for the lightning of the divine response to fall in a particular spot, and then back behind us, beyond the horizon, we hear the low rumble of thunder.

Like tonight (or last night) when I got home from the first presentation.

There was a message on my cell phone. I figured it would be from Cynthia or Katie, but it was my brother-in-law, Joe. He said they went to liturgy at the cathedral in Wichita again last Sunday, and they're going to go once again this weekend. He said they want to learn more about the Faith.

Sunday, April 22
✠ *The Myrrh-bearing Women*

It's late, and I'm tired, but it's a good kind of tired.

All the visitors came back for the presentations on Saturday. Later that afternoon, I taught the catechumen class, and we served Great Vespers.

This morning I got a slow start, but as I was driving to church, the sun came up in a bright blue sky, and that same clarity and radiance were present all through Orthros and the Divine Liturgy. When we did the forty-day memorial for Mrs. O at the end of liturgy, the light became especially focused and luminous. Then there was church school, and several people wanted to talk or do confession, but the same light was shining, and when I got home, it glowed softly while Cynthia and I had lunch.

Brendan came by around 5 PM. He's been down in San Antonio all weekend for his reserve duty. He took me out in his new car with the heated seats and temperature-sensitive steering wheel and sun roof and satellite radio and phone in the dashboard. It was fun to be with Brendan and fun to ride around in the car. I'll bless it for him in the morning, but now I'm going to bed.

Monday, April 23
✠ *George, the Great Martyr*

Brendan left this morning. I blessed his car before he took off. It was raining, but we stood out on the driveway, and I said the prayers and splashed the holy water on the car as the rainwater splashed all around us.

Today is St. George's Day, and I can never think of St. George without also thinking of Fr. George Preda. He was a Romanian archpriest. We served together at the parish in Wichita Falls. When I knew him, he was in his mid-eighties, but he was at liturgy every single Sunday morning.

Fr. George was cadaverously thin. He wore a faded black suit and a grey fedora. He carried a briefcase that held a blessing cross, his liturgy book, and the cuffs for his vestments. He would always arrive at the church during Orthros, and we could always tell when he was in the building because the smell of Vitalis would suddenly become stronger than the smell of the incense.

He spoke seven languages. He had lived in this country for more than forty years, but the older he got, the more pronounced his Romanian accent became. In fact, when we were serving together, a number of times I wondered if I hadn't somehow wandered into a bad Dracula movie.

Fr. George often lost his place in the service. We frequently had to remind him what to do next. But he was, without fail, kind and cheerful and patient. And each Sunday, at the end of the liturgy, he would do something for which I will always be grateful: After all the servers had gone to coffee hour, he would turn to me, put both his hands on my shoulders, look straight into my eyes, and say, "Be valiant!" Then he would take off his vestments, put on his black suit jacket and grey fedora, and head off to coffee hour.

The first time he did that, I was startled. The next few times he did it, I was uncomfortable. Then I just started to get annoyed. But somewhere along the way, I came to cherish that moment of blessing. Because that is what it was—a blessing. And I needed a blessing, because those were hard years: I was working three jobs; we were still new to the Faith; most of our friends and family thought we had lost our minds.

So I needed a weekly blessing. But not a wimp-ass, let's-feel-sorry-for-ourselves kind of benediction. I needed someone to take me by the shoulders and get right in my face and tell me to be brave. Which is what Fr. George did just about every Sunday for three years.

Fr. George Preda did a lot of remarkable things in his life: He traveled across Europe ministering to refugees following the Second World War; he started several parishes in this country; he taught at a number of universities; he edited quite a few liturgical books. So what he did for me in those last few years of his life doesn't even have a place on the list of his accomplishments. But it kept me going week after week, and now, every Sunday, as I commemorate him at the proskomidia, I not only say his name, I also whisper to myself, "Be valiant!"

Wednesday, April 25
✠ *Apostle and Evangelist Mark*

Today I drove over to Round Rock and took Cynthia to lunch. As I opened the door to the restaurant, we both happened to notice our reflection: I was wearing my cassock; Cynthia had on black pants and a dark blouse.

"Oh, my God," she said, "we look like the Addams Family!"

I told her that wasn't true because she was a whole lot better looking than Morticia. For some reason, we couldn't remember Gomez's name, but, as we were finishing our meal, a couple sat down in the booth across from us.

They were also dressed in black: the man had on a muscle shirt and leather biker pants; the woman had on a fringed jacket and chaps. They both had multiple tattoos and piercings, and they were both draped in chains.

They had us in the "creepy" and "kooky" categories, and they may have even been more "mysterious and spooky" than we were. But as Cynthia and I walked to the car, we agreed that, when it comes to being "altogether ooky," less is definitely more.

Friday, April 27
✠ *Symeon, the Kinsman of the Lord*

"Let us rise early at morn, and at the break of dawn . . ." It's about 5:30 in the morning. I'm waiting for Katie to arrive from San Antonio. This is the day she's moving, so I'm not going to the church for any services.

I just finished Orthros here at the house. I love this time of the morning, when the darkness is just beginning to fade, and the light is just beginning to shine. A quiet, unfolding expectancy is at work throughout the beginning of the day.

There is also freedom. There's a poem by William Stafford I used to have my middle school students memorize; I've forgotten most of the poem, but the last few lines go like this:

If you are oppressed,
Wake up about four in the morning.

Most places, you can usually be free,
At least some of the time,
If you wake up before other people.

That's so true. In fact, it was when I began to get up early on a consistent basis that my spiritual life began to really fall into place. But it's not just a matter of discipline and consistency. There is also something deeply powerful about this time of day. It's the hour when the myrrh-bearing women went to the tomb and discovered that the world had been recreated; it's the hour when the Lord God would walk in the Garden of Paradise.

Awake, O my glory; awake, O psaltery and harp;
I myself will awake at dawn.
I will confess Thee among the peoples, O Lord,
I will chant unto Thee among the nations.

Saturday, April 28
✠ *The Nine Martyrs of Cyzicus*

Yesterday, Katie and I finished cleaning her apartment, and then we loaded a U-Haul truck and drove back to Cedar Park. When we got to our house, we unloaded a few things that she will be using while she's at home. This morning, I drove the truck over to a storage facility and, with the help of some guys from the parish, unloaded everything else into a unit we have rented.

Now that I'm home, I'm thinking back over the last 24 hours, and a couple of things disturb me. To begin with, I'm good at moving. I pack well; I feel at home in a U-Haul truck. A few months ago, I wrote about the importance of staying put and living in place, and I believe all that, but I also need to own up to the fact that, deep down, I'm just a good old American nomad. While we were driving back from San Antonio, I was counting up how many moves Cynthia and I have made (ten) and how many times I moved before I even got out of high school (seven). I'll be fifty in five months, so that averages out to roughly one move every three years of my life.

So, in the words of Bilbo Baggins, the road not only "goes ever on and on"—it also runs right through my soul. But I am now also leasing a storage unit. These storage facilities are all over the place—in fact, when we were looking into renting some space, we discovered that there are five within ten miles of our home. The reason so many of these things exist is that we Americans just have too much stuff.

But I don't want to fall into that trap. Right now, we are just about the only people in our subdivision who can actually park two cars in the garage. That's because everyone else uses their garage for storage. Katie will be going down to the Hogar Raphael, an orphanage in Guatemala, for a couple of months, and we're going to keep her stuff in that facility while she's there. Then she'll move in with us, get a nursing job, and pay off the bulk of her school loans. All together, that should take about nine months. Then she will get her own apartment; we will empty out the storage unit, and our participation in that part of our super-sized American culture should be at an end.

But when I depart this life, I don't want anyone to have to clean up after me. I don't want anyone to have to go through piles of papers; I don't want anyone to have to rifle through closets and desk drawers. I may be a wanderer, but I'm going to do my best to travel light. And when I do make that last big move, there will be no boxes, no packing, no trucks, and no storage units; there will only be light and the rush of eternity and the emptiness of desire and the fullness of joy.

Sunday, April 29
✠ *Sunday of the Paralytic*

This is from *Hymn of Entry*, the text we are using in our Paschal book study:

> Life in the Divine Liturgy means conscious and complete annihila-
> tion; that is why it also means embracing a mystery which surpasses
> us. It is labor and rest. It is death and life . . . You fall into the void.

I'm glad there are people who can write like Archimandrite Vasileios; otherwise, I don't think it would be possible to communicate what the liturgy is really like.

Because standing at the altar is like standing at the edge of a high cliff. It makes you dizzy to look down, but then you feel compelled to get as close as you possibly can to the edge because the height is exhilarating, and the view is indescribable, and you feel like you could jump or fly but, of course, that also sends your stomach flip-flopping all over the place, so you get down to business and focus on the work to be done. You say the prayers and intone the exclamations and provide direction to the altar servers, and then you make an entrance or you turn and bless the congregation, and all of a sudden you realize that the edge of the precipice is twenty or thirty yards behind you, and for a moment, you end up looking at yourself looking at yourself, suspended over the abyss, and you swallow hard, and just for that moment you feel the way Wile E. Coyote in the *Roadrunner* cartoons feels after his ACME jetpack has run out of fuel. But then the music or your prayer rope or the next thing that has to be done calls you back into focus, and before you know it, you're back on the cliff and you're taking off your vestments and the energy is draining out of you, and someone wants to ask a question about fasting, and someone else needs to get an icon blessed, but your heart is still pounding in your chest, and every once in a while you tap your foot to make sure the ground beneath you is solid.

Monday, April 30
✠ *Apostle James, Brother of St. John*

Last week, we got word that WH, Cynthia's brother-in-law, died. We had been expecting the news for some time. Cynthia has spoken to EH, her sister, several times, but since WH wasn't at all religious, they aren't going to have a service. A reception will be held at the retirement facility where they lived this coming Saturday, and we are going to attend, but beyond that, it's difficult to know what to do.

I always liked WH. He was a commercial artist and a wonderful painter. He and EH were always kind and encouraging to Cynthia and me, and I've always included him in my daily prayers. But he was contemptuous of religion and dismissive of most religious people.

I read the Akathist for the Departed every Friday evening as part of Small Compline. There's a line in the service where we pray for those who have not received a Christian burial. I've always thought that referred to those people who were overtaken by circumstances beyond their control. But now, with so many people choosing to depart this life the way WH is, that intercession is taking on an entirely new meaning.

And so there's yet another reason I'm so thankful for the prayers of the Church. Even when I don't know what to say, the Church provides me with just the right words to offer at just the right time.

MAY

I love the services for this day because it was during this feast that I first knew that I had to become Orthodox.

It was while I was in seminary in the mid 1980s that I first began to seriously come to grips with the history of the Church. I took several courses in Early Christianity and did a lot of reading on my own, and what I discovered was that the Faith of the first centuries was very different from the Faith in which I had been raised. There was just a vast disconnect—not only in doctrine, but also in spirituality.

Most of my fellow seminarians dealt with that disconnect quite easily— "that was then, this is now." But I also had a number of friends who, like me, wanted to somehow bridge that gap. A few years after leaving seminary, we even formed our own community, a community that held together for over ten years. We went on retreat every few months; we supported each other and had fun together. But we also tried to learn from the experience of the ancient Church: we studied doctrine; we adopted a rule of fasting and prayer; we practiced a form of confession; we even wore albs when we were on retreat together.

Several members of the community subscribed to *Touchstone* Magazine and, in the spring of 1995, *Touchstone* sponsored a conference in Aiken, South Carolina. The conference featured an amazing line-up of speakers: Fr. Richard John Neuhaus, Bishop Kallistos Ware, Peter Kreeft, J. I. Packer. A friend of mine from the community, DT, suggested we attend the conference, so he and I drove from Dallas to Aiken.

During the trip, we talked a lot about our lives as United Methodist pastors and our membership in the community. Neither of us had any illusions about the problems facing United Methodism, but we had hoped that the community we had founded would help us resist all the careerism and cynicism and theological trendiness. However, after five years as a community, we were beginning to have our doubts: We had thought that what we had been doing was drawing on the resources of Christian history; but in fact, we were starting to realize that what our community had done was to take various elements from a living organism, rearrange them, and then expect them to come to life again. Borrowing the doctrine and spiritual disciplines of early Christianity and applying them to our lives and our work had seemed like a good idea, but it just wasn't working. Our community was functioning like a spiritual Dr. Frankenstein; we had collected all these parts and put them together, and now we were trying to artificially bring them to life.

What shocked us, though, was the realization that we were simply doing what Protestants have always done—trying to reinvent the Faith in a way that worked for our particular situation. We were, of course, aware that Christian communities existed in which the Faith of the early Church was being lived as an ongoing, daily reality. But given our current commitments, neither DT nor I could imagine how it might be possible to access that reality. As we pulled into Aiken, we joked that since John Wesley had taken the Methodists out of the apostolic succession 250 years earlier, perhaps it would be possible for us to just show up again, like a couple of ecclesiastical Rip Van Winkles: "Hey, we're back!"

That first evening of the conference, there was an Orthodox Vespers service. I had never been to an Orthodox service and was only vaguely aware that there was such a thing as the Orthodox Church. But DT and I went, and that was when my life changed completely and forever. I cannot point to a particular moment or to a specific feature of the service, but after it was over, I knew that what I had experienced was the historic Faith, that what I had participated in was the Church, and that it was a lived and present reality.

And I was completely miserable. Because I was a United Methodist pastor, and I was committed to my work, and I had a family, and, yeah, sure, my denomination had problems—lots of problems—but I certainly wasn't looking to make any major life changes. I was just attending a conference. I was just looking for some support and encouragement. I was just going to do the best I could in my particular corner of the Kingdom. But after actually having the opportunity to live the Faith for those brief moments during that service of Vespers, after experiencing how "nothing in the Church is arbitrary, or isolated or alien or mechanically added," how "each part lives with the rest in an organic unity and is embodied in the whole," how in the Church, "all things flow and proceed from the knowledge of the Holy Trinity," I knew that any reasons I might offer for not embracing that Faith as soon as I could were nothing but excuses.

That was the spring of 1995. Two years later, in the spring of 1997, Cynthia and I and the kids left United Methodism, and we were received into the Church. In August of 1999, I was ordained to the holy priesthood. Those four years were filled with fear and uncertainty and pain and all kinds of false starts and missteps. But next to marrying Cynthia, it was the best thing—the bravest thing and the most foolish thing and the truest thing—that I have ever done.

That's why I love this beautiful little feast. Because the light that shines from both Pascha and Pentecost shone on my life that day in Aiken, South Carolina, and now the Faith is no longer something I have to assemble or somehow put together on my own; it's a gift. So each year, I thank the Father, Son, and Holy Spirit for that gift and for bringing me and my family into the Church.

Thursday, May 3
✠ *Timothy and Maura, Martyrs*

I'm sitting at one of the picnic tables out behind our building. I'm looking out across the property, and I'm thinking about trees. We had a tree survey done about a year ago as part of our preparation for our new building, and there are over seventy trees on these four-and-a-half acres.

My favorite tree is the one I'm sitting under right now. It's a big live oak; I have no idea how old it is, but I can tell that it's a gentle and patient tree. We have placed several tables under it—actually, the tables are pretty much in the tree since many of its thick branches run close to the ground. The low branches also make it easy for kids to climb around in the tree, and a wooden seat has been wedged into some of the higher branches.

Psalm 1 compares the righteous man to a great tree "which is planted by the streams of the waters, which will bring forth its fruit in its season, and its leaf shall not fall." I think the prophet and psalmist David must have been sitting under this kind of tree when he wrote those words. As far as the other end of the comparison goes, he certainly wasn't thinking about the likes of me. Since Pascha, I've started reading a commentary on the Book of the Prophet Isaiah, and in today's lection was a quotation from a homily by St. Augustine. In that homily, the saint addresses his parishioners as "holy seedlings" and "fresh young plants." That's me.

Cynthia's growing some spices at the house. She's got them in three little pots on one of the windowsills. Right now, the plants are all bright green, but they're also fragile and tiny. And spiritually, that's pretty much where I am, fragile and tiny. This tree that I'm sitting under is squat and gnarled; it's been through withering heat and splintering cold; it's got bark that's rough and thick; it's probably got roots that go all over the property. But I'm a tender little sprout, just clinging to the surface of the spiritual life.

Still, I'm hoping that one day I'll grow up to be the kind of man David was writing about. In addition to that commentary on Isaiah, I've also started working my way through the *Philokalia* again. A few days ago, I saw this sentence in a homily by St. Peter of Damascus: "The knowledge and the practice of the soul's virtues have as their goal the preparation and planting of the trees of Paradise."

So who knows? Maybe the delicate shoot that is my soul will one day become a spiritual sequoia, a massive and towering tree of Paradise that grows by the River of Life.

Elder Amphilocius of Patmos once said that "whoever plants a tree plants peace, hope, and love." In light of what St. Peter wrote, I guess the reverse is also true: by practicing "the soul's virtues," I am nurturing and cultivating that tree in the Kingdom. Of course, the soul's virtues are basically just a compost mix—in fact, the way you get peace, hope, and love is by spreading the manure of this life around that spiritual sapling.

Last summer, we hired a service to fertilize our lawn. The grass was looking pretty bad, and we knew some people who had used this service, so we contracted with them to spread fertilizer several times during the year. But then I also went to Wal-Mart and bought twenty two-dollar bags of cow manure and spread it on the grass. It was pretty rank for a week or so, but boy, did our grass get green.

It works the same way with "the preparation and planting of the trees of Paradise." You gotta pile on the poop. Which is actually the very thing the gardener recommended in the parable in Luke 13: The lord of the estate wants to cut down a particular tree, but the gardener says, Lord, this year also, until I dig about it and put on manure."

Which puts a whole new perspective on all the crap in my life: When I'm wondering if the money is going to stretch all the way to the end of the month, when I'm tired of listening to people complain, when I don't seem to get anything done, when I think about all the heartaches some folks have to endure, I need to remember that those things aren't stressors; they aren't problems. They are the rich and fecund mix that is going to turn the holy seedling of my soul into the kind of tree that you can't even take in unless you step back and look straight up and crane your neck and squint your eyes, since the trunk stretches all the way into the heavens, and the branches are hidden by the clouds.

Friday, May 4
✣ *Pelagia, Martyr*

This afternoon a young couple stopped by the church. He had on a muscle shirt and shorts; she had on a T-shirt and jeans. He was from Waco; she was from Moscow. They said they had "been together for a while." They also said they had come to pray and light some candles.

Reader MT showed them to the nave. They picked up a few candles and went in. But in just a moment or two, the woman came back out. She left the building and went over to where they had parked their truck. When she came back in, she was holding a Dallas Cowboys cap. She put the cap on, adjusted her hair, made the sign of the cross, and went back into the nave.

After a little while, it was time to get ready for Vespers. I went into the nave, and the couple was still there. They hadn't yet lit any of their candles. When I came in, the woman approached me and asked which of the icons were of Christ Jesus and which were of the Mother of God. I explained all of that to her, then she went ahead and lit her candles.

All this time, the man had been sitting on one of the benches with his head in his hands. I walked over and asked if there was anything I could do. When he turned to me, it looked like he had been crying. He said that he had been looking for work and that he thought he had actually found a job, but then he was told he had failed the drug test.

We talked about that for a few minutes, and I assured them of our prayers. Then they thanked me and left.

When I was a Protestant, I would have regarded that couple's behavior as superficially religious and even downright superstitious. And even as an Orthodox priest, I wouldn't disagree entirely with that assessment. But what I have now come to see is that people are always reaching out to the Most Holy Trinity. They may not know how to do it very well—they may show up wearing official NFL headgear and have no idea as to whom they're looking at when they stand before an icon. But at least they show up; at least they are looking.

I'm thankful that St. John's is the sort of place where people can do that kind of searching. I pray that it always will be. And I pray that the Holy Spirit will continue to work in the lives of that young man and woman, and that they will show up again and do some more searching.

Sunday, May 6
✠ *Sunday of the Samaritan Woman*

Liturgy this morning was pure joy. I'm thankful that I have this experience of freedom and gratitude and happiness at the very center of each and every week. I'm especially thankful after a day like yesterday.

Cynthia and I drove up to Dallas to attend the reception for Cynthia's brother-in-law, WH. We had lunch with Cynthia's sister, EH, and it was good to be with her and to get a sense of how she's doing. After lunch, we went back to EH's apartment and looked at some of WH's art. I had forgotten how beautiful his watercolors are. Then we drove around a bit so EH would have some time to get ready for the reception.

The event itself was held in the community room of the retirement facility where EH lives. EH and WH have always been very sociable people, so just about everyone in the complex turned out. They prepared food and made nice flower arrangements for all the tables.

WH had two sons by previous marriages, and they both came to the reception. The younger son, who is my age, brought his current girlfriend; the older son was there with his wife and one of his daughters. A woman who is a cousin to EH and Cynthia was also there, and they had us all sit at a long table up at the front of the room. At the back of the room they laid out the food, and they put up several large photographs of WH.

The program began with the Pledge of Allegiance. (EH told us that's how all the events at the retirement facility begin.) EH then read a nice statement, thanking everyone for their help, and she also said a couple of touching things about WH. Then WH's older son spoke: he also thanked everyone for their care and concern. The next person to speak was a woman who lived at the facility: she introduced herself as "WH's girlfriend," and she told a funny story about herself and WH. The last person to speak was the daughter of a lady who lived at the complex; this woman was in the military—in fact, she was dressed in fatigues since she had just come from work. She talked about her recent tour of duty in Afghanistan and how WH would always listen when she wanted to talk about her experiences.

EH had asked me to pray at the end of the program. She explained that, just as the programs at the facility always begin with the Pledge, they also always end with a prayer. However, the man who typically offered the prayer was out of town, so she asked me if I would "fill in."

I went up to the microphone, which was on a low stand in front of the head table. I bent over and introduced myself. I told everyone that I wasn't sure what prayer they normally used at the conclusion of their programs, but I thought I would say one for WH. Then I asked them all to pray with me:

With the saints, give rest, O Christ, to the soul of Thy servant, in a place of brightness, a place of verdure, a place of repose, whence all sickness, sorrow, and sighing have fled away. Pardon every sin which he hath committed, whether in deed or word or thought, for Thou only art beyond sin, and Thy word is truth, and unto Thee do we ascribe glory, along with Thine Unoriginate Father, Thine all-holy, good, and life-giving Spirit, now and ever and unto ages of ages. Amen.

We then had chicken salad sandwiches and carrot sticks and brownies and some tangy yellow punch.

It was around 6 PM when we started home. However, between Waxahachie and Hillsboro, the traffic came to a complete stop. We could see flashing lights up ahead, and after a few minutes a wrecker and an ambulance drove by. Some time later, helicopters began to arrive. The accident must have been bad, because we sat there on the highway for an hour. Eventually, everyone just turned off their motors. Folks got out of their cars and wandered up and down the side of the road.

a and I rolled down the windows and put our seats back. We talked about WH and EH and the reception; we commented on everything that was going on around us. But eventually we got quiet, and the sun started to set. Cynthia dozed a bit, and I got out my prayer rope and watched the wind blowing the tall grass out on the median.

By the time the traffic began moving again, it was dark. We drove on through the night, pulled into the garage about 10:30, and went straight to bed.

But what gives all that coherence and meaning and structure is the fact that I was able to get up in the morning and serve the liturgy. Without the template of the liturgy, days like yesterday become simply random collections of experiences—some of them silly, some of them tragic, some of them just boring. But when I offer it all up on the altar, as I did this morning, then it all takes on a dignity and significance that it otherwise never would have.

Because I simply do not know what to think about the folks in the car accident or the woman who told the funny story about WH. I'm not sure how it all fits together with the chicken salad sandwiches or the prayer I offered or the fact that all those people were standing there saying the Pledge of Allegiance. I don't know what any of it has to do with all those folks standing around their cars out on the highway, and the long grass bending silently before the wind. So I fall down before the altar, and I place it all in the hands of Christ Jesus, and it begins to make sense in a way that doesn't require an explanation.

Tuesday, May 8
✠ *Apostle and Evangelist John*

Today is also St. Arsenius's Day. He's always been a big help to me.

Whenever a service is especially lengthy, or when a meeting drags on, or when the line for confession is long, I often find myself wishing I were somewhere else. St. Arsenius was a monk in Egypt, and whenever he would lose his focus, he would always ask himself, "Why did you come to the desert, Arsenius?" So I ask myself a similar question: Why did you become a priest, Wilcoxson?

I don't really ask the question. It just pops into my head whenever I start to get bored or distracted or ungrateful. And I think that happens because the holy father is praying for me.

Wednesday, May 9
✣ *Prophet Isaiah*

Things have been pretty busy the last couple of days. The semester is winding down over at the community college, so I have one last round of papers to grade. I've got to write a column for the newspaper. There's a parish council meeting on Sunday, and that always means extra emails and phone conversations. The book study meets tonight. Then there have been a lot of people who have just needed to talk about the pain in their lives.

But this afternoon I got to spend time with two young people who have been visiting the parish. Their curiosity and wonder were energizing.

And on the way home, I drove past several highway embankments that were covered with tiny yellow flowers. It looked like sunlight had been crumbled up and scattered across the grass.

Thursday, May 10
✣ *Apostle Simon*

I'm in Bastrop. Cynthia is doing a training at the employment office. I'm sitting outside in a nice little wooden gazebo.

It rained on us pretty heavily as we were driving here, but now that storm has moved off to the east, and the setting sun is shining on the back side of the tall thunderclouds.

They look like a whole range of white and massive mountains; there are vast canyons filled with air and light, and deep, shadowed chasms that are still rain-swollen and storm-dark.

Earlier, I was working on my sermon. There's a road in front of the employment office, and I walked down that road until it came to a dead end right beside a pasture. There was a fence covered with primroses, and on the other side of the fence, six young horses. I thought I would try the homily out on them.

At first, I think they were a bit startled. They looked at me for a few minutes, tails completely still, eyes blank, and grass hanging out of their mouths. Then they went on about their business, one by one moving slowly across the pasture. The last one to walk away was a pretty mare; she had white markings on her legs, and before she followed the others, she braced those legs, lifted her tail, and peed in my direction; it was a solid, steady, steaming stream that went on and on and on and on.

I'm hoping the sermon works better on Sunday.

Friday, May 11
✠ *Cyril and Methodius, Equals to the Apostles*

I just got home from the N family slava. It's a tradition they have borrowed from the Serbs, and they get better at it every year. We do a Litya, and then they serve everyone dinner. This year I ended up at a table that was mostly single guys, so we ended up talking about guy stuff—music, movies, and every once in a while, politics. It was a very enjoyable—and just a naturally Orthodox—evening.

Cynthia stayed at the house in order to officially welcome Katie home. Our daughter is now a real-live nurse graduate. She'll take her RN exam in a couple of weeks, but the whole thing has just kind of snuck up on me. She's been working towards it for so long, and then, all of a sudden, there-it-is-she's-done.

Cynthia is a good mother, though, and she wasn't in the least caught off guard. She made signs on the computer:

YOU DID IT!

WE'RE SOOO PROUD OF YOU!

and had me tape them up around the house before I left. Right now the two of them are in the living room watching a couple of chick movies, and they were kind enough to tell me I didn't have to hang around. So I came in here and read the Midnight Office, and then I thought I would write a little, but now that I'm done with that, I think I'm going to turn in.

Sunday, May 13
✠ *Sunday of the Blind Man*

It has, as usual, been a busy weekend.

We did Mother's Day yesterday. Katie and I got up early and cleaned the house. Then we took Cynthia out to a nice restaurant for what we thought would be an early lunch. But apparently, brunch is a really big deal in Austin, so the restaurant was packed out, and the girl at the hostess station expressed utter dismay at the fact that we didn't have a reservation (although she managed to do that in a way that still allowed her to remain remarkably aloof; we were all impressed). Nevertheless, we got a table without any problem and had a good time.

There were a number of confessions last night, but there were also quite a few people missing at liturgy this morning. Church school was fun on a number of levels: our "guitar guys," JD and RK, do a wonderful job every week (this session the featured song was "Seek Ye First the Kingdom of God"; I told them it made me feel like 1974 all over again). Also, the young people in the class are remarkably candid and relaxed. Then it was on to the parish council.

I'm tremendously proud of our council. That's because it's actually conciliar—in the most Orthodox sense of the word. I know many priests who have conflicted relationships with their councils. I know many councils don't do much of anything. But that's not how things work in our community. The council and I work well together; I actually enjoy going to the meetings (well, as much as anyone can enjoy going to a meeting—but still, that's saying a lot). And thank God, no one on the council has any interest in just sitting around and talking; everyone knows all kinds of stuff has to happen in order to keep our community going.

So everyone files a report, via email, before the meeting. We come to the meetings well-informed, and we stick to the agenda once we are there. The discussions are honest and healthy and helpful. We know how to fight; we know how to have fun. That's all the result of several years of hard work, but I'm just thankful that I'm part of a community that was willing to do that kind of work.

Next Sunday we'll be commemorating the First Ecumenical Council. It may sound like a silly exaggeration, but I would put our parish council right up there with the holy fathers who gathered at Nicea. After all, as Archimandrite Vasileios says, "Every problem of the Church is the problem of the personal salvation of each of the faithful." The Nicene Fathers discussed the formula for determining the date of Pascha; today we discussed how folks should be reimbursed for the expenses they incur while volunteering for the parish. But it's all about salvation. Every little detail. It's all about our salvation.

Monday, May 14
✠ *Isidore of Chios, Martyr*

Every week I have this fantasy that I'll get some time to myself. I start out the week thinking that if I work hard enough and schedule things effectively, then all the prayers will get said, and all the visits will be made, and all the emails will get answered, and all the sermons and columns and articles will be finished up, and the lawn and the bills and the laundry will all get squared away, and then I'll have an hour or two to do just what I want to do: read, watch a movie, go to the library, whatever.

That happens once or twice a year. And I'm starting to realize that's a good thing. Because, after all, time doesn't really belong to me. I've been given a certain number of hours on this planet, and since I'll be fifty in a few months, I'm actually burning through them pretty quickly. But every one of them is a gift from the Father, Son, and Holy Spirit, and I can either turn around and give them to someone else, or I can use them on myself.

And truthfully, it's always healthier, it's always more fulfilling, to give it away. I guess that's what our Lord and Master meant when He said that it's more blessed to give than to receive. After all, I have a wonderful job, a job I really love. I have a family that is even more wonderful. So this idea of "me time" is just a demonic trap to make me work even harder and enjoy it even less.

In this morning's lection from my Isaiah commentary, St. Ambrose put it this way: "No one can say that he can acquire more by his own efforts than what is granted him by the generosity of God." I'm not going to get more time because I work harder or smarter—but I will enjoy the time I have if I use it the way the Most Holy Trinity intends that it be used. Because, let's face it, the people with the most "me time," the people who have no responsibilities and no relationships that eat into their time, are either homeless or in nursing facilities. And they're not happy at all. They just wish that someone would come around and claim a little of their time.

Tuesday, May 15
✠ Pachomius the Great

Tonight at Vespers we started the Leavetaking of Pascha.

Tomorrow, we will give the feast back to the Most Holy Trinity, but it's no accident that the Paschal troparion, "Christ is Risen," ends on an unresolved note. It always sounds as if the song is going to start all over again. But that's because it does.

In fact, the hymn never ends because Pascha never ends. It's like George Herbert once wrote:

Can there be any day but this,
Though a million suns to shine endeavor?
We count o'er three hundred, but we miss;
There is but one, and that one, ever.

Wednesday, May 16
✠ Leavetaking of Pascha

Today is Brendan's nameday. Brendan the Navigator is a good patron for our Brendan. Both chose wild and wandering paths to sanctity; both of them are brave and adventurous; both of them have bright red hair. And I know that the same Spirit which guided St. Brendan through all kinds of perils and temptations and wonders will also guide our Brendan in all his voyaging, bringing him at last to the fair and calm haven that is the good will of the Most Holy Trinity.

Thursday, May 17
✠ *Feast of the Ascension*

This has always been one of my favorite feasts, although I'm not sure why. I think it may have something to do with all the metaphysical paradoxes that are involved in the Ascension: Christ Jesus returns to heaven, although in His Divine Nature, He never left:

> The Father receiveth Him whom He had eternally with Him in His bosom . . .

Christ Jesus has a body like ours, and that body is now at the right hand of the Father who is bodiless . . .

> Thou wast taken up in glory from the Mount of Olives, O Christ God, in the presence of Thy disciples, and didst sit down at the right hand of the Father, O Thou Who dost fill all things with Thy Divinity.

Christ Jesus has departed from us, but He is with us always . . .

> Thou didst ascend in glory, O Christ our God, departing not hence, but remaining inseparable from us and crying unto them that love Thee: I am with you and no one can be against you.

Those realities delight my mind—but it's not as if they were theological brain-teasers. I've never enjoyed Rubik's cubes and crossword puzzles and those sorts of things. I figure if I want to tackle something complicated and perplexing, I can always balance my checkbook. I love the mysteries of the Ascension because they fill my mind with wonder.

After liturgy, I went with several members of the building committee to meet with a number of representatives from the city. This was our initial planning conference for the new facility. There was lots of talk about setbacks and rights of way and hammerhead turnarounds and impervious cover. And it all had a kind of Rubik's cube/crossword puzzle/it's-Saturday-morning-

and-that-means-it's-time-to-balance-the-checkbook quality to it. Not too long ago, I read these words in the book we are using for our Paschal study:

> This holy intoxication and sober calm creates, with awe and with love for mankind, the architecture of the Church. . . . The unity of the faith and the communion of the Holy Spirit is present throughout this liturgical world as it lives, prays, builds, paints, and sings.

And, I suppose, as it talks about water quality and sidewalk escrow accounts. So the same wonder that accompanies my contemplation of the Ascension should characterize my approach to the building program.

To help with that, I just finished writing down a list of all the challenges, problems, and issues that were raised in the meeting, and I'm going to pray for them daily. I'm going to pray that they will be resolved quickly and easily, but I'm also going to pray for an Ascension perspective on the whole project. I want to be able to see the new facility from the best vantage point of all—from "where Christ sits at the right hand of the Father."

Saturday, May 19
✛ *Patrick, Hieromartyr*

We just got back from Katie's graduation in San Antonio. My father was in San Marcos, accompanying my younger sister, Alice, and her two boys to a piano competition. We picked him up at their hotel, and then we drove down to Trinity University, where the graduation was held.

Brendan was in San Antonio for his monthly reserve duty, and his girlfriend D was in town as well, so they met us at the graduation. We all got to sit together and watch Katie walk across the stage. She looked great in her cap and gown, but she was also third from the end out of 175 graduates. So we all decided that if she ever starts to seriously consider further education, she should also seriously consider marrying someone further up the alphabet.

The ceremony itself was pretty raucous. It started out quietly enough, and things were fairly decorous while the PhDs and MSNs received their diplomas. But once the BSN graduates started walking the stage, the whole event took on a WWF quality: there were airhorns and cowbells and signs and shrieks and groups of people dancing and doing the Wave. Lots of pride. Very little dignity.

After the ceremony, we went to a nice Italian restaurant that Katie had picked out. My father bought us all dinner. My mother had stayed in Dallas for my nephew's high school graduation, but she sent Katie an antique brooch that my father had bought for her when they were stationed in Scotland back in the fifties. Brendan and D gave Katie a PDA that can be used to download medication reference resources. We passed the presents around and ate a lot and talked a lot, and then we had to get on the road. We dropped my father back at his hotel in San Marcos and made it into Cedar Park by 8 PM.

Sunday, May 20
✠ *The Holy Fathers of the First Council*

This morning I was back out on the property practicing my sermon. When I was done, I looked down, and there was a large tortoise between my feet. I wasn't sure how long he had been there (he was hiding in his shell), but I went ahead and picked him up because I didn't want him to get run over by a car (our parking lot is small, and lots of people end up parking under the trees).

I walked over to the edge of our property, and then went a few yards into the thick brushy trees. As I was setting the tortoise down, movement exploded all around me. I couldn't see anything, but I could hear several deer racing through the branches and leaping through the tall grass. The sudden noise startled me, and I ended up stumbling over some cactus and ripping the hem out of my cassock.

The Lives of the Saints are filled with the stories of holy men and women who, through their ascetic striving, were able to restore the innocence of Eden and interact with animals the way Adam did. But, to paraphrase Mr. Dylan, that ain't me. I was trying to help the tortoise, but he's probably in counseling now—and the deer are most likely telling stories about their narrow escape from the vicious, flesh-eating human.

So that got me to thinking: If, despite our best efforts, our relationship with the animals is marked by fear and misunderstanding, do the angels encounter the same sort of thing when they try to assist us? How many sightings of ghosts and aliens and Bigfoot-type creatures had their origin in some poor guardian angel just trying to do his job? How many times have I reacted to angelic intervention in the same way the tortoise and the deer responded to my attempt to help?

It will be interesting to read the file my guardian angel has kept on me.

Entry: Tried to help subject with spiritual solace, but he remained in bed, under the covers, only occasionally sticking his head out.

Entry: Attempted to make contact with subject as he was sitting on front porch. He got up slowly and then walked quickly into the house. He later appeared at the window with a phone, telling his wife he thought he heard someone "moving around out there."

Monday, May 21
✠ Constantine and Helena

Brendan and his girlfriend, D, spent the night with us last night. It was unexpected, and so we had to scramble a bit to figure out what we were going to eat and where everyone was going to sleep, but as it turns out, we had a very nice time.

Brendan and D have been a couple (or they've been going out or have been together—I don't even know how to describe relationships between single men and women anymore) for a year and a half now, but we've only been with her twice before. Previously our impression had been that she is personable and intelligent and has a nice sense of humor. That was confirmed with this visit, but we also learned that she genuinely appears to care for Brendan. In fact, she described him in ways that left Cynthia and Katie and me incredulous; she used words like "sweet" and "thoughtful" and "patient."

It's not that Brendan is never sweet or thoughtful or patient when he is around us. But if Katie and Cynthia and I were to make a list of Brendan's good qualities, those wouldn't be in the top ten. The good qualities we see are his strength, his dogged perseverance, his honesty, his (sometimes stunning) generosity, his loyalty to his friends, his quick appreciation for irony, and his impatience with all things fake and superfluous. But apparently some other things should be added to the list.

After Brendan and D left this morning, I got to thinking about how hard it is to be a different person. It's even harder to be a different person at home, because all those relationships are based on the person you once were. The way everything works at home, the very air you breathe when you are there, just slowly but surely turns you back into the person you've always been.

So we need to cut Brendan some slack. I need to stop expecting him to be the person he has always been and give him a chance to be the person he is when he's with D. She obviously brings out the best in him. We should too.

Tuesday, May 22
✠ *Basiliscus, Martyr*

It's 9 PM. I'm sitting in a Walgreen's pharmacy waiting on a prescription.

For the past couple of weeks, Cynthia has been making on-site visits to child care centers that are located in elementary schools. At some point during those visits, she contracted pink eye. Her eyes have been bothering her for several days now, but we finally figured out what it was earlier this evening. Thank God, she was able to get an appointment at an after-hours clinic. We drove to the clinic together, and we didn't have to wait too long before she saw the doctor. Cynthia's at home now; I'm waiting on the prescription. Maybe I'm also waiting to get pink eye. We'll see.

In this week's chapter from *Hymn of Entry,* Archimandrite Vasileios writes:

> In the end, the faithful will thank God only for great suffering, for complete perplexities. In other words, everything will be swept away by the fire of praise. And the cooling wave of unbearable fire will leap up from the painful occurrences, the temptations and thorns we did not wish to undergo, considering them obstacles, a curse, making our lives miserable.

That sounds a little dramatic when applied to pink eye, but if it doesn't work at all levels, then it just doesn't work at all. So, here goes: Thank you, Christ Jesus, for this mess. Thank you for after-hours clinics and doctors and nurses and prescriptions and insurance. Thank you for Cynthia, for the work she does, and for her determination to keep going. Thank you for the possibility that I might get to share in her misery. Thank you for all the inconvenience. Thank you for the fatigue. Thank you for the expense. Thank you for the Lou Rawls song they're playing over the loudspeaker—which isn't exactly the fire of praise the archimandrite had in mind, but it's pretty good accompaniment for my lame little litany.

Thank you, Christ Jesus.

✠ *Friday, May 25*
✠ *Third Discovery of the Head of the Forerunner*

St. Isaac of Syria once wrote that "words are an instrument of the present age; silence is the mystery of the age to come." Apparently, though, the Father, Son, and Holy Spirit feel that the best way in which to use these instruments of the present age is through poetry—because that is the primary way in which They communicate to us.

Of course, Holy Scripture contains many different kinds of writing: law codes and letters and histories and gospels and collections of proverbs. But a significant portion of Scripture is simple poetry, and even those histories and letters and gospels and proverbs contain a tremendous amount of poetic material. Apparently, then, something about poetry makes it especially suited for divine communication.

Which makes all the more frightening the realization that most Orthodox communities no longer read the appointed psalms and canons in worship. The reasons typically have to do with time: including these materials makes the services too long. But if poetry is the primary way in which the Father, Son, and Holy Spirit speak to us, then we need to be familiar with that mode of communication. And the only way we can be truly familiar with the poetry of Holy Scripture and the poetry of the Church is by listening to it.

Even reading these materials at home is a second-best substitute. Occasionally, I will hear someone attempt to justify the absence of psalms and canons from the services with this observation: "Well, they can always buy a Menaion and read them at home—or, hey, they can probably even find it all online for free." But poetry isn't meant to be read silently. It should be read aloud or chanted. That's why we don't have service books at St. John's. Because we simply want people to learn how to listen.

In addition to all that, without extensive, firsthand experience with poetry, we will invariably wind up expecting the Father, Son, and Holy Spirit to speak to us on our own limited terms. And that means we will try to funnel all divine speech into the modes with which we are most comfortable:

the study guide and the theological treatise. Neither of those forms appears in Holy Scripture, and, until quite recently, they were only rarely used in the Church. That's because they oversimplify; they flatten everything out into a one-dimensional rationality, and that's the point when we turn into fundamentalists.

Of course, there is another possibility: If we no longer listen to the psalms and canons, then we will no longer have a context in which to interpret these materials. The services actually provide a highly disciplined setting in which all sorts of powerful images can be safely handled. But if we try to use these images or interpret these materials apart from the liturgical setting, the end result is poetic promiscuity. That occurs whenever we use the images inappropriately or whenever we try to manufacture our own. This is precisely why theologians like Bulgakov and Florensky are now so popular among feminists. Those priests were formed and fashioned by the services of the Church; most of the people who now read their books were not. But, as Charles Williams has said, "when words escape from verse" and symbols become "autonomous," then, spiritually, they become "deadly."

The ongoing reading of the Psalter and the canons in the services can save us from all this. The Father, Son, and Holy Spirit speak to us in poetry because, whether we know it or not, poetry is the meter of our lives. The verses we speak in our services reverberate in the blood-beat of our hearts and in the pulsing power of the sun and in the rolling rhythm of the tides. All the muscles of creation are at work in those words, and we must not try to diminish the energy they produce—neither can we afford to simply loose that energy on the world. It is the services that should give us access to the energy of the images, and it is the services that should protect us from it.

Monday, May 25
✠ *Monday of the Holy Spirit*

Today is also Memorial Day, so Cynthia has a holiday. Reader MT and I also took the day off, since this past weekend was so busy. And it was nice to sleep in. There was some slow, steady rain and some far-off thunder. The house was cool and dark and quiet.

Now I'm sitting on the hood of the car. It's parked in the shade of a tree on the far end of one of the lots at the mall. After Cynthia and I got up, we took care of a few things around the house, then we went out and got some lunch. Cynthia had a couple of things to return at the mall, so I thought I'd find a spot and do some writing.

The services this weekend were perfect. On Saturday morning, we offered the liturgy for the departed. When we pray for the dead, we are expressing the kind of commitment St. Paul describes in 1 Corinthians 13: "Love bears all things, believes all things, hopes all things, endures all things. Love never ends."

There's a quiet confidence in that hymn, a deep-down solid kind of strength, and that's what the liturgy was like on Saturday morning: our community gathered to pray for those who have gone on before us, because in Christ, our community, our commitment, our love for each other will never end.

Katie and Cynthia and I got some lunch together after the liturgy, but by 3 PM, I was back up at the church. I heard the life-confession of one of our catechumens, KS, and he and I also visited for a while. At 5 PM we had a good group for Orthodox Instruction. Great Vespers for Pentecost was . . . well, it was Pentecostal in the fullest sense of the word. The service was filled with a calm exhilaration. All the chanters were there, and they were singing well. Lots of people were in the nave, and they had full hearts and strong voices. But instead of producing some kind of shrill excitement, all that intensity was focused within the service, and within that living, liturgical structure, time became a single, still point, and worship wasn't something we were doing—it was who we were, and we became something that language can't convey. We became praise.

It was the same way yesterday morning. At the end of a fiery and contemplative Orthros, we chrismated two catechumens, KS and RC. Then the nave filled up, and the music began to swell, and all through the liturgy I felt as I did when I was four, and my father was teaching me how to ride a bike. Or rather, I felt as I did when everything finally kicked in—that all-of-a-sudden moment when the steering, the balance, and the pedaling become the rush of freedom.

The street on which we lived also circled a small park. I remember my father running alongside the bike and then giving me a big push, and I launched out into that uncertainty pedaling as fast as I could. And I didn't fall. And then I realized I wasn't going to fall, and the wind was on my face, and I was flying past parked cars and other kids, and I hit that circle and rode around the park—all the way around the park—and then I came back and pulled up in front of our house, gasping for breath, my heart pounding, a big grin on my face, and then a moment later, I was off again.

And that's how liturgy works on a great feast like Pentecost. The angels help us up and get us going, and they keep us steady for a while, but then, before you know it, we're on our own, flying through the heavenlies. The wind of the Spirit lifts our hearts, and we can barely keep up, our feet won't stay on the pedals because the wheels that are propelling us are the wheels of the four living creatures, the creatures the prophet Ezekiel saw, and of course they go wherever the Spirit goes, wheel within wheel, straight, without turning, lightning-flash fast, and we are riding along with them and on them and through them, soaring in the freedom for which Christ has set us free.

It was like that all day long—not just in the liturgy, but at the pot-luck and in the talent show as well. We just raced through the celebration and rolled through the feast, exulting in the glorious liberty of the children of God.

Shoot, a few times during the talent show we even let go of the handlebars.

Tuesday, May 29
✠ *Theodosia of Tyre, Martyr*

I'm sitting here at my desk, looking over what I wrote yesterday at the mall. I'm sure that, to some, it's going to appear a bit much. But I'm going to stick by it. Because freedom is not the sum total of all our options and choices; it's not defined or qualified by our abilities or our circumstances. In its essence, freedom is one of the energies of the Most Holy Trinity; it is a gift of the Spirit. And the only way to directly experience freedom as a pure, spiritual reality, as ontological boundlessness, is by participating in the Divine Liturgy.

Thursday, May 31
✠ *Hermias, Martyr*

When we went to Katie's graduation, Brendan's girlfriend D took several family pictures for us. Katie's now using one of them as the screensaver on her laptop. The picture turned out well: nice composition, great color, sharp focus. But Brendan forgot to take off his ultra-dark wraparound sunglasses.

So in the photo, there's this plump priest with a muddy brown beard; there's a startlingly attractive woman with a fun smile; there's a joyful young lady whose red hair looks even more radiant up against her black cap and gown; and then there's this tall, well-dressed, very buffed, super-cool blind guy.

JUNE

Friday, June 1
✣ *Justin the Philosopher, Martyr*

This morning during Orthros it started to storm. Thunder and lightning and rain rattling back and forth across the metal roof of the altar. So we joined our praises with the storm's hymn until it passed by, and when I walked out to the car, everything was dripping and silent and holy.

Saturday, June 2
✣ *Nicephorus the Confessor*

Earlier this week, when I went to the grocery store, I bought several large sunflowers. I put them in a tall vase, and then I set the vase on the counter that divides our kitchen from our living room.

They've been there for several days now, lighting up the room with their soft flames. They look like a Van Gogh constellation of golden stars, and every once in a while, a petal, like a slow, silent spark, will fall onto the counter or the floor.

Sunday, June 3
✣ *All Saints*

This morning, at the beginning of liturgy, we had a baptism, and at the end of liturgy, we did a memorial service.

The baptism was for SM and KM's infant son, SM. The memorial was for Mrs. O—her ninety-day service. So there was birth and there was death, but in the Church, those experiences are transformed into one single reality—resurrection. And in offering those services, our community is not simply marking significant life events or ritualizing important transitions. We are ourselves living the resurrection. We have been "born of water and the Spirit," just like SM and KM's baby boy. And, like Mrs. O, "we are dead, and our life is hidden with Christ in God."

Monday, June 4
✠ Metrophanes, Patriarch of Constantinople

Today Katie is taking her RN exam. Brendan has a job interview. So this morning, Cynthia went to Orthros with me. As it turned out, it was just the two of us; I did the service, and Cynthia prayed, but at the end, in the Gospel reading, Christ Jesus spoke to us. The lesson was from Matthew 7:

> What man is there among you who, if his son asks for bread, will give him a stone? Or if he asks for fish, will he give him a serpent? If you, then, being evil, know how to give good gifts to your children, how much more will your Father who is in heaven give good things to those who ask Him?

Tuesday, June 5
✠ Dorotheus of Tyre, Hieromartyr

I'm teaching one section of composition at the community college this summer. The class meets on Tuesday and Thursday evenings. I like night classes because we always have a good mix of older and younger students.

Several of the men in this particular section are probably close to my age. One of them is Hispanic. He sits in the back of the room. He is a diesel engine mechanic, and he always comes to class in a dark blue uniform shirt that has his name printed on the front of it.

The other night we were preparing for the first essay of the semester. It's a short personal experience piece. I asked the man—his name is RH—what he was going to write about.

"I have two little girls," he said, "I think I'll write about them."

I did the composition instructor thing and encouraged him to narrow the topic.

"What kinds of things do they enjoy doing?" I asked.

"They like to color in those books," he said, moving his hand back and forth with an imaginary crayon in it.

"And do they tear the pictures out and give them to you?"

He smiled and nodded.

"And do you take them to work and magnetize them to the tool drawer?"

He shook his head. His lip quivered just a tiny little bit.

"No," he said. "I fold them up and put them under my pillow."

And that settles it.

I don't care what anyone says.

This world is a beautiful place.

Wednesday, June 6
✠ *Hilarion the New*

There are now birds in our subdivision. When we first moved in, five years ago, there were none. I guess the trees are tall enough, and the hedges are now thick enough for them to nest in.

There are barn swallows and mockingbirds, and, of course, the occasional grackle. I've even seen a few blue jays and a robin.

Anyway, I'm glad they're here. I wouldn't want to live somewhere that birds don't want to live.

Thursday, June 7
✠ *Theodotus of Ancyra, Martyr*

This is the fourth day of the Apostles' Fast. During this fast, I always do the mid-hours along with the regular hours. Those little services contain some wonderful prayers, like this one from the mid-hour of the third hour:

> Grant Thou speedy and lasting consolation unto Thy servants, O
> Jesus, when our spirits are despondent. Be Thou not parted from
> our souls when they be in affliction; be Thou not far from our minds

when we are in perils, but do Thou ever anticipate our needs. Draw nigh unto us, draw nigh, O Thou Who art everywhere present, and even as Thou art ever with Thine Apostles, thus do Thou also unite Thyself unto us who long for Thee, O Compassionate One, that, being united with Thee, we may praise and glorify Thine All-Holy Spirit.

Katie got the word yesterday that she passed her RN exam, and she was also hired at one of the local emergency rooms—all of this in the midst of getting ready to leave for Guatemala for three months (the nuns at the Hogar Raphael have told her she's going to be the "school nurse"). So there has been a lot of chaos at our house and even more rejoicing.

Brendan is coming through tonight on his way to his two-week reserve tour. He'll be flying out to Georgia tomorrow. His interview didn't go as well as he had hoped, but the commander went ahead and passed his file up to the next level. So that part of the story is still ongoing.

But wherever we all are in this story, and however the chaos may finally unfold, it will be good to be together tonight, and to be with the One who is ever present with us, and yet is always also drawing nigh unto our hearts.

Saturday, June 9
✠ *Cyril of Alexandria, Columba of Iona*

Christ Jesus must have been listening on Thursday when I wrote down that prayer—especially the part about not parting from us in affliction and anticipating our needs.

Brendan arrived Thursday afternoon as planned, and he and Cynthia and Katie went out to dinner while I was at school. Both Brendan and Katie were scheduled to leave early yesterday morning, but during dinner, Katie got to feeling badly. She had been to the doctor almost two weeks earlier, but she felt she needed to go back (especially since she will be out of the country for several months).

So after dinner, Cynthia and Katie went to an after-hours clinic and then to the pharmacy to drop off Katie's new prescription. Brendan went back to the house. I got home close to 8:30 PM, and he was getting ready for bed since he had to be in San Antonio by 7 AM. We only talked a few minutes, and then he turned in. Cynthia and Katie didn't get back until around 9:30.

We then had a long discussion about whether Katie should leave in the morning. At first, she was determined to get on the plane, but she eventually changed her mind when we pointed out that it wasn't going to help the nuns if she got down there and they had to take care of her.

I went back out and got Katie's prescription, and then we all got to bed around midnight. Brendan was up at 4 AM, getting a shower and packing his stuff. I got up and gave him a hug as he was leaving. It wasn't at all the kind of family time I was hoping for, but for now at least, everything seems to have worked out.

Speaking of family, EH, Cynthia's sister, stayed with us last night. She was down in Kerrville to scatter her husband WH's ashes, and she stopped by on her way back to Dallas. She came to Vespers last night and bought a teapot at the bookstore. Cynthia cooked a nice dinner, and we stayed up late and talked (actually not too terribly late, but we were pretty tired after the short night we had on Thursday).

EH seems to be doing well. WH was sick for a long time, and she had many months to prepare, but she is also just a cheerful person. She had to leave today right after lunch, but she said she would come and stay with us again later this summer.

Sunday, June 10
✠ Alexander and Antonina, Martyrs

This morning, between Orthros and Divine Liturgy, we chrismated MH. She had a white veil on her head and a big smile on her face. At the end of liturgy, we blessed Fr. Deacon BL and Shamassy JL on their thirtieth wedding anniversary. They had gold crowns, and after the blessing, they kissed each other.

The whole day was like that. Happy people. Holy work.

Monday, June 11
✠ Bartholomew and Barnabas, Apostles

A few days ago, I was writing about all the birds in our subdivision, but this afternoon, as I was leaving the house to go to Vespers, a buzzard was standing right in the middle of the street. I pulled up to within a few feet of him, but he didn't move until I honked the horn. Then he just shrugged his wings and waddled over to the curb.

It was then that I noticed two other buzzards on the roof of a house. They were sitting together on the ridgeline, all hunched over, watching the buzzard who was down on the curb. As I drove away, I glanced in the rearview mirror, and that bird was already walking back out into the middle of the street.

They were all gone by the time I got back—and I never did see any evidence that anything had died. Perhaps they were just having a little buzzard fun. Maybe it was a gang thing: Y'know, let's go creep out some of those subdivision humans.

Tuesday, June 12
✠ *Onuphrious the Great, Peter of Athos*

I can't say that I actually enjoy fasting, but it does help me pray better. St. Peter of Damascus talks about "body prayer," and that's how fasting works for me—especially when it comes to intercession. When I'm fasting, I don't just think about the folks I need to pray for; I feel their emptiness in my emptiness, I experience their hunger in my hunger. And that's what prayer is like at the most basic level—emptiness and hunger that are offered up to the Most Holy Trinity.

My stomach rumbles, and with my stomach, I remember those who are sick: the wife and mother who will soon have surgery for breast cancer; the wife and mother who is waiting to find out if she has breast cancer; the woman who is in the end stages of breast cancer; the woman who has lupus; the women who have fibromyalgia; the young man who has stepped on a nail; the daughter who has kidney stones; the granddaughter who is autistic. I drink a big glass of water to stop the stomach rumbles, and with each gulp, I remember the widows and the widower and the single parents who are part of our community. When my head feels a bit light, I offer that lightness up for the couples who are fighting and the kids who can't seem to get their lives together. As I sit down to clear my head, I offer up that lack of focus for all those who have stressful jobs and all those who can't find a job.

That makes it all sound a bit mechanical. But the reality is much more organic. When I fast, I am needy in a way that goes straight to the core of what it means to be human. And in that need, I can better appreciate, I can better understand, I can better identify with the needs of others. Which, of course, is just what Christ Jesus has done in the Incarnation. So I put on fasting the way our Lord and Master put on our human nature; I empty myself the way He emptied Himself; I hunger for that for which He hungers—the salvation and healing of my people.

Wednesday, June 13
✠ Aquilina, Martyr

This evening, I was sitting in the altar, listening as AL read the psalms, and a gecko was sunning himself on the windowpane just opposite me. He didn't move the entire time, but this tension, this energy, just radiated from him.

I wish I were like that when I pray. Still, and yet absolutely, totally, completely focused and alive.

Saturday, June 16
✠ Tikhon, Bishop of Amathus

Over the last several days, I've spent at least twenty hours in the car. I've been to the Parish Life Conference and back, and I'm absolutely worn out, but there were many good things about the trip.

The drive, for one. I was in the car by myself, and I didn't bring any CDs or play the radio, so it was just hours and hours of silence. There was road noise, and I stopped a few times to get gas or something to eat, but other than that, it was just me and my prayer rope and rain on the windshield, and that odd combination of flying through landscapes while also sitting still.

The keynote address was given by Dr. Tristram Engelhardt. He's a brilliant man; I've read his book on bioethics, but I've never heard him speak. In person, he looks like a combination of Gene Wilder and Ho Chi Minh; he sounds like what I would imagine General George Pickett would sound like if he were alive today and giving lectures. Dr. Engelhardt spoke on the subject of the culture wars, and he managed to be both scholarly and pointedly frank. He even used the word *masturbation* twice. (The first time he used the word, Fr. JH, the priest sitting next to me, turned and whispered, "Did he just say what I think he said?")

It is also always good to see the other priests in our diocese. I don't know many of them well, but they are men of dignity and piety and learning. To be sure, there is some joking around, and every once in a while, conversations about what is going on in the archdiocese become gossip about what is going on in the archdiocese; but on the whole, they conduct themselves with a cheerful gravity, and I'm just thankful they let me hang out with them.

Then there is Bishop Basil. He sets the tone for the entire event. He is friendly, but he doesn't pretend to be everyone's best friend. He is enthusiastic, but never emotional. He is relaxed during the meals, focused during the meetings, and prayerful during the services, and that is as it should be.

But the best thing about the whole trip was pulling into the driveway, stepping out into the evening, walking through the front door, and feeling Cynthia's arms around my neck and hearing her voice in my ear: "I really missed you. I'm really glad you're home."

Sunday, June 17
✠ *Third Sunday after Pentecost*

Today is also Father's Day. When I went into my office, I found a nice card that Cynthia had put on my desk. My parents were in San Antonio for the weekend, and they drove up for the liturgy this morning. We only got to visit briefly during coffee hour because they wanted to get back on the road, but it was a blessing to be with them at the Eucharist and to hug them afterwards.

Katie left for Guatemala early Friday morning, and we agreed she's only going to call on Monday evenings, so I won't hear from her until then. Brendan called after coffee hour, though: He was out in the field waiting on the next helicopter, and he hadn't had a shower in five days, but he told me he loved me and that he would take me to a movie when he came back through town.

There are an awful lot of dad things that I've never done very well, but every single Sunday night, while I'm reading Small Compline, I also read the

Akathist to the Mother of God, Nurturer of Children. My kids are grown now, but that doesn't make the dad role any easier. I know it's not my job to give them advice or evaluate what they're doing. And I don't want to project my worries and fears onto them. But they're still my kids, so every Sunday night, I place them before the Mother of God, because she and her Son know how to love people in a way that creates freedom—freedom from dependency and expectations, freedom from the past, freedom for growth and maturity, freedom for the future.

Monday, June 18
✠ Leontius, Martyr

Katie called from Guatemala. She said everyone has been welcoming, but so far, she feels pretty useless. I told her she was right on schedule. If you're going to do ministry well, it takes a long time to get ready for it. It took Christ Jesus thirty years. She'll probably start to figure out what she's really there to do right about the time she's ready to leave. We talked about all that before she left, but being useless is tough when you've got a brand new degree and a brand new license, and you're ready to fix everything that's broken in the world.

And speaking of useless, ever since Katie left, Shelly, our aged dog, has been moping around like Eeyore.

Tuesday, June 19
✠ Jude, Apostle

Lest I appear at all wise, this exchange was also part of last night's phone conversation with Katie:

"So how was Father's Day down there?"

"They don't do Father's Day here."

"Really? Why not?"

"Dad . . . They're orphans."

"Oh. Right."

"That would be pretty twisted, don't you think?"

"Uh . . . yeah . . . definitely."

Wednesday, June 20
✠ *Methodius of Patara, Hieromartyr*

Since I've been back from the conference, a lot of people have been asking me how it went and if I learned anything new. When I tell them it was all very quiet and not a lot happened, they seem a bit disappointed.

But I'm not. That's because I remember all those years I attended Annual Conference as a United Methodist pastor. The atmosphere was very much like a political convention: there were issues and reports and personalities; there was vote-swapping and caucusing and parliamentary maneuvering. And on top of all that, there was the process of appointing pastors to parishes, a process that generated an unbelievable amount of gossip and glad-handing and career angst. Then every four years, there was General Conference, the national meeting in which just about everything was up for grabs—what the denomination believed, how it was organized, where it was headed. I don't miss it a bit. But it's not just that I found the politics so objectionable. It's that the political structure was all-consuming: It's easy to be a United Methodist pastor and spend an inordinate amount of time attending strategy sessions and planning meetings and candidate forums and renewal conventions. And of course, none of that has anything to do with actual, hands-on ministry.

Now I know some Orthodox get caught up in this kind of nonsense. One of my favorite books of recent years is *The Journals of Fr. Alexander Schmemann.* I keep a copy of it on my desk, and in the book, Fr. Alexander goes on at great length about his loathing for those sorts of activities:

> I talked with Fr. N about the Church. So many intrigues, offended ambitions, fights and mainly the extraordinary pettiness of all these problems. All of it because the Church is perceived as a continuous, feverish activity. Multiplication of departments, commissions, meetings, assemblies. A flow of documents, memor-anda, information. Money is needed for these activities; to get money, one needs constant action. A sort of vicious circle. In its present situation, the Church is a caricature of the world, with the difference that in the world, fights, institutions and so forth are real. In the Church, they are illusory because they are not related

to anything. For salvation, this fussy activism is not needed; for joy and peace in the Holy Spirit, not needed either.

So this kind of craziness is certainly present in Holy Orthodoxy, but as Fr. Alexander points out, it's not an essential part of who we are. Who we are is the Church, and in the Church, the big questions have already been settled. We know what we believe; we know how things should be organized; we know how the Kingdom is unfolding in our midst. So at the Parish Life Conference, we adopted a budget and heard some reports and made some plans, and it was all very calm and peaceful. And I am looking forward to being similarly bored for many years to come.

Thursday, June 21
✠ *Julian of Tarsus, Martyr*

When it comes to denominational politics, I have noticed something: When clergymen become Orthodox, they often have a hard time letting go of their former battles. At conferences and retreats, men who served together in a particular denomination will often gather to rehash old conflicts or to express their outrage over current developments. Whenever I overhear that kind of talk, it always reminds me of those passages in *Gone with the Wind* where Scarlett O'Hara gets frustrated with the Confederate veterans; they were living in the past and continually re-examining the "what ifs": "What if Jackson had not been killed? What if Great Britain had come into the war?"

That's what those clergymen sound like. I used to be disappointed that there weren't any other former United Methodists in our diocese. Now I'm actually a little grateful, because I don't want to end up in an ecclesiastical version of a Confederate Veterans Society. Because on this point, at least, Scarlett was right: The war's over, boys. We lost. Time to move on.

Friday, June 22
✠ *Eusebius of Samosata, Hieromartyr*

There's something in me that doesn't get along well with vestments. To begin with, I never can get everything to line up properly. My belt keeps slipping up and down over my stomach, my epitrahelion is always hanging to one side, and my phelonion is constantly trying to turn itself around. It's as if all that stuff has a life of its own.

Then there are the cuffs. If I lace them up tightly, the blood stops flowing to my hands, and the rest of the day, I end up with marks on my wrists and forearms. If I loosen the laces, then they start unraveling, and the cuffs slide up and down my arms.

But the most hazardous parts of my vestments are the buttons or baubles on the epitrahelion. Those things get caught in the holy doors and on the cross frontlet of the altar and on the drawers of the proskomidia table. I'm probably the only priest who ever got whiplash during a divine service.

So what does all this mean? I'm not sure, but I do know this: If they ever make me an archpriest and give me one of those pectoral crosses, I'll probably end up impaling myself on it.

Sunday, June 24
✠ *The Nativity of the Forerunner*

Today is our parish feast day.

Last night at Great Vespers, a number of people joined us from St. Elias and St. Sophia. Fr. DB served with me, and Fr. JB from Transfiguration Greek parish was in the nave with his family. The highlight of the service came during the Litya, when Fr. DB sang "Rejoice, O Virgin." He has such a rich and strong voice. Afterwards, I asked him to bless all the young people who were leaving for camp.

This morning's services were quietly joyful. Lots of people are out of town, so attendance was low, but Orthros was golden, and the Divine Liturgy was even brighter. We then had a potluck, and most everyone sat outside under a sky that was big and blue.

Monday, June 25
✠ *Febronia, Martyr*

Brendan stayed with us last night. He was on his way back to Wichita Falls after his two-week reserve tour. He and I went to see *Ocean's Thirteen,* and we both came away thinking that George Clooney and Brad Pitt have ceased to be cool and have simply become smug.

Before and after the show, Brendan talked about how frustrated he is with the fact that his life "isn't going anywhere." We've tried to talk about this before, and it usually doesn't work out well, and it didn't last night. But this morning at Orthros, I realized what I needed to do.

When my father graduated from high school in 1947, he started college right away. He didn't last long—maybe two semesters. Then he dropped out and went into the military. However, at some point in his early college career, a salesman talked him into buying a class ring.

After doing twenty-five years in the Air Force, my father went back and got a teaching degree from the same university. In fact, he graduated the year I started college. And through all those years, he held onto that class ring. He gave it to me when I graduated from college, and this morning, during the Praises, it occurred to me that it was time to give it to Brendan.

He was getting ready to head out when I got home, but I went and found the ring, and then I asked him to sit down with me at the kitchen table.

"Look," I said, "we don't have any family heirlooms, and I'm not sure this qualifies as one, but either way, I'm now passing it on to you." I told him about his grandfather's starting and stopping and starting again. And then I reminded him that I had done the same thing.

"You're twenty-eight," I said, "and you're not sure where you're headed. You know where you'd like to go, but you're not sure how to get there from here. Well, when I was thirty-eight, I realized that my life was headed in the wrong direction and that I really wanted to be somewhere else. So I had to back up and start over. Everyone told me I was nuts and that I should just shake it off and keep going, but I knew I couldn't do that. So I left United Methodism, and we became Orthodox."

Then I handed him the ring.

"And this," I said, "brings me to what I really want to say: Life doesn't run in a straight line. I guess some people figure out what they want to do right away and are happy to do it all the rest of their lives. Well, good for them. But it doesn't work that way for most of us. We wander around, and eventually, we just figure it out.

"So stop beating yourself up about all this. You're not on any schedule. If you keep saying your prayers, and if you live the way Christ Jesus wants you to live, He'll get you where you need to go. And on those days when you have a hard time keeping your perspective, just get the ring out and remember that you come from a long line of wanderers."

Brendan nodded his head. We stood up. He gave me a hug. Then I walked him out to the car. On the way, we started talking about a funny scene from the movie we watched last night. Then he got in the car and drove away.

About twenty minutes later, the phone rang. It was Brendan; he had forgotten his combat boots. He said to just throw them in the closet, and he would get them on his way back through next month. Then he added, "I love you."

"I love you, too," I said.

Wednesday, June 27
✠ *Sampson the Hospitable*

Yesterday I spoke at a nursing seminar about adolescents and faith. MK, a woman in our parish, is on the staff at the University of Texas Nursing School, and she asked me to participate in a presentation she was making.

So I've been thinking about adolescents and all the tasks they have to accomplish at that particular stage of faith development: They have to begin constructing an identity; they have to start coming to grips with history; they have to begin focusing on others. Of course, most people never complete those tasks. Spiritually speaking, they remain adolescents their entire lives.

And that explains a great deal about American Christianity. In this country, the most popular forms of Christianity are very self-focused: the emphasis is on how to overcome bad habits or how to achieve your personal potential. These versions of the Faith also don't deal with history effectively: either they ignore it, or they react against it by presenting themselves as something entirely new and different, or they have some idealized version of the past that they want to reproduce in the present (1950s culture or the America of the Founding Fathers).

Adolescent spirituality even explains how Americans do worship. Because right now, the most popular forms of worship are simply bigger and better versions of what youth groups were doing twenty-five years ago: an informal setting, skits, live music, and a brief, personal talk. I don't know if church growth experts are deliberately embracing this approach, but the end result is that they are treating adults as if they were still teenagers.

So does grown-up Orthodox Christianity stand a chance in this country? Probably not in the short term. But patience is an adult virtue, and sooner or later, the kid version of the Faith will be revealed for what it truly is.

Saturday, June 30
✠ *The Synaxis of the Holy Apostles*

Today Cynthia and I went to the movies. Cynthia is a huge documentary fan, so we saw Michael Moore's lat*est*, *Sicko*. It is about the health care crisis in this country, and it is better than I thought it would be. It includes some of Moore's typical cheap shots and a great deal of oversimplification. But the film was much more mature than a lot of Moore's other efforts, because, over and over again, he kept coming back to one basic question: Do we really want to be the kind of country that doesn't take care of its citizens?

Of course, his solution is primarily structural—change the system (although there were a few profound moments when he focused on personal responsibility). But the Church has a solution that goes even deeper, a solution that requires the most difficult kind of change there is: a change of heart.

Tonight we will be commemorating Cosmas and Damian of Rome, two of the holy unmercenary healers. They were ascetics and physicians, and their asceticism led them to the conclusion that they should not charge anything for their work as physicians. As we sing in their troparion, "freely did [they] receive, freely did [they] give." So, once again, the Church is way ahead of the cultural curve.

JULY

This is what my Sundays are like.

I get up at 5 AM. Just like every other morning, I take a shower and get dressed, only instead of putting on a black T-shirt, I put on one of my clergy shirts. Normally, I say the Jesus Prayer when I'm getting ready in the morning, but on Sundays, I generally run through my homily.

After I'm ready, I let the dog out and change her food and water. By then, it's usually around 5:30. I go into my office and read through the following services: Small Compline with the Canon of Preparation for Holy Communion, the Midnight Office with the Canon to the Most Holy Trinity, the Hours and the Typika, and the prayers before Holy Communion. Just before I read the pre-Communion prayers, I make my prostrations.

That takes me up to about 6:30. I drive to church, and while I'm driving, I go through my sermon. When I arrive at St. John's, I walk back under the trees until I'm standing in the tall grass on the far side of our property. Then I go through the homily two more times.

I go inside, reverence the icons, and say the prayers that accompany the entrance into the church for the Midnight Office. I reverence the altar table, then double-check the page markers for the Gospel lesson and the Epistle reading. After that, I generally go back outside and sweep off the front sidewalk. Some nice shade trees overhang the main door and the walkway, but they also generate a lot of leaves and twigs and bugs.

Once that is done, I go back inside, sit in the altar, and pray the Jesus Prayer. Around 7:15 to 7:30, Fr. Deacon BL and Shamassy JL arrive, and then the chanters start to come in. We greet one another and quickly review the service, but there's usually not much time for small talk, because we begin Orthros promptly at 8 AM.

During Orthros, Fr. Deacon BL and I do the kairon; we then put on our vestments and do the proskomidia. Sometimes I help the chanters, but generally, Orthros is just a beautiful atmosphere in which to pray—it's like breathing the air of the Kingdom. Then at 10 AM, there is the Divine Liturgy and all the mighty wonders that weekly accompany that experience.

After liturgy there is often church school or a meeting, but there are always folks to visit with: some people want a blessing or a prayer for healing; others need to talk about a personal problem or an issue in the parish. I always try to introduce myself to visitors and follow up on folks I have spoken to during the week. Every once in a while, someone will need to do confession. Sometimes, it is just a cyclone of interaction—and the whole thing is made more intense by the cramped quarters in our facility. But the only thing I dislike about this part of the day is the fact that I am the center of so much attention. A lot of times, people are actually waiting in line to talk to me, and that's just embarrassing. When I'm serving at the altar or preaching, I'm up there in front of everyone, but I'm not the focus of what's going on—Christ Jesus is. However, during coffee hour, I'm frequently the main attraction, and that's uncomfortable.

Unless there's a parish council meeting, I'm usually back home by 2 PM. I'll eat a little something, and I might turn on the TV or read a bit, but then it's time for one of Sunday's best blessings, the post-liturgical nap. Cynthia and I turn off the phones, and then we lie down together and quickly go to sleep. And that is as much an act of worship as Orthros or the Divine Liturgy. As Charles Peguy has written:

I don't like the man who doesn't sleep, says God.
Sleep is the friend of man.
Sleep is the friend of God.
Sleep is perhaps the most beautiful thing I have created,
And I myself rested on the seventh day.
He whose heart is pure, sleeps.
And he who sleeps has a pure heart . . .
But they tell that there are men . . .
Who don't sleep. What a lack of confidence in me.
I pity them . . .
They have the courage to work. They haven't enough virtue
To be idle.
To stretch out. To rest. To sleep.

We typically get up around 4 PM—though every once in a while, we sleep as late as 5. We then fix a meal or go out and get something to eat. After that, there are usually bills to pay or papers to grade, but then comes what is, without a doubt, the hardest part of the day: At some point in the evening, I go back into the office and read through the following services: Vespers, Small Compline with the Akathist to the Mother of God, Nurturer of Children, and the Midnight Office for Weekdays.

I call those services the Angel Laps. St. Paul often compares the Christian life to a race, and what I do on Sunday evening is join the angels for a few extra turns around the Great Track. I don't enjoy those services, but the week has started, and it just doesn't make sense to say, "Y'know what? I've already served Orthros and Divine Liturgy today, so I've done enough," when everyone else in the world is dealing with all the fear and boredom and anxiety and resignation that accompanies the beginning of the work week.

So I get back out on the track for one more round of services, but it's not at all pretty. I'm usually tired, and my feet are often sore, so I end up sitting down a lot, and by the time I actually make it across the finish line, they've turned off the big time clock, and the announcer's booth has been dismantled, and most of the spectators have gone home. I huff and puff and just put one word in front of another all the way to the end. It's not dignified or majestic like Orthros and the Divine Liturgy; it's not anywhere near as crisp or focused as my preparation for those other services. But it's real prayer—slow, slogging, sweaty prayer. And that's a good way to start the work week.

Monday, July 2
✛ *The Deposition of the Robe of the Mother of God*

They are building a shopping center about two miles from our house. It's going to have a Super Target and a PetsMart and a multiplex theatre and an Amy's Ice Cream Shop. Which is almost exactly the line-up of stores in some shopping centers about ten miles from our house.

Now I'm not one of those people who is against any and all development. In fact, I think those people who want progress to stop at the border of their particular little enclave are just silly. These new stores will provide a lot of folks with fairly good jobs, and hopefully, they will actually help to reduce the amount of time people spend in their cars.

My question is this: Why does development have to be so boring? And, good grief, I'm the kind of person who actually enjoys the Same Old Thing. I rarely, if ever, try new stuff. When we go to a restaurant, I order what I ate the last time. I wear black clothes every single day. I keep a schedule that hardly ever changes. So I'm not exactly Mr. Cutting Edge. But it concerns me that so much of our commercial culture is so repetitive.

The problem is that commercial culture is the only form of culture most people know. I mean, let's face it, throughout history, the vast majority of folks have eaten the same food and worn the same clothes and shopped in the same locations. But when that dull uniformity starts to intrude upon the mind and heart, then evil is at work. The Holy Fathers refer to this evil as sloth or ignorance or forgetfulness, but its main symptom is a comprehensive absence of beauty.

After years of television and internet and canned music, people lose the ability to think or have conversations or express themselves with any degree of accuracy or originality. But many of them still recognize beauty when they see it. They often don't know how to respond to it, but they realize that they are in the presence of something that is real and personal and powerful and unique. They realize that they are in direct contact with something that transcends the categories of this world. Here's how Eugene Peterson describes it:

> The distinctive thing about beauty is that it reveals, reveals the depths of what is just beneath the surface, and connects the remote with the present.

But, he adds:

> Beauty that is salvation is virtually unrecognizable to those who are indifferent to transcendence, to the organic connections between above and below, between far and near.

But that's why I continue to teach at the community college. And that's why I read a poem out loud at the end of just about every class. Because it's one important way that I can engage in cultural disobedience. It's one way I can actually provide my students with a few moments of beauty.

Now a lot of them just endure it. Many of them simply look at me with uncomprehending eyes. But from time to time, one of them will—almost involuntarily—let out a "wow" or even a "damn." And once or twice every year, one of them will come up to me after class, after everyone else has left the room, and quietly, shyly, even apologetically, say, "Could I get a copy of that?"

Tuesday, July 3
✠ *Hyacinth, Martyr*

In preparation for our trip to England and Scotland next month, I'm reading St. Adomnan's *Life of St. Columba*. Talk about cultural disobedience. Columba spent over thirty years on a rocky island at the edge of the world, and his main occupation was prayer. But his community also copied manuscripts. In other words, St. Columba and his brothers worked hard to give the world opportunities to experience beauty—and this was in a time and place when the existence of civilization itself was very much in doubt.

That gives me a lot of hope. That makes me glad that Cynthia and I are going to Iona.

Thursday, July 5
✠ *Athanasius of Athos*

To celebrate the Fourth, Cynthia and I went over to Fr. Deacon BL and Shamassy JL's house for dinner. After dark, we sat out on their upper deck and watched the fireworks. Some of them were being set off legally by various municipalities, but most of them were being fired off illegally by folks out in their backyards. Either way, it was a lot of fun. There were sizzles and pops and thuds and the occasional Boom. There were bursts of color and erratic flashes and sudden, flaming arcs. We stayed until late, and then we drove home through the night, as all around us, the darkness continued to zip and crackle and sputter.

This past couple of weeks, I have been going to the hospital to visit GT. He's one of the older folks in our parish, but he's also one of the newest. He was raised up north in a Russian parish, but he stopped attending services after he left home. He got married and had a daughter; his wife and daughter were active in Presbyterian congregations, but he did not participate with them. Last year, his wife died, and not long after that, GT starting attending liturgy in our parish several times a month.

Late last week, I got a call from GT's son-in-law. GT had fallen, and by the time they discovered what had happened, he was pretty disoriented. He has been in the ICU all week, and he is now doing much better. I've been by several times to pray with him, and I also got a chance to visit with his daughter. That encounter resulted in an interesting conversation.

She: "It's nice to meet you. Actually, I've been wanting to talk to you and ask you some questions. You see, my husband and I are Bible-believing, evangelical Protestants, and we just don't know anything at all about the Orthodox Church."

Me: "Well, what would you like to know?"

"What you believe. What you teach. Do you have a statement of faith? I guess what's behind all this is that I'm just worried about my father's eternal salvation. I don't know if he has a relationship with Christ Jesus. I mean, until recently, he's just never gone to church, and I've tried to talk to him about his salvation, and he's never been very receptive. And now all this has happened. So I'm just worried, and I'm wondering how you guys look at all this."

"We can talk about that, but first, let me thank you for being concerned about your dad's salvation. That's very important, and I'm glad it's important to you."

"Well, he's my dad. I love him."

"Which is why you want to know who he's been hanging out with. You asked about a statement of faith. Are you familiar with the Nicene Creed? Do y'all ever use that in your services?"

"Ah . . . yeah, sure."

"OK, well, that's what we believe; that's our statement of faith. Now, as to your dad's salvation: Just the fact that he's coming to services indicates that he's taking that seriously. And it's always nice when people can actually talk about their faith and let their loved ones know that they've got all that taken care of. In fact, I was a hospice chaplain for a whole lot of years, and I always encouraged the people who were dying to let their family members know where they stood with the Lord."

"That's what I need to hear."

"And I really hope you do—and y'know what? If you will pray for the opportunity, if you will ask Christ Jesus for the chance to have that conversation, it may happen."

"I hope it does. That's what I've been praying for."

"But here's the thing: Just because your dad is too embarrassed to talk to you about the subject doesn't mean he isn't talking to Christ Jesus. Remember, it's a real blessing when folks can talk to their loved ones about spiritual matters, but ultimately, they are not accountable to us. The One they have to reckon with is Christ Jesus. And as far as I can tell, based on what I've seen, your dad is coming to grips with that. It would be nice if he had done that earlier in his life—"

"Yes."

"—but, thank God, he's doing it now."

The conversation then shifted to other things. After a few minutes, I assured GT's daughter of our parish's prayers. I promised her that I would visit again soon.

As I left the building, I thought about what a great job I have. How many other people get to hear about the love of a daughter for her dad? Who else gets to look all the way into eternity? Are there others who get to spend the day talking about prayer or the Nicene Creed?

Perhaps there are. Maybe they do. But when I pushed open the door and stepped outside, the light struck my face like the grace that came upon me at my ordination, and I thought to myself, "I'm a priest of the Most High."

Sunday, July 8
✠ *Sixth Sunday after Pentecost*

Last night at Great Vespers, the evening sun set the windows to glowing and the dimly gilt cloth on the altar began to radiate a rich warmth.

This morning, as I was out under the trees, a doe was moving silently through the tall grass. As the sun came up, she turned to the light, and the dull bronze of her coat began to shine with the day's first fire.

Later, at the end of the liturgy's first litany, as I lifted my hands for the exclamation, the faded gold of my phelonion began to burn with a deep brightness. The folds almost flashed as I lowered my hands and turned the page of my service book.

The light that illumined the altar cloth and the doe's coat came from the sun that shines upon this world. But the light that briefly touched my vestments came from another place, a place that is beyond the stars, a place which shines with the golden life that is the glory of the Most Holy Trinity.

That doesn't make me a mystic; it doesn't even make me special. The glory of the Father, Son, and Holy Spirit is reflected in all the evenings and mornings of this world, but that glory becomes brilliant in the services. And that's actually what we pray for:

Raise up our thoughts to Thee, O One God of threefold light.
Hasten to lift up the minds and hearts of those who praise Thee,
and make us worthy of the splendor of Thy Light, O Lord.

Transform and transfigure Thy servant; change me from crime to virtue, O Trinity who alone are not subject to change, and make me shine with the reflection of Thy Light!

I read those hymns this morning when I went through the midnight office, so the grace that made the gold of my vestments shine was simply an answer to prayer. It was a foretaste of the inheritance of the saints in light; it was a glimpse of that moment when we will all shine like the sun in the Kingdom of the Most Holy Trinity.

Monday, July 9
✠ *Pancratius, Hieromartyr*

PZ called today. He's a retired priest and a dear friend. During our conversation, he referred to a priest who has just recently been deposed for child abuse. I hadn't heard about the situation, but apparently, it has been in the news for some time. I think at first there were two allegations/accusations, and now there are four or five. At any rate, the priest has left the country. The bishops of his archdiocese are publicly divided over the matter, but enough were convinced of his guilt that they convened a spiritual court and removed him from the priesthood.

The priest in question has been a fixture in this part of the country for close to thirty years; he's married and has grandchildren. I met him several times, and he was always gracious and friendly. After I got off the phone with PZ, I looked up the news stories on the internet: the parish is divided; the bishops are sending mixed messages; everyone has hired attorneys.

Just this past weekend, I had a long conversation with one of our members about the still-unfolding mess at the Christ of the Hills monastery in Blanco. The men of that community once had a very positive impact on many of the people in our parish. So when the accusations of drug use and pedophilia and fraud began to emerge, a lot of folks just shut down, spiritually speaking. They felt stupid and embarrassed; they were confused and angry. And they're going to have to keep dealing with all that for some time, because the legal proceedings have just barely begun, and every time there's a new development, it's all over the local media.

And then, to top it all off, last night Cynthia and I watched a documentary called *Deliver Us from Evil*. It is a well-made film about a pedophile Irish priest who molested hundreds of children while his superiors in California moved him from parish to parish. It included a lot of interviews with the priest, who is now out of prison and back in Ireland. He is obviously a sociopath; he has yet to come to grips with what he has done. The film also had a number of moving interviews with some of his victims and their families.

But there were also many interviews with clergymen who were trying to deny that they had any responsibility in the situation, or who were actually trying to capitalize on the situation in the name of reform. Ultimately, they all came across as only a little less disgusting than the pedophile—although, in the case of the reforming clergymen, I'm sure that was not the filmmaker's intention.

The whole thing just scares me. In the movie, at the time the abuse was occurring, the parents of the victims appear to have been genuinely oblivious to what was going on. If the accusations against the priest in this part of the country are true—and his archdiocese obviously thinks they are—then he was able to deceive people for even longer than the guy in the movie did. The men in the monastery at Blanco were so out of control they got caught relatively quickly, but even though they apparently didn't work very hard at concealing what they were up to, they still managed to deceive a lot of smart people.

Of course, every time one of these situations comes to light, there are always those people who say, "Well, I always knew something wasn't right," or "Y'know, I just had this sense that he wasn't who he claimed to be," or "Shoot, it was obvious. I don't know why everyone couldn't tell what was going on." But I hardly ever believe them. Perhaps they did suspect something; if so, then they should have spoken up, and they should have continued to speak up until some sort of action was taken. But most of the time, I think they're just trying to cover up their own fear. They don't want to believe that evil is so close by; they don't want to admit that they can be fooled the way everyone else was fooled.

But I think fear is an appropriate response. To be sure, it must eventually be tempered by faith; after all, when St. Peter tells us that our adversary the devil is prowling for prey, he doesn't say, "Be suspicious and never trust anyone"; he says, "Be sober; be watchful." But that kind of vigilance begins with fear—the realization that evil is real and that everyone—absolutely everyone—is a potential victim.

Tuesday, July 10
✣ *45 Martyrs of Nicopolis*

Last night I visited with a young couple who got married about six months ago. It was kind of a check-up visit; I just wanted to see how they were doing.

This past weekend, we blessed CF and OF on their first anniversary. It was a beautiful little service—the whole choir showed up on a Saturday afternoon—and later, they had a nice reception.

But for some reason, during both of those events, I couldn't stop smiling. It probably wasn't very noticeable at the anniversary blessing, but, last night, I was afraid the couple I was visiting with might think I was somehow amused with them. So several times I assured them that wasn't the case.

But the truth is, I wasn't exactly sure what was going on. Then I ran across a poem by Bill Holm; the last stanza goes like this:

But the dark secret of the ones long married,
A pleasure never mentioned to the young,
Is the sweet heat made from two bodies in a bed
Curled together on a winter night,
The smell of the other always in the quilt,
The hand set quietly on the other's flank
That carries news from another world
Light-years away from the one inside
That you always thought you inhabited alone.
The heat in that hand could melt a stone.

I don't know if it's a dark secret, but it's certainly not something you can explain. That kind of love is something you just have to experience. And, of course, it takes years—decades—before you can experience it. But that's why I couldn't keep from smiling: because I know that one day, that "news from another world" will reach both of those couples, and then they, too, will understand how the "sweet heat" of another's touch can burn right through the heart's core and on into the next world.

Wednesday, July 11
✣ *Euphemia the Great Martyr*

I just finished *The Life of St. Columba*. It's full of great stories, and of course, everyone always talks about the episode where he takes care of the heron or the scene where the horse cries. But I guess I'm just perverse. Because as powerful as those tales are, my favorite story in the whole book is about the hunting stake that just won't quit.

It seems a poor man came to the holy man. St. Columba gave him a sharpened stake that he could use as a trap; the stake would never harm a human, but St. Columba assured the poor man that he and his family would never, ever lack for meat. And the saint's words were true; the poor man set up the stake in the woods, and every morning, when he went out to check on the trap, he found an animal impaled upon it: stags, wolves, even stray seals, and they were all of "amazing size." The poor man had so much food, he began to sell what he couldn't use to his neighbors, and thus his family prospered.

However, all of this good fortune made the poor man's wife anxious. She became convinced that something was going to go horribly wrong, and so she nagged her husband until he dismantled the trap. But there wasn't any place the man could put the stake; it just kept on doing its job. He submerged it in a river; it impaled a huge salmon. He stuck it up on the roof of his cottage; it impaled a great raven. Finally, in desperation, the man chopped up the stake into little pieces, and he and his family resumed their former life of poverty.

St. Adomnan, the abbot who collected all the stories, has a few scolding sentences for the poor man and his wife, but, other than that, there's no moral attached to the story—and, to me, that makes the tale even more enjoyable. But, then, like I said, I have a pretty bizarre sense of humor: to me, there's something funny about that poor guy trying to figure out what to do with his blessed stick.

Thursday, July 12
✠ *Proclus and Hilary*

Speaking of guys who struggle with great powers, this morning we discovered that the battery in one of our cars was dead. So I called AAA. But while I was waiting for the serviceman to arrive, I realized that I would probably need to get the car out of the garage in order for him to jump the battery.

The car is a small one—a Corolla—so it was no trouble at all to push it out of the garage. But I didn't reckon on the fact that our driveway is slightly sloped, so before I knew it, the car was almost to the street. And who knew it was so hard to jump into a moving car? Those guys on TV and in the movies make it look so easy.

Fortunately, there was no traffic on our street, and I was able to get in and hit the brake before the car hit the other curb.

First I couldn't start it, then I couldn't stop it.

So, hey, just think about the damage I could do with a magic hunting stake.

Friday, July 13
✠ *Synaxis of the Archangel Gabriel*

Today I called my friend JH. His wife, MH, just finished her next-to-the-last chemo treatment. She is then scheduled to have surgery at the end of August, but this week, the doctors also told them that after the surgery she will need six weeks of radiation.

JH sounded weary. We talked about the situation and how he's holding up, and then he asked about our summer. For a split second, I thought I wouldn't mention our trip to England and Scotland, but we've been friends too long to play those kinds of games. So I told him what we had planned, and I added that we would pray for both him and MH at each holy site we visit.

The other night, Cynthia and I were watching a young actress who was being interviewed on TV. She began the conversation by saying that she had just returned from her "vakay." Cynthia and I just looked at each other.

This will be the longest and most expensive trip we have ever taken. But I'm really glad that it's not a "vakay." God willing, we will get some rest, and we will have a wonderful time. But we will also be worshipping at some of the most sacred spots in Western Europe, and we will be taking a long prayer list with us.

What we will be doing is going on pilgrimage. I think that's something all the hard-working, long-suffering, underpaid and short-lived people of this planet can understand. But I'd hate to try to explain to them what a "vakay" is—and even worse, I'd hate to have to explain to them why I think I deserve one.

Sunday, July 15
✠ *The Holy Fathers of the First Six Ecumenical Councils*

Years ago, when I was in seminary, Cynthia and I were driving somewhere, and we pulled into a truck stop to get some gas. I started the pump; Cynthia went inside to pay. I was pretty distracted with school stuff, and I think by then I was also already serving a parish. Anyway, I wasn't paying attention to what I was doing, and before I knew it, my shoes started to feel wet, and

I smelled gas. I looked down at my feet and saw a small fuel slick spreading quickly across the pavement. I glanced over at the counter inside the truck stop, and Cynthia was smiling at me and shaking her head.

I shut off the pump and wiped off my shoes with a paper towel. When Cynthia came back out, we got in the car, and then she leaned over and kissed me on the cheek. "You were just far off in some nice quiet spot," she said.

This morning in the liturgy, I missed my cue at the end of one of the litanies. I had already offered the prayer, but then I got distracted with everything that needed to be done after the service, and before I knew it, there was this moment of silence, and I suddenly realized I was standing in a pool of praise. I quickly sang the exclamation, and as I did, I looked up at the icon of the Mother of God on the back wall of the altar. She didn't shake her head, but I know she was smiling.

Monday, July 16
✠ Athenogenes, Hieromartyr

It's been a busy day. This morning after Orthros I mowed the lawn. Then I got cleaned up, read the Hours and Typika, graded papers, answered emails, and wrote an article for the newsletter.

And it doesn't look like the rest of the week is going to slow down: in addition to writing my homily, I've got to do a column for the newspaper, I've got a parish mailing to get out, and I've got four visits to make (I'm trying to work in one more, but I haven't been able to connect with that person yet). Then on Saturday, I'm scheduled to go and serve liturgy at the mission station in Fredericksburg.

Every once in a while, the thought will occur to me that if I weren't doing all these services I'd have a lot more time. But it's only the services—it's only the regular and ongoing contact with the Most Holy Trinity—that makes all the rest of the stuff meaningful. You would think writing and teaching and helping folks out and running a parish would be full of significance and very fulfilling, but after a while, all those activities easily become just a list of things that have to get done.

Only life can sustain life. Prayer—the services—that's how I stay alive. And the busier things get, the more prayer becomes absolutely critical.

Sunday, July 22
✚ *Eighth Sunday after Pentecost*

This weekend has been full of blessings.

Like this morning, there was fog. And it was pretty thick, too. When I pulled into the parking lot, I couldn't see the other end of the property. When I walked out into the trees, the fog closed in behind me and actually curled around under my feet. It all burned away quickly once the sun got up, but for a few minutes, I was back there practicing my sermon, and it was like preaching in a chapel of clouds.

And then later in the morning: We always close the holy doors and the curtain during the pre-Communion prayers. I was standing by the altar as Fr. Deacon BL got the chalices ready. The choir and congregation were singing, the altar servers were going about their business, and Fr. Deacon BL and I were reciting the Paschal troparia:

Shine, shine, O New Jerusalem, for the glory of the Lord has risen about Thee. Dance and be glad, O Zion, and delight thou, O pure Theotokos, in the rising of thy Son.

How divine, how beloved, how sweet is Thy voice, O Christ, for Thou hast faithfully promised to be with us to the end of the age. Having this as the anchor of our hope, we the faithful do rejoice.

And it was still the eighth Sunday after Pentecost, and it was still the back side of July, but as we stood there before the altar in the presence of the Holy Gifts, it was also Easter, our weekly participation in the eternal Feast of the Resurrection; so we pulled back the curtain and opened the doors, and then we took up the chalices and stepped out into the never-ending day of the Kingdom.

Monday, July 23
✚ *The Prophet Ezekiel*

This morning I mowed the lawn. It didn't take any longer than it usually does, but it was really muggy, and afterwards, I was just worn out.

After I got a shower, I sat down in the old green chair in the office. And then I remembered a picture Cynthia took of me thirty years ago when I was sitting in the same chair: I was just out of college, and we were waiting to move up to Indiana for graduate school. I got a job on an oil pipeline, and Cynthia snapped the picture after my first day out in the field. I was sunburnt and banged up, and I smelled like a walking gas can.

Once I got all cooled down, I got ready to read through the Hours and Typika. I thought about that picture again and that job on the pipeline, and I started to chuckle. Back then I thought working outdoors would be a nice break between college and graduate school, but in that heat and under those conditions, I didn't last a week.

I remember walking into the field office to tell the foreman I was going to look for another job. He was working at his desk, and at first, he didn't even acknowledge that I was there. He finally looked up at me, but he didn't say anything; he just chewed his gum slowly and deliberately. Then he shrugged his shoulders and went back to his work.

"Well," he said, "if you just ain't hoss enough . . ."

And it's true. I wasn't. But as I started the Hours, I made a metania for all of us guys who just never have been hoss enough, and another one for all the real men who have to put up with us.

Tuesday, July 24
✠ *Christina, Great Martyr*

A lot of family stuff has been going on.

Brendan came through over the weekend; he stopped by on his way to and from San Antonio. He said his girlfriend, D, is going to be transferred to Michigan in a few months, and they are trying to figure out what that means for their relationship. He bought Cynthia a small iPod since her birthday is this coming Saturday.

But there weren't any instructions with the iPod, so when Katie made her regular Monday night call from Guatemala, she talked Cynthia through the basics. Katie sounds like she's settled in, and she's actually doing a little nursing as well.

Speaking of things medical, my sister Alice called late last night to say that my father had been taken to the emergency room with heart problems.

But she left the message on my cell phone, and by the time I heard it this morning, everything was sorted out and under control. Pop is in the hospital, but he's doing all right; they just want to keep an eye on him while they swap out some medications.

And then yesterday, we got our invitation to the birthday party for Mrs. E, Cynthia's mom. We had received an email about the event, but this was the official, printed invitation. Mrs. E is going to be ninety, and one of Cynthia's half-sisters has put together a pretty extravagant evening; everyone is supposed to meet at a country club, and they will have champagne and a buffet. But Cynthia and I have mixed feelings about the whole thing. On the one hand, we're glad that everyone is going to get together and that Mrs. E is going to have a nice party; on the other hand, the invitation indicated that we're expected to chip in on the cost of the evening—even though we weren't consulted when the event was planned. Looks like this one is definitely going to be material for prayer.

Wednesday, July 25
✠ *The Dormition of St. Anne*

Today is Cynthia's nameday. I sang "Happy Name Day" to her when I brought in her glass of juice at 5:15. She reached up and grabbed my arm and pulled me down on the bed next to her. We lay there for a few moments, then she put her hand on the side of my face and kissed me. I took her hand in mine, and our fingers intertwined.

Right there in the dark, I started to smile. I was thinking about how much I love this woman—and I was also thinking of a poem. It's one that Cynthia and I both like. I often read it to my students as well. It's by Sharon Olds, and it's about a man and woman who get in bed after flying cross-country:

> We . . . laid our bodies
> delicately together, like maps laid
> face to face, East to West, my
> San Francisco against your New York, your
> Fire Island against my Sonoma, my
> New Orleans deep in your Texas, your Idaho

bright on my Great Lakes, my Kansas
burning against your Kansas your Kansas
burning against my Kansas, your Eastern
Standard Time pressing into my
Pacific Time, my Mountain Time
beating against your Central Time . . .

Apart from the goofy eroticism, what I like about that poem is that it expresses how I feel when I'm with Cynthia: we are every place and all times. In fact, the only problem with that poem is that the geography is too limited and the chronology is too cramped. Because when I look into Cynthia's eyes, the Pre-Cambrian Age shifts and cracks and slides into the Renaissance. When she puts her arms around my neck, she also encircles Canberra and Caracas and Casablanca. And when we kiss, way, way out in the middle of the South Pacific, the water begins to bubble and boil.

OK, maybe that's just a little over the top.

But that's the way it feels. And, besides, in the midst of all that hyperbole, there is one thing that is absolutely, positively, one hundred per cent true: Cynthia orients me to my proper place in the universe. When I come through the garage door at the end of the day, and she calls to me from the kitchen or the bedroom, a smile begins to curve across my face, and it's like dawn breaking across the turning curve of the earth. When she talks to me about her day or how she feels, my thoughts change like seasons, and my heart begins to turn on its axis like an orbiting moon. That's because Cynthia's my emotional GPS; she's the organizing principle of my life.

And it was that dynamic that finally helped me to understand Psalm 118. I know, that's an odd transition, but Psalm 118 is one of the basic components of my spiritual life; it's read every single weekday in the Midnight Office and every single Saturday at Orthros, and on Sundays, it's often read twice. So that long poem is a fundamental part of my relationship with the Father, Son, and Holy Spirit. But back when I was a Protestant, back when I only read it every once in a while, I thought it was just a lengthy and tendentious glorification of a lot of rules and regulations. I couldn't see how it was possible to get so excited about statutes and commandments. And I wasn't able to look at the psalm differently even after I began reading it on a daily basis.

Then, at some point somewhere along the way, it occurred to me that just as Cynthia is the ordering principle of my life, the Divine Law is the reality that harmonizes this entire cosmos:

For ever, O Lord, Thy word abideth in heaven.
Unto generation and generation is Thy truth; Thou
    hast laid the foundation of the earth, and it abideth.

By Thine ordinance doth the day abide, for all
    things are Thy servants.

If Thy law had not been my meditation, then
    should I have perished in my humiliation.
I will never forget Thy statutes, for in them hast
    Thou quickened me.

It's the testimonies and judgments of the Most Holy Trinity that structure and sustain this universe, and it's Cynthia who gives my life form and fullness—but there is no tension between those functions, because what Cynthia does for me is an image, an icon, of what the Divine Law does on a cosmic level.

All of that is reflected in the fact that Cynthia's patroness is St. Anne, and that brings me back to where I was at the beginning of all this: Today is Cynthia's nameday. Her middle name is Anne, and St. Anne is the mother of the Mother of God, and what mothers do is hold within their very being the connected nature of all things. They nurture that connectedness, and they draw everything and everyone around them into that connectedness.

The reason it took me so long to get a handle on what Psalm 118 is all about is that my life tends to be so fragmented and isolated. My natural inclination is to be self-contained on just about every level—emotionally, physically, mentally, even spiritually. But Cynthia pulls me out of that; she's my heart's true beacon, and through her love I participate in the great intimacies that run through this world like veins through a body: touch, laughter, speech, tears, listening, silence.

I think that's what Florensky and Bulgakov were trying to get at with their writing about Holy Wisdom, Sophia. They understood the deeply feminine and maternal dynamic of the Divine Law, and they tried to express that in the theological construct they identified as Sophia. But as brilliant as those men were, they had a difficult time making Holy Wisdom anything more than an abstract concept.

I will never be anywhere near as smart as those two guys, but I apparently have an advantage they didn't have: because every evening I sit down to dinner with a woman who keeps me connected with the rest of this creation; every night I sleep with a woman who unites me with the deep wisdom that is at work in this world; and every morning, I say "I love you" to a woman who is a mother of all that lives, of all that is truly alive.

Thursday, July 25
☩ *Hermolaus, Hieromartyr*

Last night we did an unction service for RT. He was diagnosed with prostate cancer about a month ago, and he'll be having surgery in a couple of weeks. But right about the time he got his diagnosis, I preached a sermon in which I talked about praying for the sick. I encouraged people to make use of the unction service, and so RT took me up on that. He sent me an email; we scheduled a time, and last night, between RT's friends and the members of our community, over fifty people were at the service.

And it was an unbelievably powerful experience. Normally, when the service is offered during Holy Week, everyone receives the anointing with oil. Last night, the only person who was anointed was RT. But that didn't exclude everyone else who was there—on the contrary, because we were all there for one person, and because all the prayers and petitions were applied to him, the service had a focus and intensity that was compelling and energizing. We were a community of Christians who had come together to do some uniquely Christian work: we were praying for our brother, and in those prayers, we became bold and strong and "terrible to adversaries."

Even our habitual Orthodox tardiness contributed to the dramatic quality of the experience. Our community is like every other Byzantine parish—folks straggle in throughout the services. But tonight that actually had a positive and profound impact on what we were doing. It's like all those movies where the hero is facing down the bad guys all alone. But then someone walks up and stands with him. A few moments later, someone else steps forward. And not long after that, a couple of others join the group. Then more and more people start to show up. And pretty soon, the hero isn't alone anymore: he's got all sorts of folks with him, and you just know everything's going to be all right.

That's the way the service felt last night. As we prayed and sang the responses, more people joined with us, and the prayer became more fervent, and the responses got louder. But it wasn't just RT's friends and the members of our community who kept showing up; it was the saints as well: As we chanted the troparia for St. James and St. Nicholas and St. Demetrius and St. Panteleimon and St. John the Theologian and the Holy Unmercenary Healers, each of those holy ones took their stand with us. We all lined up together and looked out into the darkness, and we said, "This is our brother. You mess with him, you mess with us."

Sunday, July 29
✠ *Tenth Sunday After Pentecost*

Katie called yesterday; she's been diagnosed with typhoid fever. She told us that she started to feel bad on Wednesday, and then she went to the doctor on Thursday. She's still waiting on the test results, but the doctor told her— through an interpreter—that he's certain about the diagnosis. He also said they had caught it in the early stages.

Katie's been in her room at the orphanage since Thursday. Apparently, if it's caught early, typhoid fever isn't life-threatening to adults, but it can be deadly to children at any stage. So she's basically on quarantine. And even though the disease isn't life-threatening for adults, it makes you all kinds of miserable. We're talking fever, weakness, a rash, and an inability to keep anything down.

Considering all that, Katie was doing remarkably well when she called. But of course, we sprang into parent mode: Cynthia got on the computer, and I called a doctor named CL who is a member of our parish. Cynthia found a lot of good stuff on the computer (as I was dialing the phone, she shouted from the computer room: "It says here that if it's caught in the early stages, it's hardly ever fatal!")

The doctor was even more helpful; he did some research, called us back, and patiently answered all our questions.

So our anxiety level has been lowered somewhat. When we talked to Katie, we told her that she needed to think about coming home early, and she said that she and the nun who runs the orphanage were already considering that. Nevertheless, the services this weekend were a glorious blur, and tonight at dinner, Cynthia said, "In the last forty-eight hours, I've used the words 'typhoid fever' more than I ever have in my entire life. I don't think I like those words. I don't want to use them anymore."

Monday, July 30
✣ *Silas, Silvan, Crescens, Andronicus, Epenetus,*
Apostles of the Seventy

Yesterday I was talking to WH, a member of our community. Church school was over, and we were standing together in the hallway just off the kitchen. We discussed a couple of different issues, and then he said, "Hey, I just want you to know how much I appreciate the job you do. You're just a great shepherd to this herd."

As he spoke, I happened to be looking towards the kitchen, and in the ever-so-brief time it took for him to say those few words, this is what I saw: Several people were busy cleaning up from coffee hour, and as they worked, they were kidding and joking around. Over in one corner two guys were arguing politics; over in another corner three were people talking theology. Someone was also trying to use the kitchen phone; they had the receiver on one ear and a finger in the other ear. Through the middle of it all walked two men carrying guitar cases. While I watched, the back door opened, and two little kids came in; they were finishing up their coffee hour snacks and bouncing a ball at the same time. Through the open door, I saw several other kids playing on the riding lawn mower that was parked next to the building, and back beyond all that, a group of young people were heading out into the trees for an Air Soft BB gun battle.

I then turned and expressed my appreciation for the compliment.

WH thought for a moment. Then he smiled.

"I think I just said 'herd.' I guess the traditional word is 'flock,' isn't it?"

"Yeah," I said, "but in our case, 'herd' works, too."

Tuesday, July 31
✠ *Holy and Just Eudocimus*

Katie called tonight. She and the nun in charge of the orphanage decided it would be best if she came back early. But the doctor told her she needed to rest for a few days and continue her antibiotic before she gets on the plane. So she's planning on flying back Thursday.

At this point, she's ready to come home, but she's also feeling like she's letting everyone down. "I just really started to feel useful and then I got sick," she said. Also, having to stay in her room is starting to get to her; it's a nice room, and she certainly understands the importance of not spreading the disease, but she's a social person, and being isolated isn't easy.

So there were quite a few sniffles throughout the conversation. At several points, there were also a number of sobs. We were all on the speaker phone together, then Cynthia took the receiver and spent a long time saying a lot of encouraging things to her. By then, though, it was getting late, so Cynthia handed me the phone, and then she went on in the other room to get ready for bed.

"Hi, it's me."

"H-h-hi."

"How 'bout if I say a prayer?"

(Sound of nose blowing)

"Ooookay . . . that's fine."

So I went in the office, and I stood in front of the icons, and I prayed. And the arc of that prayer rose higher than any satellite; its words flashed back and forth across the universe. And Katie and I weren't the only ones who shared in that prayer: Cynthia listened; Brendan heard it as well, and of course, every syllable of it was received in the heart of the Most Holy Trinity, that Family in which the love of every family shines like a bright and pulsing star.

No telecommunication company on earth can match that calling plan. That's because we've got a cosmic connection.

AUGUST

Last night we started the Dormition Fast. I had to teach, so I just read the services, but this afternoon, before Vespers, I switched out the altar cloths. The coverlet we put on the altar during this season is beautiful: It's a deep blue, the kind of blue you only see in the crevasses of glaciers, or in a clear autumn sky, just before the sun sets.

There are many reasons I love this season, but one of them is definitely the color. To me, blue is a tender color; it's a mixture of sadness and hope. In his book, *The Pillar and Ground of Truth*, Florensky devotes an entire chapter to "The Symbolism of Sky-Blue and Dark Blue" in an attempt to account for the extraordinary power of this color. He marshals all of his impressive erudition and surveys everything from psychometric phenomena to Goethe's theory of colors to Zhukovsky's translation of Homer. He considers Giotto's frescoes and the carvings on St. Ignatius's tomb and Byzantine miniatures and Japanese paintings. But there's one phenomenon he didn't take into account, so I would like to add one small footnote to his already lengthy list of notes: I would like to add the musical form, the blues.

I like James Baldwin's description of the young man at the piano in "Sonny's Blues." He's improvising with some other musicians, but what he's looking for through the music, what his hands are hunting for on the keyboard, is freedom—freedom from weariness, freedom from failure, freedom from pain. And when he finds the notes, when he hits the right rhythm, what he's playing is more than music; what he's playing is hope.

Through his narration, Baldwin makes it clear that this hope is as delicate as it is short-lived. ("And yet I was aware that this was only a moment, that the world waited outside, as hungry as a tiger, and that trouble stretched above us, longer than the sky.") But the significant thing is that the music that expresses this hope is called "the blues." I mean, I can't imagine anyone ever referred to this music as "the yellows" or "the purples." It's the blues for a reason—because that color expresses, it symbolizes, the kind of hope that is born of sadness.

The same dynamic is at work when a good chanter sings a hymn in one of the minor tones. And I think I'm like most converts—I was surprised when I discovered that most of the hymns of the Great Feasts are in these minor, almost mournful, tones. I was expecting upbeat, fast-paced, positive music such as you typically find in most modern Protestant and Roman Catholic hymnody. But, as a friend of mine once remarked, "The Church understands that one of the times we cry is when we are especially happy." So there's a profound correspondence between what the Church does in her chanting and what jazz musicians do in their sessions: there's the same improvisation, the same search for freedom in the phrasing and in the rhythm, and there's also the same wisdom, a wisdom that understands that hope is not optimism, but transformed sadness.

The Church, then, has her own blues; the music we pray to is liturgical jazz. And, as a priest, that makes me a blues-man. I've got a beautiful set of blue vestments that Cynthia and Brendan and Katie gave me for Christmas a couple of years ago. They are just a few shades lighter than our altar cloths, and they are trimmed in gold. But it's not just the liturgical color that makes the priesthood blue; it's the intensity of the soul-work.

When I was a United Methodist pastor, my homiletic idol was Janis Joplin. I wanted to preach the way she sang: I wanted to pour myself into every single word ("You really only need to do one thing well/You need to be a good man, to one woman/just one time/and that will be all there is"); I wanted every single phrase to explode with power ("I can see you got a little cryin' left to do/ So come, come on, come on, come on, come on, come on, and cry, cry, baby"). But, of course, Janis was just imitating all the great African-American blues singers. And all those African-American blues singers were just imitating the preachers they had listened to when they were young. So there's some gospel at work in all that, and I wasn't too far off the mark in my choice of role models—and I wasn't half bad at that kind of preaching, either.

But it can easily turn into a kind of religious performance art. So I left that behind when I converted, and I discovered that the soul-work of the priest is expressed in ways that are every bit as compelling and just as high-energy, but far more subtle: I'm talking about the way the priest serves the liturgy or the way he makes a prostration or the way he holds a baby just before the child is baptized. But what really makes the priest a blues-man are his tears. Here's what St. Isaac of Syria has to say about tears:

All just men have left this world in tears. If the saints wept and always had their mouth full of tears . . . who would not weep? . . . If those who were victorious wept here below, how is it that one who is full of ulcers would keep from weeping? A father, certainly, who has before him the body of a beloved child, does not need to be taught which thoughts will arouse tears in him. Your soul lies before you, dead through sin, and it is worth more to you than the whole world. . . . Let us then ask insistently that Our Lord give them to us. If we receive this gift, more excellent than any other, we will attain to purity through tears. And if we do reach it, that purity will not be taken away from us.

This is the ultimate, personal expression of hope as transformed sadness: the priest weeps because of his sins, and in so doing, he weeps for the sins of the world. But those tears are themselves a sign of freedom from sin, and thus they are also a sign of hope. They are drops of purest blue; they are just about the most precious gift a priest has to offer.

But blue is also the iconic color of the Mother of God. Her color is blue—she is Our Lady of the Blues—because she understands the sadness of the world, and because she gave birth to the Hope of the World. And in fourteen days, when we celebrate her departure from this world, we will honor her as the first fruits of her Son's Resurrection, and we will share in that hope that transforms all sadness.

That feast is also the anniversary of my ordination to the priesthood. Come August 15, I will have been the Church's blues-man for eight years. I'm not much good at it, but as I prepare for the feast, I'm going to be asking the Mother of God to give me the freedom I need in which to find the notes and the rhythm to the music of hope.

Friday, August 3
✠ *Isaacius, Dalmatus, Faustus*

For the last several days, I've been working my way through the Song of Songs. We're going to be reading it during this fall's Theological Seminar. The Seminar is entitled "Men, Women, and the Kingdom," and we are going to be dealing with the relationship between men and women in the Church.

Of course, the Song is a wedding poem, but the Holy Fathers interpret it as a dialogue between Christ and the Church, and that takes us straight to the imagery St. Paul uses in his letter to the Ephesians when he talks about marriage as an icon of the relationship between Christ and the Church. That makes the Song an expression of some very powerful realities, and of course, those realities are expressed in some really erotic language.

I remember the first time I actually read the Song. I was at a missions conference sponsored by InterVarsity Christian Fellowship. I believe the year was 1976; the conference was held on a university campus in Urbana, Illinois, and it was a wonderful event. I got to hear Billy Graham and John Stott and Elisabeth Elliot. But the conference lasted an entire week, and one afternoon I had some time on my hands; so I picked up my Bible and found a big chair in the lobby of the dorm where I was staying. I opened the book and looked at the Table of Contents. I saw the Song and realized that I had never actually read it. I had a vague impression that it was poetry, and that certainly appealed to me, so I turned to the beginning of the Song and started reading.

After a few minutes, I started to shift around in the chair. Then I started glancing up at the people who were walking back and forth through the lobby. I think I even looked over my shoulder a couple of times—because I couldn't believe what I was reading. I mean, I was holding a Bible in my hands, but I was reading about lips and breasts and navels and thighs and gazelles jumping over mountains of incense. And the truth is, I didn't know what to do with all that except to worry that someone might happen along and catch me reading it.

I'm afraid that's the way most people still react to the Song: They just don't know what to do with it. When Cynthia and I were first married, we read a popular Christian book about marriage, and it treated the Song as a sex manual. I think most biblical scholars regard it as something of a cultural and literary curiosity. But it's poetry; it's part of the canon of Holy Scripture; its purpose is to help us come to grips with some of the foundational realities of this life—men, women, sex, love. And what those realities express is nothing less than the deep mysteries of the Most Holy Trinity.

Saturday, August 4
✠ *Eusignius, Martyr*

Katie's back, and she appears to be doing all right. She got off the plane late Thursday night—red hair, red shirt, red ribbons on all her bags—and, except for a trip to the doctor, she slept most of the day yesterday. But today she's up and around, and she and Cynthia are even talking about going to the movies.

The doctor told Katie just to keep taking her antibiotics. They'll do some tests next week to see if the bacteria have all cleared out, but that should be the end of it. And Katie has even begun to figure out why the experience worked out the way it did. She eventually wants to do nursing in a developing country—her goal is Africa—but what better way to learn about health care in that part of the world than to get sick while you're there?

Monday, August 6
✠ *Feast of the Transfiguration*

Every year on this feast, we go over to the parish of the Transfiguration and participate in their services. And it's always a pleasure to do so, because they have such a beautiful temple. Their building does what all Orthodox temples should do: It unites the spiritual and the material, and expresses that union in ways that are simple and clear.

For example, there are three tall windows in the back of the apse. This morning during the liturgy, whenever I looked up, I saw high clouds racing through a bright sky. But the floor of the temple is covered with marble tile. So whenever I looked down, I saw those same high clouds and that same bright sky. And the whole time, I'm standing in front of the altar upon which our Lord and Master is present, and we are surrounded by clouds and brightness, just as the apostles were on Mount Tabor.

Now that's the way to celebrate the Feast of the Transfiguration—right at the point where heaven and earth are being united, right at the point where this entire creation is being transformed, right at the point where "mercy and truth are met together, righteousness and peace have kissed each other"; where "truth has sprung up out of the earth and righteousness has looked down from heaven."

"Lord, it is good for us to be here!"

Tuesday, August 7
✣ *Dometius, Martyr*

I dread having to participate in concelebrated services. That's because there often seems to be a direct correspondence between the number of priests and the level of decorum during the service: the more priests, the less decorum. Especially when they all get behind the iconostasis, the atmosphere is often that of a golfing party: there is casual conversation, there is good-natured teasing and joking around; and when it's necessary, they actually engage in the activity for which they ostensibly got together in the first place.

Thankfully, it wasn't like that at yesterday's liturgy. There were four priests: Fr. JB, the pastor of the Transfiguration parish; Fr. MS, who serves a Greek community in Ft. Worth; Fr. DB, from St. Elias here in Austin, and myself. The service was dignified and radiant because all the clergymen were attentive and prayerful. That's the way worship is done in the Kingdom; that's the way it should always be done.

Thursday, August 9
✣ *Matthias, Apostle*

RT had his surgery today. During the procedure, I went to the hospital chapel and read through the evening services. Hospital chapels can be really interesting places; this one certainly was.

It was about the size of a large bedroom, with twelve or so chairs with kneelers attached to them. In the back of the room was a studio piano. Up at the front stood a table with a white cloth spread haphazardly across it. On one side of the table was a small set of electronic votive candles; the lights in the candles flickered furiously. On the other side of the table, seven objects were attached to the wall. The objects were enclosed in Plexiglas cases arranged in the form of a cross. At the top of the cross was a crucifix; underneath the crucifix was a Star of David, a small figure of Krishna, a statue of the Virgin of Guadalupe, and a statue of Shiva. A statue of Buddha and a picture of Ganesh formed the bars of the cross.

The front of the room was entirely taken up by a large, square painting. The canvas was almost completely filled by a big, luminous disc rimmed with bright yellow. At first I thought it was meant to be an eclipse of some sort. But after sitting in the room for a while, I decided that it was a giant magnifying glass, and that I was under it.

Judging by the decorations, the chapel was intended to be used primarily by Hindus or Zoroastrians. But no representatives of those groups came in while I was reading the services. At one point, though, three children came in, a boy and two girls. The boy looked like he might be in middle school; the girls might have been old enough for elementary school. They all looked at me. The boy smiled and nodded, and then they all went up to the front of the room and knelt down.

The boy turned to the girls.

"Do you want me to say it?" he asked in a stage whisper.

The girls nodded.

The boy bowed his head, and the girls did as well.

"Father, please let there be no brain damage . . ."

There was a long awkward pause. The boy looked up, and so did the girls. The boy shrugged; both girls nodded. Then they all got up and left the room.

RT came through the surgery just fine.

But I've also been praying that there wasn't any brain damage.

Saturday, August 11
✠ *Euplus the Deacon, Martyr*

It's about 10:45 PM. I just finished reading Great Vespers. It's been a long day, but it also turned out to be a good day.

Cynthia, Katie, and I left this morning at 8 AM and drove to Dallas to see my family. We had a nice lunch; my brother Brigham, his wife LuAnne, and their son Ben joined us. Everyone seemed to be doing well, but my father was moving very slowly. During his last hospital stay, he contracted pneumonia; he's officially over that now, but it's left him pretty tired. My mother told us that she is worried about him, since he's never been one for sitting around ("he only reads for information, you know"), and she's afraid what will happen when that's all he can do. But he certainly brightened up whenever we talked about our trip: He had that "let's hit the road" gleam in his eye, and later on, he went back in his office and found some British currency left over from their last trip. "I wish I were going with you," he said as he gave me the money.

About 3 PM, we said goodbye and drove over to Euless. The birthday party for Mrs. E was a pleasant surprise: The setting wasn't quite as fancy as the invitation had suggested, several of her old friends showed up, and we watched a slideshow with photos of Mrs. E that went all the way back to elementary school. That was a big hit, and the food was nice, too. There wasn't a lot of really personal interaction, but at least everyone got along. We headed home about 6:45 PM and pulled into the driveway about 9:30.

Like I said, it turned out to be a good day. I'm thankful for that, but I'm also very tired.

Sunday, August 12
✠ *Eleventh Sunday after Pentecost*

This morning after liturgy, I was cleaning the chalice after consuming the holy gifts. I don't do that very often, not since Fr. Deacon BL was ordained. But Shamassy JL's father died this past week, and he is in Mississippi with her.

Anyway, I poured some wine into the chalice, and then I drank it. Actually, though, I didn't really drink it; I just stood there with my mouth full of wine. And as I stood there, I remembered one of the main reasons I was so happy when Fr. Deacon BL was ordained: I don't like wine. I mean, I really don't like wine. In fact, as I was standing there, steeling myself to swallow the stuff, I started to retch. But I stamped my right foot, and down it went. That was a technique I devised when I was a kid and I had to eat my quota of Brussels sprouts. The amazing thing is that it just came back to me so effortlessly and instinctively.

I suppose that also says a great deal about my level of maturity. I'm less than a month shy of fifty, but I'm also a genuine Beverage Wimp. I've never liked the taste of alcohol or tea or coffee. Now, as an Orthodox priest, you can get by without drinking very much alcohol—but coffee is another matter. Real Orthodox priests—especially Antiochian priests—drink coffee. In fact, I sometimes wonder: If the metropolitan had known that I wasn't a coffee drinker, would he still have approved my ordination?

So on this score—as on many others—I'm something of an embarrassment. A few years ago, I was at a restaurant with several priests. I was sitting next to Fr. MK, my ordination sponsor. Everyone else ordered wine or a mixed drink with their dinner; I ordered a soft drink. When the beverages arrived, the waitress served everyone else first, then set the glass with the soft drink down in front of me. There was a straw in it.

Fr. MK turned to me.

"Good God, if you insist on ordering that sort of thing, at least drink it like a man."

Monday, August 13
✠ *Leavetaking of the Transfiguration*

I just finished reading *The Voyage of St. Brendan*. It was included in an edition of a *Life of St. Cuthbert* that I was reading in preparation for our pilgrimage. I had only read selections from the *Voyage*, so I decided to go ahead and read it the whole way through. I'm glad I did, because it's full of wonderful things.

Like the battle between the sea monsters. An obvious precursor to all those Godzilla versus the Atomic Tyrannosaurus movies.

Better yet, though, was the fact that the *Voyage* takes place in a world full of monks. Just about every island St. Brendan and his companions stop at is populated by monastics; some are hermits, and some live in communities, but their various rules and ascetic practices express in clear and concrete ways what every rule and all asceticism are designed to do: transform the environment in which we live by transforming us.

But what was most wondrous of all was the encounter with Judas— St. Brendan encounters this sad villain on a deserted island. But contrary to Dante, in this tale Judas still receives mercy from Christ Jesus, and St. Brendan even prays that he might have some additional respite. The demons, however, don't get it: "How can you evoke the Lord's Name over His own betrayer?" they cry. I love that line. It's a breathtaking vision of just how far-reaching the Lord's mercy is—and a clear rebuke to those of us who would want to restrict it.

Tuesday, August 14
✠ *The Forefeast of the Dormition*

We will be leaving tomorrow after the liturgy, but today we are rushing around trying to take care of all those last-minute details. But all of our rushing is happening in a world that "has been mystically adorned in the immaterial Spirit," because the Dormition will begin tonight, and that will be a blessing, because we will depart on our pilgrimage on the day we commemorate the Mother of God's departure from this world.

Wednesday, August 15
✠ *The Feast of the Dormition*

It's been a truly beautiful feast day.

LH is a woman who frequently brings flowers to church. This weekend she must have found a good deal on gladiolas, because we had four big vases full of them. And by the time we began Great Vespers last night, the stalks were creaking under the weight of pink and gold and orange blossoms. The colors stood out even brighter against my blue vestments and the blue altar cloths. Then, when the service was over, I drove home as the sun was setting, and the sky was clear blue, streaked with pink and gold and orange.

This morning we had a hushed Orthros and a Divine Liturgy that was quietly jubilant. Then we drove to the airport, and now we are flying through the air, just as the apostles did on their way to be with the Mother of God. As I look out the window, it's blue sunlight as far as the eye can see, and the hymn for the feast is still ringing in my heart:

> In giving birth, thou didst keep thy virginity, and in thy repose thou didst not forsake the world, O Theotokos. Thou art the Mother of Life, and thou hast passed over into Life. And by thine intercessions, thou dost save our souls from death.

Thursday, August 16
✠ The Icon Not Made with Hands

Actually, it may still be Wednesday. I don't have a watch, and Cynthia is asleep. We are on the flight to London, and according to the screen the man next to me is watching, we are 35,000 feet above the Atlantic and just about directly south of Greenland.

There are a lot of those screens on the plane. Some people turned them on the moment they sat down and have been watching them ever since. The man across the aisle from me has been watching Indian musicals for at least four hours, and the little girl further up the aisle has been watching episodes of *South Park*.

They turned off the lights in the cabin some time ago. I slept for a while, but I can only do so much of that while sitting up. I brought C. S. Lewis's *That Hideous Strength* to read on the trip. We're going to be using it in this fall's Theological Seminar, but it's also a great book to travel with.

After Brendan's first trip on an airplane—I think he was in high school—I asked him what he thought. "It's a bus with wings," he replied. I've never heard a more accurate description. But this international flight also reminds me of that old submarine movie, *Das Boot*: lots of people with compromised hygiene in cramped quarters loaded down with all kinds of stuff for an unbelievably long period of time—and the turbulence even adds a slight depth-charge ambience to the entire experience.

Thursday, August 16
continued

We arrived at Gatwick Airport outside London about 7:30 AM UK time. We walked endlessly through the airport, then boarded a train and rode to Victoria Station in downtown London. From there we took a taxi to Liverpool Station, and on the way, we got a quick tour of London: we drove past Buckingham Palace and through Trafalgar Square and along the Thames. From Liverpool Station we took a train to the small town of Witham. At Witham, we got into a taxi driven by an affable man named Dean, and he took us out to the Monastery of St. John.

When we walked onto the monastery grounds, we saw a group of monks installing a mosaic on the walls of the church. They were intent on what they were doing, but one of them stopped and showed us where to drop our luggage. Then he took us to a room he described as the old refectory and brewed some tea for Cynthia. By then it was about 11:45 AM, and Cynthia was feeling very tired. But the women's guest mistress was with a group of pilgrims from London, so we walked around to try to stay awake.

After a bit, one of the sisters came looking for us. Her name was Sister S, and she found a nice big chair for Cynthia to collapse in. But soon after that, Sister P, the guest mistress, arrived and whisked Cynthia off to a room in the women's quarters. I went to lunch in the new refectory. Counting all the monks, nuns, novices, pilgrims, and visitors, about seventy-five people were in the room. We ate salad and potatoes and bread and pasta while one of the brothers read a homily on the Dormition of the Mother of God.

Now all the monastics are back at their jobs, the pilgrims have just about all left, and I'm sitting on a bench just under the wall, watching the sunlight filtering through the trees and flickering across this notebook. This community is a remarkable place, and I'm going to try to write more about it when my body isn't several time zones behind my mind.

Friday, August 17
✠ *Myron, Hieromartyr*

It's about 6 AM, and I'm standing on the sidewalk on Folly Street in the village of Tolleshunt Knights, waiting on a ride to the monastery. It turns out that the men's quarters were full, so late yesterday afternoon, they took me to the home of a couple in this village, which is just down the road from the monastery. They have a spare bedroom, and they were pleased to have me stay with them.

They have an electric shower in the bathroom. The woman was showing me the bathroom, and she said, "Well, I suppose I need to show you how to operate the shower. In we go." We stepped into the shower; she showed me how it works; we stepped out, and then she said, "Now I can go tell all my friends that I've been in the shower with an American priest."

I went to sleep about 6:30 PM and woke up about 5 AM, when the sunlight started to show through the curtains. One of the nuns is going to pick me up for the morning service, but before she gets here, I thought I would write a bit about the monastery.

It straddles a narrow road, and it sits on the top of a ridge that has a long and gentle slope. The men's quarters are on one side of the road, the women's on the other. On the women's side is the main refectory along with a guest house and dormitory, large gardens, greenhouses, and an orchard. There are also several outbuildings and one or two nicely shaded arbors. On the men's side of the road is the original building, which was once a rectory, St. Silouan's Church, the old refectory, a guest house and dormitory, a building which used to be a dormitory but which is now used for offices, a small house where Fr. Sophrony used to live, a parking lot, a couple of garages, and the chapel where Fr. Sophrony is buried.

Yesterday afternoon Cynthia and I fulfilled the only responsibility Bishop Basil gave me for our pilgrimage. When I sent him an email to let him know that we were leaving, he asked me to pray for the clergy brotherhood at Fr. Sophrony's tomb. The crypt itself is simple and even austere. The whole thing appears, at this point, to be constructed of brick and tile. The walls are lined with large openings for other caskets; these are empty right now, and it gives the impression of a dormitory filled with bunk beds. Fr. Sophrony's tomb is in the back of the room, centered against the wall and flanked by two other, smaller tombs. Up above Fr. Sophrony's tomb is a large handwritten icon of Christ Pantocrator, and on the tomb itself sits a small oil lamp.

Before I left home, I took from my daily prayer book the lists of names for our diocesan clergy brotherhood and our parish community. I folded them up and slipped them in my back pocket, and when Cynthia and I went to Fr. Sophrony's tomb, I pulled out the lists and prayed through them.

Friday, August 17
continued

There was bread and jam for breakfast, along with bowls of tea. Cynthia and I thought the bowls would be for some sort of cereal or oatmeal, and we were a bit disappointed when everyone started pouring tea into them. At the services and the meals, Cynthia is with the women and I am with the men, so after breakfast, it was nice to walk down the road to the Norman church the monastery owns.

Sister P gave me the key; it was about the size of a small handgun. The church itself has lots of layers of plaster and whitewash on it, but the original window frames and ceiling timbers are still visible. There is also a beautiful little porch above the main door, which is on the side of the building. There were a number of gravestones in the churchyard; the most recent was from 1923—a Rev. Wilcock who was the priest of the parish for fifteen years. Cynthia and I sat in the church for a while, I prayed through my lists and wrote in this notebook for a bit, and then we walked back to the monastery, holding hands and stopping every once in a while to look at the flowering shrubs that grew thick along the side of the road.

Friday, August 17
continued

One of the sisters told me there are twenty-nine nuns and fourteen monks in the community, and they represent fifteen different nationalities. Scripture verses are inscribed on the eaves of most of the buildings, and in the new refectory, the walls are lined with life-sized icons of saints, each saint holding a scroll that displays one of his or her sayings. All the verses and all the sayings concern humility, service, and brotherly love. For example, this verse runs around the length of the refectory, just under the ceiling: "Beloved, let us love one another, for love is of God, and everyone who loves is born of God."

At lunch we had rice, green beans and carrots, salad, bread, and what Cynthia and I both at first thought were potatoes covered in cheese—but it turned out to be apples covered in custard. This afternoon, we went for another walk, this time on a narrow road that went down a steep hill. There were tall trees and fields on either side. Cynthia had found some hard candy in her suitcase that was left over from our airplane snacks. We ate that as we walked, and after all the extremely healthful food we've been eating here at the monastery, it felt a bit wild and daring.

Saturday, August 18
✠ *Florus and Lauros, Martyrs*

We are on the train to Durham. Trains, it turns out, are a great deal like airplanes: there is no leg room; there are lots of people; there's very little air that circulates. You can look at the scenery when you're riding on the train, but you have to look off into the distance; otherwise, the speed can make you dizzy. So what I'm going to do is just write a few notes about our last day at the monastery.

On the day we arrived, Fr. Zacharias suggested that, later on, we might have "a little chat." I was excited about that, because he is one of the main reasons I wanted to visit St. John's. He is the monk who spoke at our Clergy Brotherhood Retreat this past February; I've read his two books and listened to his tapes, and it was a real blessing to speak with him briefly this past spring when he was at the retreat. So having an actual appointment with him was a huge deal.

We sat in his study. The room was lined with inexpensive bookcases and crowded with stacks of paper. On the desk were more stacks of paper and some sort of commercial calendar; stuck on the wall just above the desk were a photo of Fr. Sophrony and several more recent photos of Fr. Zacharias with different monks and hierarchs. Fr. Zacharias sat in a chair next to the desk. He was holding a large bottle of water; he said the doctors wanted him to drink a lot of fluids. He invited me to sit in a chair opposite him, and then he asked me several questions about our parish.

I then told him I had some questions. Several of them were personal, and I'm still thinking about his responses. But one of the questions I asked was about evangelism: How is an Orthodox parish supposed to reach out to others?

He asked me about the size of our community. When I told him, he reacted as if our parish were quite large—in fact, many of the other monks and nuns asked about the number of people in our community, and when I told them, they all reacted the same way. But then Fr. Zacharias said, "Of course you want to be kind and friendly to all those who come to you— and God will send the ones who need to come. But the main thing is the liturgy; if you work hard at founding a community that serves the liturgy, everything else will take care of itself. That's what Fr. Sophrony did." He then told me about a prayer he now uses before each and every liturgy. I asked him if I could have a copy of the prayer, and this is what he gave me:

Behold, O Lord, I stand before Thy Holy Presence with my brethren. I beseech Thee, O Savior of all men, especially those who believe, overshadow our congregation with the grace of the Holy Spirit, fill the hearts of all my brethren with the gifts of Thy goodness, and let none of us depart this holy temple without the incorruptible consolation of Thy salvation.

He then asked if I would like to concelebrate the liturgy with him in the morning. That is probably a courtesy they extend to all visiting priests, but I was thrilled. I told him it would be a great blessing.

The only word I can think of to describe the liturgy is stillness. The nave was full; the vestments were old but well cared for; the prosphora was soft and delicate. A visiting Greek bishop—His Grace, John Zizioulas— was in the altar with us, but he simply prayed along with everyone else. Fr. Zacharias was busy throughout the entire service: The deacons were constantly handing him additional commemoration lists, and several times he had to leave the altar to check on something at the prothesis table. But none of that disrupted the careful silence of the liturgy. I was enfolded in that silence, and I did my share of the exclamations and blessings without any apprehension or even any real conscious thought.

During the liturgy I had noticed a small pectoral cross hanging from the large cross on the altar table. After the service, I asked Fr. Zacharias about the cross, and he told me it had been Fr. Sophrony's. We went back behind the altar, took off our vestments, and washed our hands. I then thanked Fr. Zacharias for the blessing of serving with him; he said perhaps one day we would serve together in my parish. I told him I would like that very much; then before I left the church, I went back into the altar, made a metania, and kissed the cross Fr. Sophrony had once worn.

Saturday, August 18
continued

We arrived in Durham close to 5 PM. The temperature here is about 45 degrees, and there's a stiff wind with rain. The part of the city we are staying in has brick streets lined with eighteenth-century row-houses—and just about every street runs up or down a hill. The angle on some of these hills is pretty fierce: There are handrails along the sidewalks, and even then, the climbing isn't easy. We discovered that when we went out for dinner. It was downhill all the way, but on the return trip, we were huffing and puffing, and we even had to stop and rest once or twice.

But here's what I really wanted to write down, since I was afraid it would slip my mind: While we were at the monastery, we saw Sister Magdalen, the author of that incredible book, *Conversations with Children*. She invited us to sit with her at tea, and we had an enjoyable visit. She then took us to see the clubhouse that she mentions so often in her book.

The clubhouse is simply one end of a car-shed that has been partitioned off. A door on the side opens out onto a nice lawn, but the space itself is about the size of a large American bathroom. There were shelves for books and some cushions that didn't match and an artificial Christmas tree in one corner. The walls were covered with snapshots and graffiti and children's artwork. So the premiere Orthodox education theorist does her work in a space that most parishes—and certainly most public schools—would consider unprofessional and substandard.

As we walked away, Cynthia remarked, "It's wonderful. It's all about the relationships she has with the children. It's all about giving them the freedom to be children."

Sunday, August 19
✠ *Twelfth Sunday after Pentecost*

The cathedral in Durham is truly magnificent.

You can see it from just about anywhere in town, but we still managed to get lost on the way there. We ended up having to hike a steep path that ran along the river, and when we were about halfway up, it started to rain. However, once we were inside the cathedral, we quickly forgot all that, because the massive pillars and the tall windows just compel your attention.

But after we had been in the church for a while, we began to realize that it has also become the repository for all sorts of interesting oddities. For example, there are lots of stained glass windows: most of them date from the nineteenth century, and for that era, they are pretty traditional. But there are a couple of big windows that were donated by the local chapter of the Masons, and a few that were given to the cathedral even more recently, and these are pretty ghastly. A number of art objects are scattered throughout the building, and these range from the conventional to the bizarre.

St. Bede's tomb is at one end of the cathedral, St. Cuthbert's at the other. St. Bede's tomb is in a relatively open area; St. Cuthbert's is a bit more secluded. There were wooden kneelers and kneeling cushions at both tombs. I used the kneeling cushions at St. Cuthbert's tomb: I prayed through my list and then leaned over and kissed the slab that covers the grave. At St. Bede's tomb I used the wooden kneeler, but while I was reading through my list, I happened to glance up, and when I did, I was gazing directly into the cheerful yet quizzical face of a little boy who was standing right up against the other side of the kneeler. An adult quickly snatched him away, but he kept looking back at me as he was towed off by the arm. I think he probably thought I was one of those strange art objects.

At any rate, the Most Holy Trinity still answers the prayers of the saints. After I finished reading through my list at St. Bede's tomb, I asked him to help us find a ride back to our bed and breakfast. The owner of the bed and breakfast had told us that cabs were hard to come by, which was why we walked to the cathedral in the first place. But Cynthia certainly wasn't up to the walk back. Still, it wasn't thirty minutes before a man came up to us. He was one of the cathedral stewards or guides, and he asked us if we had any questions. I asked about a pay phone to call a taxi; he said he was getting off in a couple of hours and would be happy to give us a ride. His name was Gerry, and he had actually been to Austin twice to visit some friends. So Cynthia and I got some lunch and walked through the cathedral museum and gift shop (they had some laminated icons for sale; the sign said they were produced especially for the gift shop by Orthodox nuns who live in

Texas!). At 3 PM, we met Gerry in the cloister and followed him to his car. He took us right to the door of our bed and breakfast.

Truly, God is wondrous in His saints!

Monday, August 20
✠ *Prophet Samuel*

We have just arrived on Lindisfarne. The train we rode on today was much more pleasant than the one to Durham; we also stocked up on snacks before we boarded. We took a cab from Berwick, and when we got to the island, we were amazed at the number of tourists. There were so many the cab driver could barely squeeze by on the narrow roads. It's now evening, and most of the people have left, because they have to get off Lindisfarne before the tide comes in and it actually becomes an island. But at the peak times, every shop and restaurant is packed, and every grassy spot is filled with people resting or eating picnic lunches.

Durham Cathedral wasn't quite that crowded, but I was still surprised at how many tourists were there—especially since it was so cold and rainy on the day we visited. Another thing the cathedral and Lindisfarne have in common is religious kitsch: coffee cups, T-shirts, postcards, key rings, coasters, charms, bookmarks, coloring books, back scratchers, stationery, air freshener, rings, nightlights, candles, refrigerator magnets—all of these things are available in the names of St. Aidan and St. Cuthbert and St. Bede (some of this stuff even displays the names and images of the saints).

At first, I was bothered and even disgusted by it all. Durham and Lindisfarne were full of people wandering around with bags full of souvenirs, gawking at the sights, snapping pictures, and then rushing on in an odd combination of haste and boredom. But then it occurred to me that this is the way it has always been when it comes to the saints and devotion: a few pious people come to pray; just about everyone else comes to play. And despite the zeal and self-righteousness of all different kinds of reformers, despite the disdain and contempt of secularism, that's the way it still is.

So I'm going to enjoy the crowds and the silliness. And who knows? I may even buy a Celtic-patterned flyswatter.

Monday, August 20
continued

Tonight we went to evensong at St. Mary's Church. This church stands on the site of the original monastic church which St. Finan, St. Aidan's successor, dedicated to St. Peter. The church is a great deal like Durham Cathedral in that it does double duty as a place of worship and a museum: in one aisle is a life-sized statue of monks carrying the body of St. Cuthbert, and in the other aisle are replicas of St. Cuthbert's coffin and a coracle, the little boats the monks used to travel between the island and the mainland. Plaques and bulletin board displays were scattered throughout the building.

A nice lady invited us to sit in the choir, but we remained in the nave. There was a general exodus of tourists who didn't want to remain for the service, but about six or seven stayed. So, counting the locals, about twelve people were at the service. Two clergymen were present, both dressed in brown Franciscan-looking cassocks with long hoods and white, knotted rope belts.

The service itself was plain and a bit lumpy, since the clergymen and the locals wanted the tourists to participate as well. But it became poignant when they started to read through the prayer request cards people had left throughout the day. There were quite a few of them, and they were like little picture postcards from other people's lives. They spoke of illness and death, young people going off to school, troubled marriages, folks looking for jobs. Some of them were written as requests for prayer with all the requisite religious language; a lot of them were more like wishes. But that desire to let Someone Else know what is going on, that desire to reach beyond the limits of this life, is further proof that devotion to the saints is very much alive and very much needed.

Tuesday, August 21
✠ *Apostle Thaddeus*

I'm sitting on top of the Heugh; it's a low promontory that rises up from the harbor and overlooks most of the island. It's about 8:30 AM; the wind is blowing; the temperature is probably in the low fifties.

The hotel we are in is pretty nice, but the bed is nothing more than a mushy mattress laid across a metal frame, and it was brutal on Cynthia's back. So she's lying down in the room resting her spine. However, she encouraged me to go out and walk around—as long as I returned with a cold Diet Coke.

I'm sitting on a wooden bench with my back against a stone wall. A plaque at the foot of the hill says this wall was part of some seventeenth-century fortifications that were constructed to ward off the Dutch (boy, it's been a long time since anyone has needed to ward off the Dutch). From this spot, I can look straight down into the ruins of the medieval monastery. To the right of the ruins is a field full of sheep. Beyond the wall that encloses the field is a farmhouse and then the harbor. To the left of the ruins is St. Mary's Church, where we attended evensong last night. The church building is surrounded by a graveyard and a wall. Just past the wall is a road, and then the land runs sharply down to the beach.

From this point on the promontory, I can also see the outcropping where both St. Aidan and St. Cuthbert would often go to pray. It is cut off from the island by the tide, and right now, the tide is in. I hope to go out there and pray before we have to leave, but I can see from here that the outcropping is almost a full acre of rocks, birds, mud, and surprisingly, quite a bit of tall grass. A rocky little hill juts out on the side of the outcropping that fronts the mainland, and a cross has been planted just in front of it.

The wind is blowing fiercely, so I'm going to stop now and go down into the village to find that Diet Coke. My patron was a holy man, but he also must have had a high tolerance for weather, both cold and wet.

Tuesday, August 21
continued

This afternoon, while Cynthia was napping, I walked across the mud to the outcropping. Cynthia had thought about joining me, but I'm glad she didn't—there were some pretty deep pools of water, and the rocks were slippery.

When I got to the outcropping, I discovered that it's significantly bigger when the tide is out. The receding waters leave exposed several sharp and rocky shelves. The birds were gone, too. The rocks on the outer rim are covered with a bright yellow-green lichen. Then comes the grass, which is thick and soft under the feet. Intermingled with the grass are all sorts of flowers: tiny pink blossoms, tall purple blooms, quite a few daisies, and even a number of what appeared to be sunflowers.

In the middle of the outcropping are some low stone walls that outline the foundations of two small buildings. The grey wooden cross is at the head of one of these buildings. On one side of the rocky little hill is a hard plastic plaque; the inscription has been weathered off it, but it appears to have contained Bible verses.

After I had been on the outcropping for a few minutes, I looked around and realized that I had it to myself. Some people had been climbing about on it when I arrived, but they had started to make their way back to the island. Out across the mud, quite a few people were moving around on the beach, but they didn't show any signs of heading my way. So I walked across the outcropping and sat down facing the mainland. I got out my list and started to pray.

The wind burned my face and numbed my fingers. It even snatched a few pages of my list, and I had to slap and grab after them to keep them from sailing out across the water. But eventually I finished with the list and got it folded up and put safely back in my pocket. By then some low clouds had settled on the mainland, and the light grey water of the sea was united with that far-off slate-colored fog. The gulls cried hoarsely as they hovered and swooped. The flowers and the grass bent over and then bobbed up again as the wind came over the rocks in gusts.

And that's when I heard it: Aidan's Song, my song, the kind of song that saints sing. Perhaps one day I will be able to sing it too, but I heard it as I sat on that little outcropping where my patron and protector once sat.

I'm not at all sure how to describe the experience, except to say that it's like being in choir, and the choir director gives you a specific assignment— not a solo, but a bit of harmony, a part that highlights or enhances other aspects of the piece. So my song is very much a part of a much larger effort. It's a tiny portion—just a few bars, maybe—of the Great Hymn that is even now being sung in heaven. But if I don't learn my part, if I don't sing it well, everything else will suffer. It will be like trying to listen to that old record player my family had: the bass in it was broken, so none of the songs sounded like they did on the radio.

Which means if I don't practice my song, then the wind and the sky and the grass and the sea and the birds won't sound the way they're supposed to. Because when I was out there praying where St. Aidan used to pray, they were all harmonizing with my heart. Or I guess it was the other way around. But even the silence of the rocks had a different quality to it because we were all praising the Most Holy Trinity. We were a Living Lauds:

Praise the Lord from the earth, ye dragons, and all ye abysses,
Fire, hail, snow, ice, blast of tempest,
Which perform His word,
The mountains and all the hills, fruitful trees and all cedars,
The beasts and all the cattle, creeping things and winged birds.

So it's like the Isley Brothers once said: "I got a song to sing / Can't nobody sing it like me!" And what that means is that I gotta get my heart in tune. I gotta get holy. I gotta sing like the world depends on it, because in a real sense, it does—

"I'm gonna count to three, and if you don't get off those damned rocks, I'm gonna smack you!"

While I had been praying, a number of people had come across the mud, and now they were walking around on the outcropping.

"Mum, what's the cross here for? Is it here for Jesus?"

"I dunno, luv . . . maybe it's for those what got lost at sea."

A couple of folks had brought dogs, and someone was trying to get a kite up, so I figured it was time to head back. But all the talking and yelling and activity didn't disrupt or drown out the song. Instead, all those noises were caught up right along with it into something greater and richer and even more comprehensive—and it's right then and there that I realized it's all supposed to be part of that Great Hymn. Every last bit of it. The only thing missing was that one holy person who can sing in just the right key and at just the right time and bring it all together.

So I walked back across the mud. A group of girls were playing with plastic shovels and pails. An older couple were sitting on a bench. A younger couple were necking on a blanket. A man was playing fetch with two very excited Labs. A little boy was peeing behind a rock. And as I walked past them, the Hymn rang out all around us, and together, just like the rocks and the sea and the grass and the sky and the flowers and the birds, we all became radiant, we all became beautiful, we all became one.

One person. That's all it takes to bring this whole world, theme upon theme, movement within movement, into harmony with the Great Hymn of heaven. My patron and protector did it during his brief, sixteen-year ministry. I want to do it as well.

So I'd better get busy.

I've got a whole lot of practicing to do.

Wednesday, August 23
✠ Agathonicus, Martyr

Today we slept in late, then went for a walk and got some lunch. After lunch we got a taxi over to Bamburgh.

In St. Aidan's time, Bamburgh was a royal city. Now it's a tiny village, but it is right next to a huge castle. We didn't go into the castle, though; we went to St. Aidan's Church. It's right on the edge of the village, and the current building was constructed on the site of a church that St. Aidan built in the seventh century. In fact, he died there: He became ill while in Bamburgh, and they put him in a shelter on the side of the church building. He departed this life while leaning against one of the wooden buttresses that supported the structure. The buttress itself survived at least two fires, and it's now part of the roof in the current building.

The spot where St. Aidan died is marked in the church by a small nineteenth-century stained glass window that is almost at floor level. A rather odd black cylinder with a cross encased in it hangs in front of the window. But there is also a wooden prayer rail with a plaque. As I stood there staring at the whole set-up, some lines from "Little Gidding" came to mind:

You are not here to verify,
Instruct yourself, or inform curiosity
Or carry report. You are here to kneel
Where prayer has been valid. And prayer is more
Than an order of words, the conscious occupation
Of the praying mind, or the sound of the voice praying.
And what the dead had no speech for, when living,
They can tell you being dead.

So I knelt down at the rail and read through my list. When I finished, we took some pictures and walked around the graveyard a bit. Then we went across the street to a greengrocer and got some ice cream. The wind was brisk, and we were both wearing coats and sweaters, but the sun was out, and it *is* the end of August, so we huddled together on a bench outside the churchyard and ate our ice cream and waited for the taxi back to Lindisfarne.

Wednesday, August 22
continued

This evening, Cynthia and I went for a walk among the boats and fishing equipment scattered all along the beach. Now she's watching TV, and I'm sitting on the floor writing in the notebook.

I just read back over the description of what I experienced yesterday on that little outcropping, and I think it comes close to capturing what actually happened. But I would add this: It's something to feel at one with all those anonymous people on the beach, but if I'm going to sing the way I'm supposed to, if I'm going to get holy and be the priest I'm called to be, then I'm going to have to learn to really love the people I'm with on a day-to-day basis, and that begins with Cynthia.

Now, I can get along with just about anyone. There's nothing at all virtuous about that; it's just my personality. And besides, we're talking love here, not affability, and the truth of the matter is that while I may appear to be completely laid-back and easy-going, I can keep a big pot of irritation or impatience simmering for a long time. I also have a tendency to worry. But you can't do those kinds of things and truly love other people—or, what's more to the point, I can't continue to do those things and sing the song I've been given. But when it comes to my heart, Cynthia just about always has the right pitch. And over and over again on this trip, she has shown me when I've been off-key.

Like just about every time we've had to wait for a train.

We might be waiting in the station for an hour, but as soon as the time approaches for the train to arrive, Cynthia will announce that she's going to try to find a Diet Coke or that she needs to use the bathroom—and off she goes. She always gets back on time, but I'm always afraid she's not going to make it, so when we're finally safely aboard and in our seats, the conversation usually sounds something like this:

C: I wish you could relax while we're making these connections. You always seem so tense, and I just want you to enjoy it all.

Me: I wish you wouldn't run off just before the train pulls up.

C: But I got here on time. I always get back on time.

Me: I know, but I just worry that you won't.

C: So stop it.

Me: Why don't you stop it?

C: You're such a whiner.

Then she kisses me on the cheek and starts to rummage around in the backpack.

Cynthia always sounds the notes that are clear and true. I may have a whole lot of practicing to do, but at least our Lord and Master has given me a good music teacher.

Thursday, August 23
✠ *Leavetaking of the Dormition*

We are on the train headed for Iona. We left Lindisfarne about 6:30 AM, and we've already changed trains twice (in Edinburgh and Glasgow). We will get to Iona about 6 PM. It's our longest travel day of the whole trip, and it gives real significance to the word "pilgrimage."

St. Aidan was, for many years, a monk in the monastery of Iona, and what we are doing is retracing the trip he took after St. Oswald invited him to come and do missionary work (Cynthia says she hopes that St. Aidan's back was in better shape than hers is). We are getting better at this train thing, though: we brought snacks, and we made sure to find seats in the back of the compartment. The trains have also been much more quiet as we have made our way north. And the scenery! We are, right now, riding through the West Highlands, running along streams, past tall forests and even taller mountains, in and out of fog, rushing past waterfalls and plunging through thick, leafy tunnels.

Friday, August 24
✠ *Eutychius, Hieromartyr*

Iona is much quieter than Lindisfarne. Of course, a lot of that has to do with the fact that Lindisfarne is much more accessible. There are tourists here on Iona—plenty of them—but there still aren't nearly as many as there were on Lindisfarne.

Our bedroom and the dining room of our hotel both overlook the sound that separates Iona from Mull. This morning was foggy, so it was hard to distinguish the sky from the sea—the sun was reflecting off both in a silvery shimmer. Sheep are grazing right below our bedroom, and just down the lane is the restored medieval monastery.

We walked through the monastery buildings this morning. All of it was constructed long after St. Columba and St. Aidan. It then fell into ruin following the Protestant Reformation, but in the 1940s a Church of Scotland clergyman moved out here. He began working to restore the buildings, and he started an "ecumenical community" which is still going today.

"What's an ecumenical community?" Cynthia asked.

"Well," I said, "it's kind of like a Protestant version of a monastery."

"Do they take vows like the monks and nuns?"

"Not really."

"Do they share everything?"

"I don't think so."

"So it's sort of like a commune."

"Well . . . I don't think they would use that word."

"Sounds sort of like a commune to me."

The community has done a nice job of restoring the church and the chapel and the cloister—they look absolutely pristine—but in the middle of the cloister is a weird bronze sculpture of some sort of Annunciation with a dove hovering over a world-womb. The chapel is dedicated to St. Michael, but the walls are whitewashed and devoid of all representational art; the room looks like it was done by John Knox's interior decorator. The walls of the church are bare stone, but the nave is full of speakers and microphones; the sacristy opens out onto the altar and is crowded with all kinds of musical instruments. And scattered throughout all the buildings are posters and brochures and flyers about global warming and fair trade and disarmament and sustainable agriculture.

Friday, August 24
continued

A shrine to St. Columba stands just outside the main entrance to the monastery church. That is where his body was originally buried. Out in front of the monastery complex is a low rocky ridge where the saint's cell was located. I prayed through my lists at both those spots, but later, walking back to the hotel, I thought about the fact that neither St. Aidan nor St. Columba has a tomb. But that is as it should be. They were both pioneers, and they both lived in unsettled times. St. Cuthbert and St. Bede lived only a few generations later, but theirs was a world of well-established communities within a culture that was increasingly Christian.

I guess I feel a stronger identification with St. Aidan and St. Columba because the community I serve doesn't yet have an actual temple—truthfully, we don't have much at all in the way of facilities. But, of course, facilities don't last long, either. After all, Cynthia and I have spent most of this trip wandering through the remains of facilities that people worked hard to build. In fact, if there's one thing I've learned from this pilgrimage, it's that hardly anything is permanent.

The monasteries St. Aidan and St. Columba started and the communities St. Cuthbert and St. Bede belonged to only lasted a few hundred years. That's a long time by American standards, but the point is this: They had a beginning and an ending; they had a definite life span. That is what will also happen to the Monastery of St. John. That is what will happen to the parish I serve. But that's all right. The goal is not to prolong the existence of a particular community or preserve a specific set of buildings. The goal is patient endurance and joy and faithfulness during the time we are given.

And, really, the only time we are given is today.

Sunday, August 26
✠ *Thirteenth Sunday after Pentecost*

We're sitting in the Edinburgh airport, heading home. We've got a good long while before we board the plane, so it's time to give out the Happy Pilgrim Awards. There are thirteen categories, and the first award to be presented is:

The Goofy American Moment Award: Has to be when we fried our hair dryer on the first morning. We had brought a plug adapter but not a voltage converter.

The Goofy British Moment Award: We're going to give this one to British TV—so it actually represents a number of moments. I thought nothing was worse than American television, but the UK has bested us in this area. Especially the commercials: They manage to combine the idiocy of ads from the fifties and sixties with the technology of the twenty-first century.

The Nicest People Award (UK): The sisters and brothers of the monastery win hands down here, but the cab drivers in England and Scotland are a close second. There was the man in Berwick who pointed out all the sights and then told us in detail about his recent holiday in Rhodes; there was the man in Bamburgh who had his young son and daughter with him and regaled us with stories about his days as a salmon fisherman; there was the man in Edinburgh who told us about ordering nachos for breakfast in Tampa, Florida, and then running into an old schoolmate in the loo of the same restaurant.

The Nicest People Award (US): We didn't run into a lot of Americans until we got to Iona, but this award goes to an older gay couple who were very friendly and outgoing. These two guys go to Iona every year from Southern California, and they were very interested in us and in our impressions of the island.

The Nastiest People Award (UK): This one will have to be divided up between a couple who ran a bed and breakfast we stayed in and acted like we were unwanted house guests, and several shopkeepers in both England

and Scotland who actually seemed to be bothered by the fact that we had set foot in their stores.

The Nastiest People Award (US): This one also has to be divided up between the loud and obnoxious tour group that took over the hotel restaurant this morning at breakfast, and the loud and obnoxious group of golfers that is here in the airport with us as we wait to board the plane.

The What They Know About Us Award: Every single person we met in the UK who had traveled to the US had been to Florida. A very few had visited other places as well (first runner-up: you guessed it, Las Vegas), but everyone wants to someday make it to Texas ("cowboys, after all," as one cab driver put it).

Weird Food Award: Forget the haggis and the black pudding and the baked beans on toast. The surprise winner here is the chips. We would call them steak fries, but they are served with absolutely everything. Cynthia and I have read *Fast Food Nation*, and the author of that book claims that most of the potatoes grown in the US are used for fries, but obviously, that man has never been to the UK.

Best Costume Award: We saw a number of kilts during our time in Scotland, but Glasgow Queen Street Station is far and away the best place to see people dressed in interesting outfits. The first time we were in the station, we saw a group of Japanese drummers get off one of the trains: They had on the white headbands and black coats and colorful sashes and the slippers with toes; they were also carrying their drums and banners. A few minutes later, another train arrived, and this one carried what I can only describe as a traveling Blues Brothers Convention: Once again, everyone was Japanese, and they were all wearing cheap black suits and thin ties; they all had fedoras and dark glasses. A few days later, we were once again in the station, and as we got off the train, we walked right into a group of women dressed as zebra-striped bunny rabbits, complete with tall ears and puffy tails.

Most Pleasant Surprise Award: Two awards here. First, the flowers and the gardens. The Monastery of St. John has gardens that are large and just gorgeous—in fact, it would probably qualify as a small farm. But just about every house in the villages where we stayed had a small garden or flowerbed, and there were boxes under every window and pots hanging from every eave and pole, and little explosions of color bursting from every nook in just about every stone wall. And then, also, the dogs. A great many people in England and Scotland traveled with dogs—mostly spaniels, Labs, Airedales, and terriers. But the animals were all on leashes, they were well-groomed, and they were unbelievably well-behaved. In fact, we only heard a dog bark once during our trip, and that was when we were outside, and the dog was a good distance away.

Strange Restaurant Encounters: Three moments deserve mention here.

(1) At O'Neill's Pub in Durham, we both ordered fish and chips. After a few minutes, the waitress/barmaid came out and said, "We've only got the one fish."

(2) At the Crown and Anchor Pub on Lindisfarne, I ordered a steak sandwich. Shortly thereafter, the bartender/waiter came out and said, " 'Fraid I've got some bad news: The last steak, she's been eaten—but it wasn't me, I want you to know."

(3) At the St. Columba Hotel on Iona, I ordered a breakfast that included sausage. Not much time passed before the waitress came back and said, "Umm, the sausage seems to be all gone—but it will be back tomorrow, I promise. In the meantime, would you like vegetarian sausage?"

Scary Plumbing Noises: We stayed in an old hotel on Lindisfarne. The bathroom was very modern, but whenever anyone in the building flushed a toilet, it sounded like someone was operating a large and noisy pneumatic drill.

And last, but certainly not least:

The Music Awards: Everyone in the UK listens to American music; the only exception we encountered was the monastery. At Durham, the breakfast cook rocked out to Rudy Valley and Steely Dan. At Edinburgh, we ate dinner to the mellow sounds of Meat Loaf. The cab drivers were all stuck in the eighties (Michael Jackson, Dire Straits, Tears for Fears). On Lindisfarne, we heard opera coming from the kitchen one night when we were at dinner, but we were later told that the chef was from the former Yugoslavia.

Monday, August 27
✤ *Poemen the Great*

We got home last night about 10 PM. The flights were grueling, but the one into Austin from Atlanta also had a peaceful and radiant quality to it. I had been thinking especially about St. Columba and St. Aidan and about the fact that they were both great sea saints. And as we flew home, I looked out the window, and there was a low layer of soft, silver clouds. Right above those, but scattered here and there across the sky, were clouds that were much taller and much darker. These darker clouds had steep ridges and deep valleys, and they rose up out of the night like islands. And shining far off and through it all were the bright orange and gold shafts of the west-setting sun.

So we sailed home across the sea sky, and I thanked the saints for their guidance and their prayers, and Cynthia slept on my shoulder.

Wednesday, August 29
✠ *The Beheading of the Forerunner*

This morning I was standing at the altar during liturgy, and another line from "Little Gidding" came to mind:

We shall not cease from exploration
And the end of all our exploring
Will be to arrive where we started
And know the place for the first time.

Two weeks ago, I was serving liturgy for the Dormition, and we were just about to leave on our pilgrimage. Now I'm back, standing before the same altar, and all the places we visited are right here as well: the tombs of St. Bede and St. Cuthbert, the island where St. Aidan prayed, the little church where he died, the spot where St. Columba's cell stood. In my heart, I can see the mist rising across the sound on Iona; I can hear the tide coming in at Lindisfarne; I can kneel before the tombs at Durham; I can look upon the little plaque at the church in Bamburgh. Because all of those holy places are connected to—they are accessible from—this altar. It's not that the trip was somehow unnecessary. Far from it. If we had not spent the money and taken the time to travel to those sites, I never would have known that they are all right here in this place called prayer.

Friday, August 31
✠ *Aidan, Bishop of Lindisfarne*

Today is my nameday. Bishop Basil and Fr. Deacon BL sent me emails; so did a number of other priests and deacons. EH sent me a nice handwritten note.

Cynthia and Katie took me to lunch, then they had a nice dinner waiting when I got home after Great Vespers for the Indiction.

They said I deserved more, but that's not true. The one who deserves more is my patron saint. There are no hymns dedicated to him in the Byzantine Menaion we use. He is mentioned in the Synaxarion, but out of the fourteen saints listed, he is number thirteen—and he doesn't even have any verses to accompany his name.

So today, I wrote a Synaxarion verse for him. It probably needs a bit of explanation, though: St. Aidan always refused to ride a horse; he felt that a bishop shouldn't be set apart from the people he served. Also, in St. Bede's *Life of St. Cuthbert,* a young St. Cuthbert is herding sheep at night when he sees St. Aidan's soul accompanied to heaven by angels, and it is this vision that inspires him to take up the monastic life.

That's the back-story for my verse. May it glorify the Most Holy Trinity, and by the prayers of the Enlightener of Northumbria, may I be granted more of his humility and love.

Holy Cuthbert saw thee winged to heaven
By the angelic powers, O Aidan;
Thou who, as a hierarch, refused to mount
Any earthly steed.

SEPTEMBER

Saturday, September 1
✚ *The Indiction*

Last night we did Great Vespers, and this morning we did Orthros and Divine Liturgy along with the Blessing for the New Year. Shamassy JL is still out of town, so it was Reader MT and Fr. Deacon BL and I doing the chanting this morning. On top of that, Fr. Deacon BL and I haven't actually served together in over a month, and we are a bit out of practice. We got through it all well enough, but it's on occasions like these that I take great comfort in G. K. Chesterton's dictum: "If it's worth doing, then it's worth doing badly."

Tuesday, September 4
✚ *Babylas, Hieromartyr*

I was thinking about all the services we did this past week, and I remembered something that happened the night before we left for our pilgrimage. We had served Great Vespers for the Feast of the Dormition, and a couple from another parish attended the service. Afterwards, I thanked them for praying with us, and they told me they had been expecting a Vesperal Liturgy. In fact, they said they were disappointed that they weren't able to receive the Eucharist. I explained to them that we always try to do the full cycle of services. They both just looked at me; the man chuckled; the woman smiled. Then they both said, "Why?"

That sort of thing happens on a fairly regular basis, but I still haven't gotten used to it. I just don't understand why doing the services in the traditional order and without abbreviation should require some sort of explanation or justification. Now, when we were received into the Church, there was a whole lot of talk about Orthodox fundamentalism. Apparently, some convert

233

communities were not only doing the entire Typicon, they were also insisting that anyone who did less was somehow less than Orthodox. That sort of self-righteousness is reprehensible. But equally reprehensible is the attitude that automatically views liturgical integrity as somehow extreme—or silly. I've met one or two Orthodox fundamentalists in the short time I've been a priest, and they were certainly unpleasant people, but on the other hand, I've run into lots and lots of folks who want the services abbreviated whenever and wherever possible.

In that regard, the whole Orthodox fundamentalism controversy reminds me of a passage from C. S. Lewis's *The Screwtape Letters*. In one of his missives, Uncle Wormwood outlines an interesting strategy for the junior tempter:

> We direct the fashionable outcry of each generation against those vices of which it is least in danger and fix its approval on the virtue nearest to that vice which we are trying to make endemic. The game is to have them all running about with fire extinguishers whenever there is a flood, and all crowding to that side of the boat which is already nearly gunwale under. Thus we make it fashionable to expose the dangers of enthusiasm at the very moment when they are all really becoming worldly and lukewarm.

So, in my experience, the threat of fundamentalism is hugely overrated; the real danger is that we will end up shortening the services (all in the name of convenience, progress, realism, flexibility, and pastoral sensitivity) to the point where we basically do what the rest of American Christianity has done—restrict divine worship to only one hour each week.

The really nutty thing is that most of the elements people want to cut out of the services don't actually take up that much time. A competent reader can get through a kathisma of the Psalter in fifteen minutes: If you're going to do Vespers at all, what's an extra fifteen minutes going to hurt? If you are already devoting an hour to Orthros, why not show up thirty minutes early and include most of the canon? And then there are the absolutely goofy abbreviations: Does it help to say twenty "Lord have mercy"s rather than forty? Does reading just three of the six psalms at Orthros make any significant difference?

Even the much-vaunted Vesperal Liturgy is problematic when looked at from this perspective. This combination of Vespers and Liturgy done the evening before the actual feast is supposed to make it possible for more people to participate in festal services, since it doesn't interfere with work or school. But it only stands to reason that if you have opportunities for worship at two different times—the evening before the feast and the morning of the feast—then you are going to have more participants overall than you will with just one opportunity. That has certainly been our consistent experience at St. John: The total number of people who attend Vespers on the eve of the feast, and Orthros and Divine Liturgy on the morning of the feast, is always greater than the total would be for a single Vesperal Liturgy. Not everyone gets to participate in the Eucharist, but more people get to participate in the feast.

So do I think people who abbreviate services are less than Orthodox? Absolutely not. As I said earlier, that is a judgmental perspective. I do, however, think the reasons they give for wanting to shorten the services are mistaken, and because of that, I believe their approach to worship is far more dangerous than the threat posed by a few fundamentalist cranks.

Wednesday, September 5
✠ Zacharias the Prophet

I think today must be Fr. Zacharias' nameday. I was thinking about him as I drove home after Orthros. When we were about to leave the monastery, we got one of the nuns to take a picture of Cynthia and me with Fr. Zacharias, and after the picture, he took Cynthia by the hand and said to her, "I'm sorry we did not get a chance to visit. But this I have to say to you: Share in the cross of the priesthood, and you will also share in its glory."

I've thought about that a lot since then. Mainly because Cynthia and I have, over the years, spent a lot of time thinking and talking about the role of a clergyman's wife. When we were United Methodists, there were two different approaches to the subject. The traditional view was that the pastor's wife was basically the congregation's assistant manager. That meant she played the piano, taught Sunday school, did secretarial work, counseled and advised parishioners, and hosted all sorts of events at the parsonage. However, in the last few decades, with the big rise in the number of ordained women, another model has emerged: the "clergy spouse." This is someone who is married to the clergyperson and participates in the life of the congregation, but has his or her own career and interests which have nothing to do with the parish or the ordained ministry.

While we were United Methodists, Cynthia tried both roles and found them wanting. She sang in choirs, accompanied various groups on the piano, played for worship services, taught/resourced Sunday school, and put together innumerable parsonage open houses, but the idea that she was basically an unpaid employee of the parish was demeaning. On the other hand, there wasn't anything appealing about the "you have your career, and I have mine" approach; you simply end up living in parallel universes.

But not long after we converted, I realized what the priest's wife is supposed to do: She's supposed to take care of the priest. Of course, many khourias and presbyteras and matushkas take on all sorts of projects and responsibilities, and there's nothing at all wrong with that. But their primary job—the way they share in the cross of the priesthood—is by ministering to the priest.

And that isn't easy. There are certain times of the year when the priest is hardly ever home. Many times, when he is home, he is just incapable of dealing with one more problem or having one more conversation. If something is troubling him, there's a good chance that he simply cannot talk about it due to the constraints of confidentiality. There are the late night phone calls, the interrupted meals, the last-minute changes to long-standing plans. There are the spiritual struggles: the fear, the frustration, the uncertainty, the temptations to pride and anger. And then there will always be a certain number of people in the parish who just flat don't like the guy.

The priesthood is a cross, that's for sure. But watching someone suffer is almost as difficult as the suffering itself. I learned that as a hospice chaplain. And I think about that every time I hear a stavrotheotokion, one of the hymns that describes the Mother of God as she stood before the Cross of her Son. Because that's the icon that best expresses the ministry of every priest's wife: watching over, caring for, being with the man you love as he suffers for the sins of the world.

Cynthia does it with great courage and dignity and beauty, and I am thankful for Fr. Zacharias's prophecy that one day, there will also be glory.

Thursday, September 6
✣ *Miracle of the Archangel Michael at Colossae*

Every once in a while, as I'm driving through our subdivision, I'll pass by a man who's practicing juggling. He strides down the sidewalk holding six white batons, and then suddenly, the batons start to spin and flash as he tosses them up and catches them in a rapid, fluid motion.

There's also a man in our subdivision who rides a unicycle. I usually see him in the same cul-de-sac, rocking back and forth on that one wheel, with his body all tense and his arms outspread.

Maybe those two guys are related. Maybe there's actually a circus camp hidden away somewhere in our neighborhood. I don't know. But it makes me happy whenever I see them. Which is why I think the world needs more circus acts—and more banjo playing and yodeling and kite flying.

It's just hard to be grumpy or worried when those sorts of things are going on.

Friday, September 7
✣ *Forefeast of the Nativity of the Theotokos*

It's been very hot and humid. And that means our altar area has been extremely hot and super sticky.

The room we use for our altar was originally an enclosed porch that had been added onto the rest of the house. We ran some A/C duct into the room and installed a pretty big vent, but there isn't any insulation, and there's no real ceiling to speak of, so it's just the broiling Texas sun and a few inches of shingles and wood and sheet metal and then me—usually in several layers of clothing and vestments.

Sometimes just stepping between the nave and the altar can mean a difference of ten to twenty degrees. And when that little room has been cookin' all day long—well, let's just say that if I were a real priest, I would emerge from that oven looking the way the Three Holy Children did when they stepped out of the Babylonian furnace: refreshed by the dew of the Spirit's breeze. But that ain't me, and tonight after Great Vespers, when I came out of the altar, I looked like Alec Guinness when he finally got out of the "box" in *The Bridge over the River Kwai.*

<hr>

Monday, September 10
✠ *Menodora, Metrodora,*
Nymphodora, Martyrs

I grow old. I grow old.
I shall wear the bottoms of my trousers rolled.

Those lines from "The Love Song of J. Alfred Prufrock" have been going through my head all day, but I've had a hard time working up any angst about this birthday. I'm fifty, but so far, the only emotions that have registered are a faint sense of guilt and some incredulity: incredulity because it's simply dumb luck that I've lasted this long, and guilt because I've got this nagging thought that I ought to be smarter than I actually am. I mean, if you've lived a full half-century, you should have picked up a little wisdom along the way—or at least some practical how-to-start-fires-in-the-open and fix-all-sorts-of-machines kind of knowledge—but I'm not there yet. Maybe I'm just developmentally delayed. Anyway, other than those two feelings, for me, fifty hasn't generated much in the way of soul-searching.

I did do a little of that earlier this summer, though. In talking to some of my friends, I learned that the careers of most of my former United Methodist colleagues have peaked. Just about all of them are serving big, important congregations. They have secretaries and administrative assistants; they supervise large numbers of staff people; they preach to hundreds on a regular basis; some of them are even getting ready to retire. And so several times throughout the summer, I wondered, "Did I do the right thing in leaving the denomination? Would it have been smarter to have just stuck it out? I could've had one of those prestigious congregations. I could be getting ready to retire!"

Those questions actually stuck with me for several weeks, but then one Sunday morning, I was standing with Fr. Deacon BL before the altar. The choir was singing the Great Doxology; he and I were beginning the dialogue that the priest and deacon read before the liturgy begins, and I remembered a scene from the movie, *The Right Stuff.* The movie is about the Mercury program and the astronauts who served in it, but it's also about one pilot, Chuck Yeager, who didn't get into the program. Sam Shepard plays Yeager, and while all the other pilots go on to achieve fame and acclaim through the space program, Yeager quietly continues setting records as a test pilot.

But the scene that popped into my mind that day in front of the altar is one that occurs several times during the movie: Shepard is sitting in the cockpit of a plane; he's about to take off, and his friend Levon Helm is helping him to get strapped in. But then at some point, Shepard always looks up at Helm and says:

"Ya got any Beeman's?"

"Yeah, I think I got me a stick."

"Loan me some, will ya? I'll pay you back later."

"Fair enough."

Shepard folds the gum into his mouth, then they close the cockpit, and he roars off to break the sound barrier or push back the altitude ceiling.

That little dialogue Shepard and Helms do reminded me of the words Fr. Deacon BL and I exchange at the beginning of each liturgy:

"It is time for the Lord to act. Bless, master."

"Blessed is our God, always, now and ever and unto ages of ages."

"Amen. Pray for me, master."

"The Lord direct thy steps unto every good work."

"Remember me, holy master."

"The Lord God remember thee in His Kingdom, always, now and ever and unto ages of ages."

Of course, what we say to each other is far more significant than the dialogue Shepard and Helms share; they're talking about gum; we're talking theology. But there are also some real similarities: In both situations, men are about to do something daring and dangerous; in both situations, men are about to soar into the heavens. And as I stood there before the altar, as Fr. Deacon BL and I finished the dialogue, I knew that even though acclaim and fame and a large congregation and a secretary and retirement probably aren't ever going to happen for me, I made the right choice. I'm where I'm supposed to be.

So I bowed to Fr. Deacon BL, and he went into the nave. I picked up the Gospel book and raised it above my head, and then we lifted off, rising swiftly—beyond all doubt, beyond all regret, beyond all looking back—into the great and luminous stillness that is the Kingdom of Truth.

Tuesday, September 11
✠ *Theodora of Alexandria*

This morning when I was backing the car down the driveway, I stopped for a moment to make sure no other cars were out on the road. I happened to glance down to my right, and a frog was sitting on the sidewalk, looking up at me. As I drove down the street, a couple of cats stuck their heads out of a storm drain and watched me pass by. When I arrived at church, I got out of the car, and a low-hanging branch caught my shoulder. I looked up at it, and I saw that the early morning darkness was studded with cold and bright stars, each and every one of them gazing down on me. As I was walking up to the building, a gecko shot across the sidewalk and raced halfway up a wall— but then, about eye level, he stopped and turned his head and watched me as I unlocked the door and went inside.

I stepped through the door of the nave and made a metania, and when I stood up, I was looking into the eyes of the Mother of God and the saints and the angels as they all watched me from the iconostasis. And then I realized: The frog, the cats, the stars, the gecko, the holy ones—they'd all been waiting on me. They were all where they were supposed to be, and they were waiting on me to take my place before the altar of the Most High.

Thursday, September 13
✠ *Forefeast of the Elevation*

The other day someone was asking me what it takes to be a priest, and I surprised myself. Instead of talking about sermon preparation or liturgical skills or counseling techniques, I simply said, "You gotta have a high tolerance for conflict."

That just sort of came out, but I'm going to stand by it. Because conflict is simply what happens when you get a lot of people together and try to be a community. Most of it is low-level, "he's looking at me!" sort of stuff, but from time to time it gets more intense, and every once in a while, it becomes downright toxic. Nevertheless, whatever the current threat level might be, the bottom line on conflict is that it is just an ongoing part of parish life.

Anyone who doubts that needs to reread 1 and 2 Corinthians and St. John's letters.

So what's the priest's responsibility in all this? To begin with, he just has to learn how to live in the midst of it. Tragically, some priests also participate in it or even initiate their own conflicts. I have heard of clergymen who were willing to do battle over what kind and how much incense should be used in the divine services. I have heard of clergymen who were physically violent.

Actually, though, the vast majority of priests tend to the opposite extreme: They do all they can to avoid conflict. The consequences of this approach aren't as dramatic, but they are often even more serious and long-lasting. If a staff person is accountable to no one, that situation probably has its roots in a priest who, years ago, was afraid to risk a confrontation. If a parish council regularly defies archdiocesan policy, that dynamic can usually be traced back to a priest who didn't want to take the chance of offending anyone.

So when should a priest step in and get involved? About as often as he does in the liturgy. The priest is responsible for the entire service, but he actually does very little (assuming he has a deacon). What he does do is absolutely critical—the exclamations, the blessings, the consecration of the gifts—but the vast majority of the liturgy is done by the deacon and the people. The priest is providing leadership and praying for everyone, but he only speaks when it is strictly necessary—and at those times, his voice should be clear and calm, and it should command.

Friday, September 14
✠ The Feast of the Elevation of the Cross

This morning, between Orthros and Divine Liturgy, we blessed the entire planet.

BT, one of our parishioners, had made a beautiful wreath for the cross, and during the Great Doxology, I took up the wreathed cross and processed out to a small table we had placed in front of the holy doors. We sang the troparion for the cross three times, then I went around to each side of the table, pausing on each side to sing one line of a litany, and to kneel while the chanters responded to the line with a hundredfold "Lord, have mercy." When I got back to the front of the table, the chanters sang the kontakion for the feast, and then we all sang the hymn, "Before Thy Cross," as we made three prostrations.

That's how we blessed the planet, north, south, east, and west. And it's one of the most profound, intensely spiritual, and truly loving things we do during the course of the liturgical year. St. Irenaeus captures something of the significance of this mystery when he writes:

> There are four zones of the world in which we live and four principal winds . . . the living creatures are quadriform, and the gospel is quadriform, and . . . for this reason four principal covenants were given to the human race: one, prior to the deluge under Adam; the second, that after the deluge under Noah; the third, the giving of the law under Moses; the fourth, that which renovates man, and sums up all things in itself by means of the Gospel.

And, of course, the symbol of that great summing up, that all-enfolding embrace, is the cross:

> Today the cross is exalted, and the world is sanctified. For Thou who art enthroned with the Father and the Holy Spirit hast spread Thine arms upon it and drawn the world to knowledge of Thee, O Christ.

> Oh new wonder! The fourfold cross reaches as high and as wide as the heavens, for its divine grace shines out to sanctify all creation.

But just because we were blessing the planet, that doesn't mean that everyone on the globe was aware of what was happening. After all, only a little over twenty of us were in the nave. And as I was processing out of the altar, I could see out of the front door, and the street was lined with cars and trucks and school buses and motorcycles. As I was kneeling on the south side of the table, I could hear the clank and rumble of construction vehicles coming from the new subdivision down the street. And as we were singing "Before Thy Cross," the phone in the kitchen started to ring.

But that's the way it was when the first cross-blessing took place: It was another busy Friday morning, and people had places to go and things to do, and I'm sure some noticed the commotion over by the praetorium—there was probably even a good deal of conversation about that strange eclipse in the middle of the day—but then, of course, there was the big holiday, and right after that, the start of a new week, with all its worries and concerns and new distractions.

Saturday, September 15
✤ *Niketas the Goth, Martyr*

All week long, Katie has been doing orientation for her new job in the ER. A great deal of it has focused on documentation, and of course, that means learning all sorts of new and interesting abbreviations. My favorite so far? UBI: Unexplained Beer Injury.

And speaking of beer, Brendan called to let us know that he is now the toast of his military police unit. It seems the base commander has decided that his installation will achieve a perfect safety record. To that end, for the last few months, every DUI arrest the MPs have made has been knocked down to a less serious charge. However, this has only made the MPs more determined than ever to make some charges actually stick, and as it turns out, Brendan was the cop who finally made the collar: an underage enlisted man, driving a stolen car, and the arrest came complete with a positive breathalyzer, videotape, eyewitness testimony, and a signed confession.

No word yet as to the base commander's mood, but there has been much celebrating in the offices of the military police.

Sunday, September 16
✤ *Sunday after the Elevation of the Cross*

Last night we did Great Vespers early so we could do an unction service for CM, a woman who is a member of our parish. Last week, CM was diagnosed with breast cancer; she's going to have surgery this coming Thursday, so we did the unction service at a special time.

We had a good turnout for the service, and afterwards, we asked CM to stand over by the wreathed cross so that folks could greet her and assure her of their prayers. But now that we've held two of these services for individual members of the parish, I've become convinced of the broader significance of what we are doing: yes, we are praying for healing; yes, we are expressing our love and support for the person who is ill. But the service also represents a strategic opportunity in the ongoing fight against evil.

I sensed that in a dramatic way during last night's service. As we were listening to the canon, I thought of the Charles Williams poem, "Mount Badon." A vast "indiscriminate host" of barbarian raiders is ranged against King Arthur and his knights. Taliessin, the king's poet, commands the reserve unit of cavalry, and in "a passion of patience" he is watching the battle, looking for the precise, decisive point at which he should commit his troop. While he waits, Taliessin thinks about Virgil, the great poet of order and civilization, and how the Roman master must have searched for words that were equally precise and decisive. Then, Taliessin sees the strategic moment he has been waiting for, and he seizes that moment in the same way Virgil must have suddenly seized upon just the right words:

> Civilized centuries away, the Roman moved.
> Taliessin saw the flash of his style
> dash at the wax; he saw the hexameter spring
> and the king's sword swing; he saw, in the long field,
> the point where the pirate chaos might suddenly yield,
> the place for the law of grace to strike.
> He stood in his stirrups; he stretched his hand;
> he fetched the pen of his spear from its bearer;
> his staff behind signed to their men . . .
> the household of Taliessin swung upon the battle . . .
> the candles flared among the pirates; their mass broke. . . .
> The lord Taliessin kneeled to the king;
> the candles of new Camelot shone through
> the fought field.

That's a wonderful description of what we did last night, because at the beginning of the unction service, during the canon, we simply wait and watch. We observe our own "passion of patience." Taliessin's struggle is ordered and expressed through the poetry of Virgil; ours, through the hymns of the Church. But then, at the decisive moment, we also enter into the battle, with Scripture and the prayers and the holy oil, striking at the heart of the "pirate chaos" that constantly threatens to engulf this world with sickness and sorrow and stupidity.

After the service, the lamps on the iconostasis burned brightly and the candles in the trays "shone through the fought field" as, one by one, we spoke to CM and gave her hugs and promised her our ongoing prayers.

Monday, September 17
✛ *Sophia and Her Daughters, Martyrs*

This morning after I got home from Orthros, I felt really tired. I wasn't sure what that was about until I remembered what yesterday was like: We did Orthros and Divine Liturgy, and right after that, we made four people catechumens—a young man named DM, and a young couple, DW and VW, along with their two-year-old son, IW. Then we did a memorial service for Shamassy JL's dad, and a wedding anniversary blessing for Subdeacon TW and his wife, PW. After all the services were over and I got my vestments off, I greeted the visitors (five of them). Then I talked to IZ about prosphora, to RT about chairs in the nave, and to LB about her upcoming trip to Russia and her family who lives there. I spoke with VK about becoming a catechumen and with MB about being VK's godmother. I blessed DZ, who was absent last week when we blessed all the young people for the start of school. I checked with MT to see how she's recovering from her surgery. I followed up on an email with KR and on RC and MC's wedding plans. I asked BL and RM about their new jobs; I talked with HB about how his job might be changing; I spoke briefly with SB about her search for a job. I talked with KS about his trip to Russia, then I tracked down Reader MT and told him that KS was going to Russia (in case he wanted to order anything for the bookstore). I got a movie recommendation from CL and listened to CM talk about an experience she had at Carlsbad Caverns. A Greek woman—whose name I don't yet know since she just recently started attending services—stopped me and told me how much her teenaged daughter is enjoying the parish. KR told me that she is planning to choose St. Elizabeth the New Martyr for her patroness. Then I did seven stewardship visits. After the visits were done, I set up the music stands and got out the books for the next morning's Orthros. As I was leaving, I spoke with KS about how we would divide up the lawn work this week, with CM about coffee hour and missions trips, and with JM about several former catechumens.

Except for the stewardship visits, that's a fairly normal Sunday. It wears me out, but then a priest is supposed to wear himself out. Since we returned from our pilgrimage, I've been rereading Fr. Zacharias's book, *Christ, Our Way and Our Life.* Having visited with Fr. Zacharias and prayed at Fr. Sophrony's tomb, I now have a much deeper appreciation for the book. Like the following passage; I read it this afternoon, and it puts my fatigue in a completely new light—the light of the Gospel, the light of eternity:

> As a prerequisite for the acquisition of the spirit of this love, one must fulfill the indispensable condition set by the Lord: "Whoever would be great among you must be your servant, and whoever would be first among you must be your slave." He expressed the same condition in the commandment which He gave to those who wish to follow Him and become His disciples: "Whoever loses his life for my sake will save it." This becomes the law of life for those who are inspired by the idea of going downward . . . to be united with the Spirit of Love, and, strengthened by the grace of the Lord, to be able to "bear the weakness of [his] weak brethren." In an ineffable fashion, his descent makes man like the Son of God, the "Lamb of God who takes away the sin of the world."

Wednesday, September 19
✠ *Trophimus, Sabbatius, Dorymedon, Martyrs*

Tonight we are going to be discussing the Song of Songs in our theological seminar. So, to put together a little introductory material, I pulled off the bookshelf that bastion of evangelical Protestant scholarship, Eerdman's *Old Testament Survey.* I got the basic information I needed, but I also had a whole lot of fun with some of the editors' analyses.

For example, in the section entitled "Suggested Interpretations," I found this observation:

> Not only is the history of interpretation full of conflicting theories, but all the resources of modern scholarship—archaeological dis-coveries, recovery of huge bodies of ancient literature, insights into oriental psychology and sociology—have produced no uniform approach to the book.

Uh, guys? It's a love poem. Perhaps if you stopped focusing on archaeology and ancient literature and oriental psychology, and instead kissed your wife or held hands with your girlfriend or just took a good long look at the next woman you find yourself standing next to in the checkout line at the grocery store, the whole thing might not be quite so mysterious.

Then there was this gem about allegory: "The allegorical interpretation is questionable because scholarly control is impossible." What these guys just don't understand is that the Holy Fathers who wrote about the Song weren't particularly interested in the historical or sociological context of the poem. Now modern scholars will acknowledge that fact; they will pay lip service to it. But what eludes them is the real dynamic that's at work in most patristic commentary—and this is especially obvious in the work the Fathers did on the Song: Their commentary simply consists of poetry they were inspired to write as a result of the sacred poem they were reading. Like this from St. Ambrose:

> After this, you went up to the priest. Consider what followed. Was it not that of which David speaks: "Like the ointment upon the head, which went down to the beard, even Aaron's beard"? This is the ointment of which Solomon, too, says, "Your name is poured out, therefore have the maidens loved you and drawn you." How many souls regenerated this day have loved you, Lord Jesus, and have said, "Draw us after you, we are running after the odor of your garments," that they might drink in the odor of your resurrection.

That kind of interpretation needs no scholarly control. It is inspired by the Spirit, and of course, just as "the wind blows where it wills and you hear the sound of it, but you do not know whence it comes or whither it goes, so it is with everyone who is born of the Spirit"—and, we could add, everyone who writes poetry in the Spirit.

Thursday, September 20
✠ *Eustathios and His Family, Martyrs*

Today CM had her surgery. I prayed with her before they took her to the operating room, and while she was there, I went to the hospital chapel to pray.

There were a lot of pews and a surprisingly large altar in the chapel, but the ceiling was very low, and there were only windows on one side of the room, so the whole effect was a bit like being in an ecclesiastical basement. Nevertheless, I felt at home there, and at first I wasn't sure why. But after I finished reading the services for the day, I was sitting there looking at the windows, and I realized what made it seem so familiar: The Greek parish I served in Wichita Falls has the same kind of stained glass.

I think it's a technique that was popular in the late 1960s and early '70s: think rough pieces of glass set in a framework of broad metal bands. In the Greek parish, one of those windows was set directly behind the altar table, so I spent many hours looking at the bright colors and the textured glass. But thinking about CM and her surgery, and reading through the services for the day (tonight we begin the Leavetaking of the Feast of the Elevation of the Cross), and remembering that window I used to look at for hours on end, reminded me of an experience I had while I was serving in Wichita Falls.

The parish could only pay me a small stipend, so I supported our family by working full-time as a hospice chaplain. In fact, all told, I did that job for over a decade. During those ten years, the organization I worked for experienced phenomenal growth: We were able to care for a great many patients and their families; we were also able to realize our dream of opening an in-patient facility. However, with the facility came pressures and complications no one had anticipated. In addition to that, our little nonprofit organization was forced to deal with a whole new range of ethical questions, such as who should have access to the limited number of beds in the facility and what is the proper use of medication at the end of life.

No one in the hospice was prepared to deal with that much change; no one was equipped to handle the new challenges we were facing. But the way the leadership chose to handle the uncertainty and anxiety was simply to clean house and start over: Everyone who had been with the organization for any length of time was forced out. This was accomplished in a variety of ways: no one was ever fired; most people were simply bullied until they couldn't take it anymore, and they left. Unfortunately, I didn't realize what was going on until only one or two other long-time employees were left, and by then I was being threatened and berated on a regular basis. I looked around for other work, but in a small town like Wichita Falls, there wasn't much a guy like me could do.

During that time, I would stop by the church every chance I got—before work, after work, on my lunch hour. But one morning in particular made a huge difference: The day before, I had been told the only reason I still had a job was out of pity for my family. I hadn't said anything about it to Cynthia; I didn't want to worry her. But that night I hardly slept at all, and while it was still very early and very dark, I got up and got ready for work and drove to the church.

I didn't even turn on any lights in the building. I didn't try to do a service. I was too tired and too stressed out. I just went straight into the altar, and there, in the dark, I knelt down and put my hands and my head on the altar table.

I was there for quite a while—and I didn't move at all. My legs started to cramp; my hands went to sleep. I didn't care; I was just too miserable. But when I did finally raise my head, I looked up at the window across from the altar table, and in the first dim light of the new day, I saw a faintly illumined cross.

Now that is what was normally in the window; the name of the parish is Holy Cross, so they had put a cross in that main window. But usually that cross was surrounded by a rainbow riot—green, blue, purple, red, yellow— every wild and crazy color combination of the seventies was enshrined in that stained glass. But on that particular morning, there was just the darkness, and the bare light of dawn shining through that cross, and me.

I got up and worked the cramps out of my legs. I shook my hands until the feeling came back into them. Then I went to work, and I stuck it out until I was transferred to Cedar Park and St. John's parish almost two years later.

I hope CM saw that same cross when she was coming out of the anesthesia. The surgeon said everything looked good, but they'll know more after the pathology tests come back next week.

Friday, September 21
✠ *Leavetaking of the Elevation of the Cross*

This morning, during Orthros, we chanted this hymn in the eighth ode of the canon:

Let all the trees of the forest shout with joy, for their nature is made holy by Christ, who planted them at the beginning and who was stretched out on a tree. At its exaltation today, we worship Him and magnify the holy wood.

It's my week to help with the yard work, so after the service, I went outside and mowed the lawn in the front and both sides of the building. The sun was barely up. There was a nice breeze. My boots got all wet from the dew. I listened hard, but I couldn't hear the trees shouting. I could tell they were praying, though, because their branches were lifted up and spread out to the sky, and all morning long, it was like I was walking back and forth through a congregational prayer, through a living assembly at worship, through a forest of great orants.

Sunday, September 23
✤ *First Sunday of Luke*

In the contemplative life, Holy Scripture is no longer simply a book; it is a dynamic dimension of everyday reality.

Like last night at Great Vespers: This weekend, we are commemorating the conception of our patron and protector, St. John the Forerunner. While the chanters are singing "O Lord, I have cried," Fr. Deacon BL and I are standing at the altar, but then during the stichera, the chanters begin to sing about the priest Zachariah and the encounter he had with the archangel Gabriel. Zachariah was standing before an altar, just as I am. The archangel Gabriel appeared just to the right of the altar, which is where our own liturgical angel, Fr. Deacon BL, is standing. Then the chanters start to sing through the conversation the holy priest has with the great angel, and that conversation also takes place in my heart as fear alternates with trust, and unexpected, unlooked-for joy leaves the soul speechless. Then Fr. Deacon BL takes up the censer, and we process out of the altar as the chanters sing, "Today the fruit of prayer has taken root in a barren womb," and I'm thankful for that conception, because that means my barren heart will also one day blossom and bloom.

Then early this morning I was out under the trees practicing my sermon, and at the other end of the property, a single deer rose up out of the tall grass. In a series of perfect arcs, he leapt three times across the field and then disappeared into the trees. And as I watched him fly through the dawn, a passage from the Song of Songs sprang into my mind:

Make haste, my beloved,
and be like a gazelle
or a young stag
upon the mountains of spices.

Just knowing that Christ Jesus loves me with that kind of strength and that He is willing to come to me with that kind of swiftness filled me with all kinds of holy energy. I turned right then and walked into the building. The services were magnificent, and I preached well, and when it came time to partake of the gifts, as I was standing before the altar and raising the chalice to my lips, another passage from the Song flashed into my mind:

Your kisses are like the best wine
that goes down smoothly
gliding over lips and teeth.

I placed the chalice back on the altar, but the sweetness of that intimacy left me thirsty for an experience of even greater union, and for the contemplation that leads, step by step, to that wellspring of joy.

Monday, September 24
✠ *Silouan the Athonite*

I love this great saint.

I have venerated his relics. I have prayed at the tomb of his spiritual son, Fr. Sophrony. I have read Fr. Sophrony's books; I made a pilgrimage to the monastic community he started. I have visited with Fr. Sophrony's spiritual son, Fr. Zacharias; I have also read his book and listened to his tapes. My archpastor, Bishop Basil, is a member of the monastery Fr. Sophrony founded. And Bishop Basil has recently announced that the speaker for next year's Clergy Brotherhood Retreat will be Dr. Christopher Veniamin, a seminary professor who is a spiritual son of Fr. Zacharias.

So I am part of the saint's spiritual inheritance; I am a member of his family; in a real sense, I am related to him.

And as I was reading back through the pages of this journal, I remembered one dramatic way in which the saint has intervened in my life. It was some years ago, when Fr. Zacharias was the speaker during our annual Clergy Brotherhood Retreat. I had read several of Fr. Sophrony's books, but it was the first time I had ever heard of Fr. Zacharias. Nevertheless, his humility and his spiritual insight were quickly apparent, and I listened carefully to all that he had to say. But one remark he made went deep into my heart.

During a question-and-answer session, one of the priests asked Fr. Zacharias about joy. I don't remember exactly how the question was phrased; I think the priest asked Fr. Zacharias about the joy that was such an obvious part of his life. But this is what Fr. Zacharias said in response: "Fr. Sophrony used to say that on Mount Athos, when a monk is gloomy, they say it's because he has not worked in the night."

I thought about that observation throughout the rest of the retreat and all during the long drive home. I thought about it so much because I was gloomy. That was right about the time I was going through all the turmoil with my job at the hospice, and I had very little hope.

So a month or so later, I wrote Fr. Zacharias a letter. I thanked him for leading the retreat. I asked him what he meant about working in the night. But while I was waiting for his response, I had the experience I wrote about just a few entries ago, where I went to the church very early one morning and, without realizing it, actually did the sort of work Fr. Zacharias had been talking about. I simply placed all my fears and uncertainty and anger and worry before the Most Holy Trinity; I offered it up, and the softly illumined cross showed me that my sacrifice had been accepted.

So when Fr. Zacharias's letter arrived, it simply explained what I had already experienced. But without that explanation, I never would have understood the full significance of what I had been through. This is what Fr. Zacharias wrote:

Dear Father Aidan, Christ is in our midst!

I read your letter carefully and reflected upon it. For me the matter is clear. You are a partaker of the holy and suffering priesthood of Christ. And as it is written of Christ that all the reproaches of them that reproached Him fell upon Him and that He became for us a curse and 'sin' in order to save us, so also upon His partakers or fellows all evil will fall on them and they will bear the burden of their fellows, console them and intercede for them. Therefore, I am not surprised that you feel crushed at times in your ministry. As St. Paul says to his Corinthian disciples: Life worketh in you and death in me. The partakers of Christ assume in their godly life the death of their fellows and transmit to them the gift of life.

Nevertheless for us not to succumb in this struggle but show Christ victorious in all things we must learn not only to weep in the night but every negative energy—as well as positive—that assails us during our lifetime we must make energy for prayer and repentance and the grace thereof will keep us ever happy in the wonderful grace of Christ's salvation. How does this transformation occur? We accept every pain out of love for Christ. More simply, we make every pain and every emotion energy for prayer by determining the thought of our presentation before God.

Please forgive me for my daring to write these words to you and pray for me a sinner. We will not forget you in our liturgy, neither your wife and children.

With humble love in Christ,
Archimandrite Zacharias

That letter was written by Fr. Zacharias, but in it, he is faithfully transmitting the teaching of St. Silouan. That's why I've hung onto it for all these years. Because it reminds me of my spiritual lineage, and every time I read it, I am thankful that I am one of St. Silouan's children and that, no matter how dark things may get, as it says in his troparion, I too am one of those "called to hope."

Tuesday, September 25
✠ Euphrosyne

Speaking of my spiritual lineage, today I get to honor another member of the family, St. Ceolfrith, abbot of Jarrow. St. Bede includes St. Ceolfrith in his book, *The Lives of the Abbots of Wearmouth and Jarrow,* but my favorite story about this saint comes from the anonymous *History of Abbot Ceolfrith.*

A round of plague had killed all the monks in the community who could read or sing, and St. Ceolfrith was left to do the services with one small boy who was being brought up in the monastery. The saint thought it was best therefore to abbreviate the services, but:

> . . . when this was done for the space of only one week with many tears and laments, he felt unable to bear it any longer, so he decided that the psalms with the antiphons should be resumed as before. With everyone trying their best, he completed this by himself with no small labor and only the help of the boy mentioned above, until he trained sufficient companions in the work of God.

Most historians agree that the boy was St. Bede. But what I like about the story is St. Ceolfrith's sensitive perseverance: In an age of complete uncertainty and utter brutality, in a time when death was a daily fact, it would simply make sense to regard the divine services as luxuries, as an optional project that should be undertaken only after the essentials of life had been addressed. But St. Ceolfrith didn't look at worship that way; he understood that it is "the work of God." And that's how we should approach the divine services.

Wednesday, September 26
✣ *St. John the Theologian*

This afternoon, I was driving to school, and I felt a piece of paper in the front pocket of my cassock. I pulled it out and looked at it: A list of names was written on a small square of purple notepaper. The names were all Russian. Then I remembered what the piece of paper was for: A Russian woman had stopped by the church this weekend and written down the names of her departed relatives, and she had asked that we remember them during a service. Reader MT had given me the list, and I had stuck it in the pocket of my cassock.

So all this week, I've been walking around with a list of dead people in my pocket. I imagine that's something that only happens to priests. But this fall, on Monday and Wednesday evenings, I've been reading Small Compline and the Midnight Office in the break I have between classes. So as I began my prayers, I got out the purple piece of paper and asked the Father, Son, and Holy Spirit to remember all our fathers and brethren who have fallen asleep in the hope of the resurrection to eternal life.

I also offered prayers of thanksgiving for CM: She got her test results back from the oncologist, and everything is looking pretty good. She still has some treatments to get through, but it appears that the cancer has not spread.

Thursday, September 27
✣ Callistratus and His Companions, Martyrs

Every morning, I get to work just about the same time as Sonic Guy.

To be truthful, Sonic Guy often beats me. I'll be driving down East Park Street, and I'll pull up at the stop sign on old Highway 183, and—zip!—he flashes right past me in his small, light-colored Ford. Before I even get to the light on the new 183, he's parked his car and is headed for the drive-in's kitchen, shoving his shirt into his pants with one hand and trying to hold onto his hat, nametag, and apron with the other. When I finally get through the light and I'm headed up West Park Street, I'll glance in the rearview mirror. By then, the big drive-in sign is on at full power, and he's racing around the kitchen, throwing switches and turning on machines.

Sonic Guy and I actually have a lot in common. We both get up early; we both wear uniforms; we're both on our feet for hours and hours; we both have to deal with lots of requests from lots of different people. And we both do important work. After all, a good cheeseburger can be as much a blessing as a good prayer. Anyone who doubts that has most likely never really tasted either.

Sunday, September 30
✣ Second Sunday of Luke

Today was glorious. We made VK a catechumen. We baptized MF, CF and OF's infant son. We chrismated KR and RT. The nave was packed.

The singing was—well, let's just say I can still hear it. It was that beautiful.

But I also realized something today. It sounds strange, but I've always enjoyed the exorcism prayers that we use when we make people catechumens, but today I finally understood why: It just feels great to be able to get angry in a way that's completely righteous—and not only righteous, but articulate and flowing.

When it comes to anger, our culture is all messed up. Some people can't control their anger, and that's why we have road rage and child abuse and workplace shootings. But a great many people can't get angry. That's not the sort of problem that's going to get you a spot on the CNN news crawl, but it's still a big deal. And a great many Christians struggle with this problem: Somewhere along the way, they've picked up the idea that anger is wrong, so they sit on their feelings. But even when they do express their anger, most of these folks hardly ever cut loose and let the fur fly. They hold back; they never close their eyes and swing for the fence.

Of course, if you never express your anger, then you forget how to do it. Rageaholics can go from mellow to white-hot in less than a minute, but the rest of us have a hard time even getting the program to boot up. For instance, I'm the sort of person who can never think of what I want to say. Several hours later, I always come up with really good stuff, but at the moment of confrontation, I sputter and stutter and say things like, "Oh, yeah? Well . . . uh . . . that just shows what you know!"

In that respect, I've always admired those people who can taunt their foes in eloquent and poetic ways. I went to high school with a kid whose nickname was Wolf City, and I'll always remember standing in a packed stairwell and watching him do the dozens with a bully about twice his size. But Wolf City didn't back down, and amidst applause and laughter, he finished the guy off by commenting that he looked like he'd "been ridin' in a runaway ugly machine." Then there's Rostand's play *Cyrano de Bergerac,* in which the great swordsman composes a "ballade of three eight-verse couplets and an envoi of four lines" while dueling with the boorish Viscount de Valvert and scoring a hit on the last line. And, of course, one of the most delicious scenes in the entire history of cinema is in *Guess Who's Coming to Dinner,* when Katharine Hepburn fires her racist gallery manager:

Then take the check, which I feel you deserve, and get—
permanently—lost. It's not that I don't want to know you, Hilary—

although I don't—it's just that I'm afraid we're really not the sort
of people you can afford to be associated with. No, don't speak,
Hilary—just go.

Of course, there's a lot of sinfulness in that sort of behavior: pride,
jealousy, resentment, cruelty. But it's not entirely sinful; otherwise, why
would we get this feeling of satisfaction when bullies and boors and racists
are put in their place? And why would we experience this elation when the
verbal fencing is elegant and precise and sharp? There must be an element of
truth somewhere in that sort of interaction.

I used to wonder about all this a great deal—until I read what the Holy
Fathers have to say about the proper use of anger: It's only rarely to be
directed at our fellow human beings; the demons are the real target. So the
wrathful have got it wrong: We are hardly ever supposed to get angry at
other people. But then, all of us wimps are also mistaken: We should be able
to smite the demons; we should be able to unload on them with anger that
is confident and inspired and uninhibited.

Now, most people are aware of the fact that the Church can help the
wrathful to become meek; what we many times forget is that the Church
can also help wimps become warriors. That kind of training takes place
in worship, and the basic equipment is the cursing psalms. For example,
in Psalm 57, when we talk about washing our hands in the blood of our
enemies, we're not talking about people; we're talking about the evil creatures
who are the enemies of our souls. When we pray Psalm 108 and wish this
on our foes:

Let his children be vagabonds and his wife a widow;
let them be cast out from their ruined dwellings.
Let his creditors search out all his substance,
and let strangers plunder all his labors.
Let there be for him no helper
nor anyone to pity his fatherless children.

—what we are doing is lashing out at the demons.

Some Christian communities are embarrassed and appalled by the
cursing psalms, and they have actually removed them from worship. But
that not only ignores the reality of human nature (after all, we do get angry;

it's just part of the emotional equipment the Most Holy Trinity has put into us), it also ignores the reality of evil (there are some really bad creatures out there, and they want to destroy us). The end result is that our emotional life is enervated, and we are left without some very important weapons.

But it's not that way in the Church. Not only do we read the cursing psalms every week at Vespers and Orthros, we also get to recite that tough, taunting poem, "God Is with Us," at Great Compline during Great Lent:

God is with us; know, ye nations, and be vanquished.
Give ear, even unto the uttermost parts of the earth.
Ye that have prevailed, even ye be vanquished.
For though ye should prevail again, yet again
ye shall be vanquished.
And whatsoever counsel ye shall take,
the Lord shall bring it to naught.
And whatsoever word ye speak,
it shall not abide in you.
And the fear of you we shall not fear,
neither shall we be troubled.
But we will sanctify the Lord our God,
and He shall be our fear.

And then there are the prayers of exorcism. Reading them is always such a rush, because there are usually a whole lot of people crowding into the nave and the narthex, and we array ourselves against all that's unfair and petty and ruthless and dishonest and ugly and mean, and we don't even have to think about the words because the Church has given them to us, so we lift up our kilts and degrade our enemies; we dis' them; we spit on them and remind them of just how sorry they are all going to be:

Depart! Know the vainness of thy might, which had no power,
even over pigs. Remember Him that commanded thee, at thy
request, to enter into the herd of swine. . . . I forbid thee by the
Saving Passion of our Lord Jesus Christ, and by His precious Body
and Blood, and by His dread Coming-again; for He will come, and
will not tarry, to judge the earth, and He will punish thee and thy

cooperating host in the fiery Gehenna, consigning thee to outer darkness where the worm ceases not and the fire is not quenched.

It's cosmic trash talk; it's a spiritual end-zone dance. And of course, the only way we get away with it is because we are shielded by mighty angels and protected by the One who is mounted on a white horse and clad in a robe dipped in blood, whose eyes are like a flame of fire, and upon whose head are many crowns.

OCTOBER

It's getting harder for our dog Shelly to get around. We've lost track, but she's either seventeen or eighteen years old. Her hips and shoulders are just about worn out, so she can't manage the steps at the back door. That means we have to take her out in the front yard when she needs to go. But because she's been a house dog for all these years, she's too nervous to walk out into the yard by herself. We have to put a leash on her and take her out in the yard and stand there while she sniffs around for just the right spot. Usually, we're talking four to five trips a day and sometimes one in the middle of the night. It's a lot of trouble, but then, a few years down the road, someone will probably have to do something similar for me. And, as they say, every dog deserves a little dignity.

Wednesday, October 3
✠ Dionysius the Areopagite, hieromartyr

Oh boy.

The holidays are here.

The people across the street from us have spread a gauze web across the trees in their yard and put a large, inflatable, purple-and-black spider on their roof.

Down the street from us, a family has lined their sidewalk with fluorescent plastic skulls and hung white plastic ghosts from the trees in their yard.

On the street that leads out of our subdivision is a house with two large, inflatable, purple-and-black spiders, one on the roof and one on the side of the house. In the yard is an inflatable jack-o-lantern about the size of a small SUV. At night, this entire display is illuminated by two spotlights.

I don't want to be a Halloween Grinch, but I don't get it.

I mean, I really don't get it.

Saturday, October 6
✠ *Apostle Thomas*

I'm a bad son.

I forgot my mother's birthday.

Here everyone has made such a big deal about my birthday, and I didn't even have the presence of mind to pick up the phone and call the woman who brought me into this world.

And unfortunately, this isn't the first time. In fact, I used to forget almost every year. Sometimes one of my sisters would remind me, and I would make a phone call or get a card in the mail, but it was hardly ever because I remembered. After we became Orthodox, it was easier to keep the date in mind, because her birthday is October 1, the day we honor the Protecting Veil of the Mother of God.

But this year I blew it again. In fact, I wasn't even aware of the fact that I'd forgotten until I was talking to her on the phone, and she mentioned something about her birthday party.

Ouch.

I am truly slime.

But as penance—and to honor my mom—I will write about an incident that demonstrates what kind of woman my mother is.

In 1969, my father was serving his tour in Vietnam. We were living in my mother's hometown in south Georgia. We were renting a large old house, and one evening, we had just sat down for dinner. Actually, the four of us kids were sitting at the table, and my mother was still doing something at the kitchen counter. But then the back door opened, and a strange man stumbled in. He was drunk, but none of us kids had ever seen anything like that. We just sat there at the table and stared.

However, my mother acted as if the man were a guest that we were somehow expecting. She greeted him and asked him if he would like to have a seat at the table. The man slurred something in response, then he started to stagger around the kitchen. My mother continued to speak to the man, but she also told Rosemary—my older sister—and me to take the younger kids to the next door neighbor's.

We were all in a state of semi-shock; I think Rosemary wanted to stay, but my mother insisted, so in just a moment, we were all outside. I waited on the front lawn; Rosemary and the two younger kids ran next door to get our landlord, Mr. Truitt. It wasn't long before Mr. Truitt came running over; he was carrying a shotgun. But at the same moment, my mother came out of the front door of our house. She had managed to get the man to sit down at the dinner table, and then he had passed out.

The police came and took the man to jail. My grandfather came over and spent the next couple of nights at our house. But even though I'm a lousy son, I know a good mother when I see one. Because that night, my mom was our protecting veil; she stood between us and danger; she was pleasant and kind, gentle and firm, and she never showed the slightest hint of fear.

Sunday, October 7
✠ *Third Sunday of Luke*

Apart from the liturgy, I think the proskomidia is just about the most profound service in the Church's typikon. Of course, the proskomidia cannot really be separated from the liturgy, but one of the things that makes this service so powerful is the fact that it is hidden. But this isn't just a matter of concealment for the sake of liturgical propriety, or—what would be far worse—an attempt to create an atmosphere of mystery. It is an expression of what St. Paul talks about in his letter to the Colossians: a manifestation of our life that is "hidden with Christ in God."

During the proskomidia, it is just Fr. Deacon BL and I behind the iconostasis. But we do the service during Orthros, while the psalms are being read. So the proskomidia, the preparation of the bread and wine for the Liturgy, becomes a service within a service. It's as if Fr. Deacon and I enter deep into the heart of the psalms, and there, amidst those very prayers, amidst the audible cries of humanity's hunger and thirst for the Most Holy Trinity, we prepare the meal.

The focus of our preparation is the prosphora loaf and the chalice of wine. They are the gifts that we will offer to the Father, Son, and Holy Spirit. But in the service, the prayers and hymns that accompany the preparation of these gifts speak of birth and death. Those two realities define what it means to be human; they summarize all our suffering. Nevertheless, in the proskomidia, we speak of a particular birth and a specific death, the birth and death of the incarnate Son of God, and that birth, that death, transform our living and dying:

> Make ready, O Bethlehem, for Eden hath been opened for all. Prepare, O Ephratha, for the tree of life hath blossomed forth in the cave from the Virgin: for her womb did appear as a spiritual paradise in which is planted the divine plant, whereof eating we shall live and not die as Adam. Christ shall be born, raising the image that fell of old.
>
> Thou hast redeemed us from the curse of the Law by Thy precious Blood; nailed to the Cross and pierced by the spear, Thou hast poured forth immortality upon mankind, O our Savior, glory to Thee.

Thus, what the offering of bread and wine symbolizes is our opportunity to be united with Christ Jesus in His birth and His death, an opportunity to unite our suffering with His and thereby join with Him in redeeming the world.

All of this is graphically expressed through the dialogue Fr. Deacon BL and I recite as I cut the loaf of bread with the spear, and he pours the wine into the chalice:

"Let us pray to the Lord. Lord, have mercy."

"As a sheep led to the slaughter."

"Let us pray to the Lord. Lord, have mercy."

"And as a blameless lamb before its shearer is dumb, so He opened not His mouth."

"Let us pray to the Lord. Lord, have mercy."

"In His humiliation, justice was denied Him."

"Let us pray to the Lord. Lord, have mercy."

"Who can describe His generation?"

"Take up, Master."

"For His Life is taken up from the earth."

"Sacrifice, Master."

"Sacrificed is the Lamb of God, who taketh away the sin of the world, for the life of the world, and its salvation."

"Pierce, Master."

"One of the soldiers pierced His side with a spear, and at once there came out blood and water; and he who saw it hath borne witness, and his witness is true."

"Bless, Master, this union."

"Blessed is the union of Thy holy things,"

"Always, now and ever, and unto ages of ages. Amen."

But the service becomes even more compelling and even more poignant when we begin the commemorations. We pray for hundreds of people at this point in the service, and each time, with each name, as I thrust the spear into the soft crust of the bread, I physically evoke the suffering of our Lord and Master, and I pray that the life of each person may be united with the Life of the One who is "alive for evermore and who holds the keys of Death and Hades."

But—and this is the most wondrous thing of all—it is precisely through suffering that this union takes place. It's through our suffering—and there's hardly anything noble about it. It's ordinary, everyday misery. A lot of it is self-inflicted; hardly any of it makes sense. But as I remember each person and every situation—the girl who just survived her second suicide attempt, the woman who's so worried that she's having trouble sleeping, the man who's not sure he can continue to stay married, the young man who can't stop looking at pornography, the woman who's just now coming to grips with how abusive her mother is; as I place crumb after crumb on the diskos plate—for the woman who isn't sure how much longer her husband is going to hang around, for the father who is going to be traveling abroad this week, for the widowers who miss their wives, for the grandmother who wonders what will happen to her autistic granddaughter, for the man who's recovering from a stroke and scared that he's going to have another one, for the women who have cancer, for the young woman who is waiting for someone to tell her what she does have—all of it is transformed. It's transformed because it has become an offering, an offering that we make in union with the sacrifice Christ Jesus has made to God the Father on behalf of each one of us.

And through this offering we are also transformed. Through this offering, we become the Church. In fact, it is through the suffering that is offered up in the proskomidia that the Church is actually gathered for the liturgy. That assembly begins before we even get to the commemorations, because before we remember all the members of St. John parish, "and those whom they love, their kinsmen of flesh and spirit," we remember the saints. We start with the Mother of God, and then we also call upon the angels and the prophets and the apostles and the great hierarchs and the martyrs and the ascetics and the holy unmercenaries. We also remember our patron and protector, St. John the Forerunner, and by the time all those saints have gathered, by the time we get to the commemorations for our particular community, I'm praying for people here in Cedar Park and for the folks who live all over Austin and for the families who are over in Leander and for the people who are waking up in Round Rock and Taylor and Georgetown. I'm praying for people who are driving in from Temple and Killeen and Bastrop and Elgin and Burnet and Kerrville.

It's a cosmic gathering. It's an assembly that spans eons and ages. And it's all focused right here on this converted ranch house on four-and-one-half wooded acres in the heart of Central Texas. Because after the bread and wine have been prepared, Fr. Deacon BL brings the censer, and I bless it, and then I pick up the metal star that covers the diskos plate. I hold it over the incense and kiss it; then I put it on the diskos and say, "The star came to rest over the place where the young child was." And just as all creation was focused on the cave in Bethlehem when Christ Jesus was born, just as the magi followed the star, so the entire Church down through history and on into eternity is coming to this liturgy; they are hurrying to join us in this celebration.

Then I place the veils over the diskos and the chalice. I say, "The Lord is king; He is clothed with majesty.... For He hath established the world which will not be moved." I say, "Thy virtue, O Christ, hath covered the heavens, and the earth is full of Thy praise." And with that, a new creation, a new heaven and a new earth called the Church is present in the world, and Fr. Deacon and I finish the prayers; we bless this new world and offer it back up to the Most Holy Trinity.

As we finish up the service, I can hear cars pulling into the parking lot. Folks are moving around in the kitchen getting ready for coffee hour. One or two people are out in front of the iconostasis, lighting candles. The altar servers start to arrive, and they look through the robes to find one that fits.

It's the same day, but it's also different. It's Sunday morning, but it's also the Eighth Day. It's Cedar Park, but it's also the Kingdom of Heaven. Because we are the Church, and the bread and the wine are ready, and we are about to join together in the Great Marriage Supper of the Lamb.

Monday, October 8
✣ *Pelagia, the Former Courtesan*

That guy that lives on the street that leads out of our subdivision has added a third large, inflatable, purple-and-black spider to the other two in his display. This one is attached to his fence. He has also placed another inflatable decoration on his lawn: a ghoul seated on a life-sized motorcycle. The biker ghoul is right next to the giant pumpkin.

Cynthia thinks maybe the guy makes inflatable yard art for a living, and this is simply his way of advertising. Katie is wondering if there is a neighborhood contest we don't know about. I'm worried that civilization, as we know it, is coming to an end.

Thursday, October 11
✣ *Philip the Deacon*

I called my spiritual father, Fr. TM, today, and we had a good, long talk. He had called me last month, but I wasn't really prepared, so we didn't stay on the phone for long.

Back when I was a Protestant, before I had a spiritual father, whenever I read about that sort of guidance, I was often left with the impression that it was some sort of arcane discipline that dealt with experiences that were primarily interior and generated insights that were almost ineffable. But now that I have been receiving that kind of guidance for the better part of a decade, I'd have to say it's really all about honesty and friendship.

I tell Fr. TM what's going on in my life: what I'm struggling with, what I'm worried about, what I'm afraid of. He listens; he talks a little about his own life. Then he tells me that he loves me and that he will be praying for me.

And that's pretty much it. Sometimes—but not often—he makes suggestions. Sometimes he tells me things I already know—and he usually prefaces it by saying, "I'm going to remind you of something you already know." When we're together at a conference or a retreat, I'll actually make my confession with him. The rest of the time, when I need to go to confession,

I call up Fr. DB at the downtown parish or wait until Fr. CH comes through to visit his family.

I suppose there are many different ways of providing spiritual guidance, and I'm sure there are all different kinds of spiritual fathers. But for me, it's all about honesty: It's about having someone in your life who knows everything there is to know about you. And it's all about friendship: It's about having someone who will take your life into their own and offer it up in union with the life of our Lord and Master.

Friday, October 12
✠ *Probus, Tarachus, Andronicus, Martyrs*

Since we returned from our pilgrimage, I've changed my prayer rule somewhat. Instead of doing an akathist or a canon at Small Compline, I've been doing the Jesus Prayer. I use my prayer rope, and I go through it four times. I'm sure I'll increase that at some point. But what prompted that change was being in the services at the Monastery of St. John and talking to Fr. Zacharias. The services reminded me of how important it is to focus my heart and keep it that way. And Fr. Zacharias talked to me about the importance of striving for no more than "a single thought."

So that's how I'm starting to simplify my spiritual life. But I think the next step in that direction will be to bring this journal to a close. At the end of this month, I will have written in these notebooks, almost daily, for a full year. It's been a lot of work, but it's also been a blessing, and along the way, I think it's been a blessing for at least a few others, as well. I know that it's brought Cynthia and me closer together, and some of the folks who have read the entries I posted on the parish website have told me that they were helped—or at least they got a good laugh—as a result of what I wrote.

But writing not only clarifies and communicates; it also complicates. This past week, I ran across a quotation by Christian Wiman, the editor of *Poetry* magazine. He observed that "most writers live at some strange adjacency to experience in that they feel life most intensely in their reaction to it." I think that's true; in fact, in many ways, this journal is just a sustained record of that kind of "strange adjacency." And as valuable as that can be, I don't want that perspective to characterize the rest of my life—because you end up experiencing everything in a tape-delayed format. So at the end of this month, after just a few more entries, I'm going to step back into my life and do my best to keep my heart focused on the really important relationships and to strive after that "single thought," to be present in the right then and there.

Sunday, October 14
✠ *Holy Fathers of the Seventh Ecumenical Council*

The day I was ordained to the priesthood, Bishop Basil told me he wanted me to learn the services carefully. He said, "Don't even try to pray yet; just pay close attention to the *Liturgikon* and learn the services really well; once you've done that, then you'll be able to pray."

I've tried to follow his instructions, but at the time, I was genuinely mystified by his idea of praying during the services. I wasn't at all sure what that was supposed to look like, because as a United Methodist pastor, the last thing I had time to do during the services was pray. There was always a hymn to lead or an announcement to make. Granted, there were sometimes a few free moments when the choir was singing the anthem, but I was still up on the platform; I was still "on"; I was looking out at all the people, and they were looking back at me. So it was next to impossible to maintain the kind of focus that prayer requires.

But the worship of the Orthodox Church provides all kinds of opportunities for that kind of focus. Like this morning at Orthros. During the canon, I got out my prayer rope and leaned back on the bookcase that we keep in the altar. I prayed along with the hymns, and after a few minutes, it wasn't so much that I was praying as that I was being prayed. And that happens a lot during the services: I become part of something much larger than myself; I become part of the Church; I become part of the worship that unites heaven and earth.

And when I'm using a prayer rope, all of that happens in a way that is intensely personal, in a way that is very hands-on. I think a lot of people have the impression that using a prayer rope during a service somehow reduces worship to the level of personal devotion. I'm sure that can be a danger, but my experience has always been just the opposite: The prayer rope doesn't narrow the focus of my piety; it blows the walls off my heart and opens me up and reminds me that I'm part of a vast, worshipping community. Because just as the knots on my prayer rope are connected to each other, through the services of the Church, every believing heart is connected. Every believing heart acquires the same rhythm of prayer. And together, we become a noetic prayer rope in the hands of the Great High Priest, and each one of our hearts passes through those hands of healing and blessing.

So even as we are praying, we are also being prayed.

Monday, October 15
✤ *Lucian of Antioch, Hieromartyr*

Last week, my sister Rosemary and my brother-in-law Joe called. Their kids are going through some rough times. And then, on top of that, Rosemary and my mother had words over the whole situation. Mom feels Rosemary's kids are being manipulative; Rosemary feels Mom is being unbelievably insensitive. They have both talked to me, but I don't think they have yet talked again to each other. They will, of course, but that clash only made a bad situation worse.

And then yesterday, Cynthia called her mom. She does that several times a month, but it's always the same non-conversation. And it's always painful.

The bottom line is that I'm sometimes at a loss to know how to pray for my family. It's not that our problems are any more complicated or intractable than the problems any other family has. It's just that I'm more familiar with them. If I knew all the intricate twists of every other family's characteristic dysfunctions, I'd probably feel just as stymied in all my intercessions. So in that regard, when I'm praying for the families in our parish, a little distance, a little ignorance is actually a good thing. Ironically, since I don't know the whole history—since I'm not an integral part of the history—I can pray with more hope and more confidence.

But with my own family, I sometimes get stuck; I sometimes get discouraged. So a couple of years ago, I decided it was time to get some help, to bring in a few ringers. I started praying to St. James and St. Jude and St. Symeon, the half brothers of Christ Jesus; I also started praying to the holy and righteous Joseph, Jacob's son. I mean, if anyone knows about family dysfunction, it's those guys. The half brothers of our Lord and Master tried to do an intervention with Him—but they all ended up as His disciples. The brothers of Joseph actually managed to sell him into slavery—but he forgave them and saved them all, along with their families.

Making those saints my daily companions in prayer has helped a lot. They remind me that every family has problems, but each family has reason for hope. And just knowing they are praying for me and the people I love sends me back to my own prayers with greater resolve and renewed strength.

Wednesday, October 17
✠ *Prophet Hosea*

This year's theological seminar is producing some intense discussions. Most of the intensity is coming from the non-Orthodox participants, but I'm glad they are there, and I'm glad we are dealing with the subject of men and women in the Church. Because our society is completely messed up in regards to gender issues, and most Christian communities simply reflect that confusion.

Of course, the controversial crux of all this is the ordination of women as pastors and priests, and that is now a foregone conclusion for most American Christians. It is the new Arianism, triumphant and secure, not because of imperial favor, but because of something even stronger—societal sanction. And those conservative Christians who are trying hard to resist this perspective are not, for the most part, doing a very good job. Protestants are simply insisting that their interpretation of particular biblical texts is correct; meanwhile, their opponents easily bypass that with scholarly appeals to social context and authorial identity and hermeneutical principles. Roman Catholics can appeal to the authority of their institutions, but that only strikes people as even more oppressive and sexist than pointing to a text that was produced in an ancient and patriarchal society.

Unfortunately, the Orthodox Church isn't doing a whole lot better. In Holy Orthodoxy, the approach is often only slightly different from that which the feminists are using. Basically, it's all about parity: "Let's allow the women to do whatever the men have traditionally done." Practically speaking, this means women can chair committees, preside over the council, chant, teach, and even preach. Of course, we still don't allow women to serve as priests and deacons, but increasingly, that appears to be an arbitrary cut-off point. After all, if we are truly serious about parity, why stop there?

But there's nothing creative in that approach. It's all about one sex mimicking the other. And ultimately, that's demonic. Because the devil cannot create; he only copies what the Most Holy Trinity has brought into existence, and that very act is also a perversion. No wonder even faithful women are getting exasperated with the whole situation. All too often, the Church is not offering them a spiritual role or a way of being Christian that is based on their unique charisms as women; what they are being offered is a knock-off, scaled-down version of what the men are supposed to be doing.

So there needs to be much more proactive, positive work done by people who are committed to the Faith and determined to discover and nurture and support the unique identities of both men and women. This seminar we have embarked on is a start, but only a start. So much more needs to be done.

Friday, October 19
✣ *Prophet Joel*

Brendan came in last night on his way to San Antonio. He parked in the driveway, so before I left for Orthros, I had to get his keys and move his car out onto the street.

I managed to operate the keyless entry without setting off the alarm, but when I sat down in the driver's seat, the entire dashboard lit up like the Starship *Enterprise*, the steering wheel moved toward me, and the seat adjusted itself in several different ways.

I sat there for a moment, feeling completely aboriginal. Then, in quick succession, I managed to activate the radio, the headlights, the windshield wipers, and the dashboard phone. Finally, I found the ignition, put the car in gear, and backed down the driveway.

Truly, this world is not my home.

Sunday, October 21
✣ *Sixth Sunday of Luke*

We have a relic of St. John Chrysostom in our altar.

It's a tiny, light-brown bone fragment—one of the altar servers once remarked that it looks like something you might find "at the bottom of a bowl of Grape Nuts." Anyway, it came to us in a small glass container, and Fr. Deacon BL installed the container in a large icon of St. John that hangs in the altar.

The relic also came to us in a roundabout way. It seems that it was, at one time, in a Roman Catholic parish in Manila. At some point after the Second Vatican Council, the priests of that community decided to dispose of all their relics, but a pious family rescued this one that we now have, and for many years, they kept it in their home. In the 1980s, the family moved to Southern California, and they ended up living next door to a family who had recently converted to Orthodoxy. The two families became friends. Eventually, the American family moved to Cedar Park, and before they left, the Filipino family gave them the relic and the papers that attest to its authenticity.

The American family was touched by the gift, but after they arrived in Cedar Park, they quickly got in touch with us and donated the relic to our community. So now, every Sunday before we celebrate St. John's Liturgy, I get to reverence his relic. Every Sunday, before I preach, I get to reverence the relic of one of the Church's greatest homilists. And even though it's something I do on a regular basis, I never kiss that glass container without coming away with this vivid sense of my participation in a community in which there is no distance at all between the saints and me—neither chronological, nor emotional, nor political, nor theological. Because St. John and I serve the same altar; we proclaim the same faith; we live in the same Kingdom.

Monday, October 22
✠ *Abercius, Hieromartyr*

This past weekend, I was blessed with another, tangible sign of just how little distance there is in this community we call the Church. Mr. O, one of the oldest members of our parish, baked the prosphora.

Mr. O is eighty-five, and he had never baked prosphora before. His wife departed this life less than a year ago. She was a tremendous cook, and I'm sure she baked many prosphora loaves over the years. But a few months ago, Mr. O decided he wanted to be able to offer some loaves in memory of his wife; however, since he is by profession an engineer, he did several weeks' worth of experiments and trial runs. In fact, his daughter, VP, told me he had spent days and days baking bread, adjusting the recipe, and perfecting his technique. But it all paid off beautifully, because on Saturday evening, he showed up at Great Vespers with four of the best-looking loaves I have ever seen.

But what made that bread so wonderful was not simply Mr. O's love for his departed wife or the diligence and care he put into the baking process. What made that bread so precious is that Mr. O is our community's link to the living history of the Church. That's because Mr. and Mrs. O grew up in Ukraine just after the Communist Revolution. Mr. O's grandfather had been a priest, but neither he nor Mrs. O had the opportunity to attend services when they were young. All they knew about the Faith is what they learned in private from their families.

When the Nazis invaded the Ukraine, both Mr. and Mrs. O were taken to labor camps in Germany. That's where they met, and after the war, they were able to find a priest and get married. They then immigrated to Brazil, but they never did feel at home there. So after a few years, Mr. O got a job with Westinghouse in Buffalo, New York. They lived in Buffalo for quite a while, then were transferred to Texas. Mr. and Mrs. O were very active in their parish in Buffalo, and they attended St. Elias, the downtown parish, after they moved to this area. But after St. John's was started in the mid 1990s, they transferred their membership to our community, since we are closer to their home in Georgetown.

But what was in many ways a matter of convenience for them turned out to be a priceless gift to our parish. Since most of the members of our community are converts, we haven't had many real connections with flesh-and-blood Orthodoxy. And that can be pretty dangerous, because the Faith isn't something you read about in books or on the internet; it is something that is lived. And if you don't have any role models for that kind of life, then Holy Orthodoxy can easily be reduced to nothing more than rules, robes, icons, and incense.

But Mr. and Mrs. O have helped to keep us from that. They have helped to make our community real. And the bread Mr. O brought this past Saturday night symbolized that gift. Because what he handed me wasn't just bread: It was all his years with Mrs. O; it was the legacy of his grandfather's priesthood; it was the memory of two people who found love amidst the hell of the Second World War; it was the loneliness and isolation of being immigrants; it was the patience and good humor both he and Mrs. O displayed in dealing with our community's enthusiasm and silliness. In other words, what he handed me on Saturday night, and what we used at the liturgy on Sunday morning, was their life, which, in turn, has become our life, and which we then, together, offered up for the life of the world.

Tuesday, October 23
✠ *James, Apostle and Brother of the Lord*

When I was in seminary, I enjoyed homiletics. My senior year, I even won a prize for preaching. A year or two out of seminary, I was selected as one of the "Outstanding Young Preachers" in the conference that I served. Back then, my sermons were literary and self-conscious. I especially liked story sermons: These were basically short stories that used biblical imagery and had an obliquely spiritual message. I managed to get some of these story sermons into a couple of magazines, and I was even thinking about trying to get a whole collection of them published.

But then one year, I started street preaching, and everything changed. The United Methodist congregation I served in Wichita Falls had a monthly slot at a local mission; we were responsible for one of the mission's evening services. Only thing was, the mission had this rather manipulative policy: If you wanted a meal, you had to attend the service. So I would often end up preaching to over a hundred tired and hungry men, women, and children— and I quickly learned to keep it short and simple.

Later on, our congregation started its own outreach project; we called it the motel ministry. Every Friday afternoon of the year, I would make the rounds of all the local bars, strip clubs, and adult theaters. I would put up posters and visit with folks. In the summer, we would do vacation church schools at a number of cheap motels, and we would have several street services.

We did that work for about five years, and during that time, I preached in motel lobbies, in parks, on sidewalks, and in between the sets of local bands. I learned a lot about preaching in that kind of environment: how to get to the point, how to talk directly to people, how to make things simple without dumbing it all down. In fact, I was once asked to do a continuing education seminar on this subject. A few of my fellow United Methodist pastors attended, and at the end of the presentation, one of them asked me,

"What would you say is your one guiding homiletic principle in this work?" Without even thinking about it, I responded, "If you can't spray-paint it on a highway overpass, then it's too complicated."

That's still the principle behind my best preaching. I haven't won any awards in a long, long time, and I wouldn't try to publish any of my sermons, but since becoming Orthodox, I've discovered that a great deal of patristic preaching works the same way. In my opinion, St. Gregory Nazianzen has the most beautiful rhetorical style of any of the Fathers. But in Constantinople, he had to preach in a little makeshift house church, and he not only had to put up with hecklers, but he was constantly wondering if the Arians were going to burst in and start pelting him with rocks. The sermons of St. John Chrysostom and St. Augustine are often quite long; that's what people in the ancient world expected from their orators. But St. John and St. Augustine weren't presenting those lengthy expositions to modern, well-behaved congregations. Most of the people they were preaching to were rowdy and uneducated. Not only that, but in Constantinople, St. John had to compete with the Hippodrome, and in Hippo, St. Augustine was working in an environment where doctrinal disagreements were settled by the "Clubs of Israel." So their preaching is consistently direct and simple, and they always end their sermons with a practical application.

So actually, I think those great saints would understand my highway overpass principle. In fact, I not only think they'd understand it, I think they'd dig it. Because they were street preachers, too.

Wednesday, October 24
✚ *Harith and His Companions, Martyrs*

That highway overpass image not only guides my preaching, it also provides my work week with a funky kind of focus.

Because every one hundred or so hours, I have to get up in front of folks and preach a sermon. So every week, it's like I'm driving along this flat stretch of West Texas highway. I'm cruising along in the light green 1972 Impala we inherited from Cynthia's mom. And then in the distance, one of those low, concrete overpasses appears just above the horizon.

Before too long, I'm there, and I pull off to the side of the road. I get a couple of cans of spray paint out of the trunk, then walk back around to the front of the car and sit down on the hood.

Then I look up at the overpass. Sometimes I end up looking at it for quite a while. I'll walk back and forth across the quiet highway, looking at the bridge from different angles. I'll lie down on the hood of the car; I'll lay my head back on the windshield, and I'll stare up at the overpass. But eventually, a smile will start to spread across my face. Then I grab a can of spray paint and start shaking it as I walk toward the bridge.

When I'm done, I walk back to the Impala and toss the empty cans into the back seat. I look up at the overpass one last time, then I pull out onto the highway and head down the road until the next bridge comes into sight.

Thursday, October 25
✠ *Marcian and Martyrius, Martyrs*

This morning after Orthros was over, I was getting out the books for Vespers. For some reason, this ongoing sequence of services is never oppressive. As a matter of fact, it's actually freeing. Because what the liturgical structure of the Church's life reflects is nothing less than eternity, and, as Robert Taft, one of my favorite liturgical scholars, has written, "For those who believe, there is no end, but only what comes next."

Friday, October 26
✠ *Demetrios the Myrrh-streaming*

I've only got a couple more entries to make before I wind up this project, but I'm at the end of a notebook, so I guess I'll have to just start a new one. That will make six notebooks in the course of the year. Which means it really is time to wrap this up.

Another, even better reason to bring all this to a conclusion: A few minutes ago, when I was getting out that last notebook, I started thumbing through some of the old ones, and the thought occurred to me, "I wonder if any of it is any good?"

It's not that I haven't worked hard on this journal. These notebooks are full of rewrites and revisions. But when you start wondering about whether what you've written will last or stand the test of time, when you start wondering if it's any good, that's when you need to put it down and walk away. Because it's like that poem W. S. Merwin wrote about his visit with John Berryman:

> I asked how can you ever be sure
> that what you write is really
> good at all and he said you can't
> you can't you can never be sure
> you die without knowing
> whether anything you wrote was any good
> if you have to be sure don't write.

Sunday, October 28
✠ *Seventh Sunday of Luke*

This morning I pulled into the church parking lot at 6:30 AM.

Daylight Savings Time doesn't end for another week, so it was still dark. But there was a big moon, and the stars were glinting, and the night was still, so I got out of the car and walked back into the trees.

And what surprised me was the fact that I could see just fine. It took my eyes a few minutes to adjust, and it's not like I could make out tiny details, but the moon was so bright, the trees and the underbrush were lit up with this soft, gentle light.

There were even shadows. The branches from the larger trees were outlined on the ground, and when I stepped into one of the clearings, my own silhouette fell across the tall, thick grass.

I stood out there for a while and practiced my sermon. Even though I do this every single Sunday morning of my life, every once in a while I get a sense of how odd it must seem. I think about what I would say if I had to explain myself to a policeman or to some of the people who live in the houses that border our property. After all, I'm up way before dawn, I'm wearing a black dress, and I'm standing out in the middle of the woods.

But then I'm sure my Celtic forebears had to deal with the same thing: "Aidan's out on his island again."

"Is that Cuthbert over there in the surf?"

"Columba? He's probably up on Sithean Mor. At least that's the first place I always look for him."

"Sorry. You just missed Brendan. He's back out on the boat."

There's nothing to prevent someone from being Orthodox in a totally urban setting, but I know that I'm a better priest because I get to pray and preach out under the trees as the world turns around and the night turns to day. In fact, I need to do that before I ever pray and preach in our liturgy.

This afternoon, after all the services, the building committee met, and we went over the final design for the new facility. As the years go by, and as we develop more of the property, I need to remember to ask the parish to leave a corner where the live oaks can get tall, and the scrub cedars can stay thick, and the grass can grow wild, and the deer can hide.

I think they'll understand.

Monday, October 29
✠ Anastasia, Martyr

This morning I read this passage from C. S. Lewis's autobiography, *Surprised by Joy:*

> One of the first results of my Theistic conversion was a marked decrease (and high time, as all readers of this book will agree) in the fussy attentiveness which I had so long paid to the progress of my own opinions and the states of my own mind. . . . If Theism had done nothing else for me, I should still be thankful that it cured me of the time-wasting and foolish practice of keeping a diary. (Even for autobiographical purposes a diary is nothing like so useful as I had hoped. You put down each day what you think important; but of course you cannot each day see what will prove to have been important in the long run.)

C. S. Lewis is one of my favorite writers, and while I would never say that this journal has been a waste of time, his observation confirms my sense that it's time to move on. That doesn't mean I'm done with writing altogether—plenty of homilies and newspaper columns and newsletter articles are still out there ahead of me—but it's definitely time to wrap up this project.

And in that regard, I feel a bit like St. Maximos Kafsokalyvitis. He was an Athonite monk who lived in a series of huts: He would build one and stay in it for a while; then he would burn the hut down, move to another location, and build a new shelter.

That's a great paradigm for the Christian life: Hang onto the essentials; walk away from the rest.

Time to burn this shack down and move on.

Wednesday, October 31
✠ *Apelles, Amplius, Stachys, Urban, Narcissus,*
Aristobulos, Apostles of the Seventy

I'm at school. The students are writing essays, and I'm finishing up this journal.

But as I do, I know that I want to apply this same sense of craft and hard work to the more important aspects of my life: my love for Cynthia and Brendan and Katie; my love for this parish; my love for the Most Holy Trinity. Because, in the end, there's only one kind of writing that really matters. And since St. Isaac of Syria understood that far better than I ever will, I'll close this journal with his words:

Life in this world is like writing letters on tablets: whenever a man wishes to do so, he can add to them or make changes in the letters. But the future life is like writings on clean rolls sealed by the royal seal, where no adding or subtracting is allowed. Therefore, while we are still in the midst of change, let us pay attention to ourselves; and while we still have power over the record of our life, which we write with our own hands, let us strive to add to it with right living and erase the defects of our former life. For while we are in this world, God does not affix His seal either to what is good or what is evil, up to the very moment of our departure from this life.

GLOSSARY

Aer ❖ Large veil used to cover the diskos and chalice

Afterfeast ❖ Days following a major feast

Akathist ❖ Hymn of twenty-four stanzas honoring the Mother of God

Analogion ❖ Lectern or icon stand

Antidoron ❖ Bread distributed following the dismissal of the Divine Liturgy

Antimension ❖ Cloth imprinted with an image of the entombment of Christ which is kept on the altar

Apolitikion ❖ First principal hymn of the day

Aposticha ❖ Hymns and psalm verses chanted near the end of Vespers and daily Orthros

Canon ❖ A long hymn, divided into nine odes, each ode consisting of numerous stanzas

Cassock ❖ A black robe which is the normal outer garment of Orthodox priests and monks; also called an endorasson

Compline ❖ A service done in the late evening; the second service of the liturgical day. There are two versions of this service: Great Compline is served primarily during Great Lent; Small Compline is done at all other times of the year.

Divine Liturgy ❖ The primary eucharistic service of the Church; offered on Sundays and feast days

Diskos ❖ Footed plate for the eucharistic bread

Entrance ❖ A liturgical procession; there are two entrances during each Divine Liturgy and one at Great Vespers

Epitaphion ❖ Large, embroidered cloth icon of the entombed Christ

Epitrachelion ❖ Liturgical stole worn by bishops and priests

Exorasson ❖ Black outer clerical robe having a full body and long, wide sleeves; typically worn over the endorasson, or cassock, during services

Forefeast ❖ Days preceding a major feast

Homily ❖ A sermon

Holy doors ❖ Central gates of the iconostasis leading from the nave to the holy table

Holy table ❖ A consecrated altar

Hours ❖ Short services done at the first hour (6 AM or right after Orthros), third hour (9 AM), sixth hour (noon), and ninth hour (3 PM or right before Vespers). These services, which are the last four of the liturgical day, are also often grouped together and done all at the same time.

Iconostasis ❖ Icon screen between the sanctuary and the nave

Jesus Prayer ❖ A short prayer consisting simply of the Name of Jesus or a sentence such as, "Lord Jesus Christ, Son of God, have mercy on me, a sinner."

Katavasia ❖ The last stanza in the ode of a canon

Kathisma ❖ Each of the twenty major sections of the Psalter

Khouria ❖ The traditional Middle Eastern title for a priest's wife

Kontakion ❖ Second principal hymn of the day

Lamb ❖ Cube of bread that is consecrated during the Eucharist

Lampadas ❖ Oil lamps

Leavetaking ❖ Final day of a festal season

Litya ❖ Short prayer service that includes hymns and litanies of intercession; can be done alone or combined with another service such as Vespers

Matushka ❖ The traditional Slavic title for a priest's wife

Metania ❖ Low bow made while extending the right hand to the floor; the sign of the cross is made preceding or following each metania

Mid-hours ❖ Short services added to the regular Hours in the weeks leading up to Nativity

Midnight Office ❖ Service offered late at night or early in the morning; third service of the liturgical day

"O Lord, I Have Cried" ❖ Musical arrangement of Psalms 140, 141, 129, and 116, used each day at Vespers. Short antiphonal hymns are sung between many of the psalm verses.

Orthros ❖ First service of the morning; fourth service of the liturgical day

Paraclesis ❖ Service of supplication to the Mother of God

Paramon ❖ Day of preparation preceding the Nativity of Christ and the Theophany

Phelonion ❖ Capelike priestly garment

Polyeleos ❖ Psalms 134 and 135 when chanted at Orthros

Prayer Rope ❖ A knotted rope used to maintain rhythm and focus during prayer; often used with the Jesus Prayer

The Praises ❖ Psalms 148, 149, and 150, read every day at Orthros and chanted on Sundays and feast days

Proskomidia ❖ Service for the preparation of the eucharistic bread and wine

Prosphora ❖ Round loaf of specially prepared liturgical bread

Prothesis ❖ Room or table where the proskomidia is performed

Psalter ❖ Book of Psalms

Shamassy ❖ Traditional title for a deacon's wife

Solea ❖ Raised area in front of the iconostasis

Stasis ❖ Section of a kathisma of the Psalter

Stichera ❖ Hymns sung antiphonally during "O Lord I Have Cried"

Synaxarion ❖ The account of a saint's life or the list of saints honored on a particular day of the year; the list of saints is often accompanied by short, poetic verses.

Theotokion ❖ Hymn addressed to or referring to the Mother of God

Theotokos ❖ The Virgin Mary; literally, the Birth-giver of God

Typika ❖ Short service done between the sixth and ninth hours

Vespers ❖ Service offered in the early evening; the first service of the liturgical day. On Saturdays or on the eve of a feast, a longer version of the service is offered; this longer version is known as Great Vespers.

Other Books of Interest

At the Corner of East and Now
A Modern Life in Ancient Christian Orthodoxy
by Frederica Mathewes-Green

Acclaimed author Frederica Mathewes-Green takes us through a typical Divine Liturgy in her little parish of Holy Cross in Baltimore, setting of her well-loved book *Facing East*. Interspersed with reflections on the liturgy and the Orthodox faith are accounts of adventures around the country. In all the places she visits and all the people she meets, Frederica finds insights about faith, American life, and what it means to be human, and she shares these insights with the wit, pathos, and folksy friendliness that have made her one of the most beloved spiritual writers in America.

"A thoughtful source of inspiration for any truth-seeker. . . . If as Mathewes-Green writes, most people have been fed a boiled down 'oatmeal version' of faith, then *At the Corner of East and Now* offers more demanding fare for those with discerning palates." —*Los Angeles Times*
Paperback, 270 pages (ISBN: 978-1-888212-34-1) CP Order No. 007609—$16.95*

We Came, We Saw, We Converted
The Lighter Side of Orthodoxy in America
by Fr. Joseph Huneycutt

Based on his popular blog and Ancient Faith Radio podcast, *Orthodixie*, Fr. Joseph Huneycutt presents a humorous look at the pluses, minuses, joys, pitfalls, and struggles of perpetual conversion within an Orthodox Christian worldview. Within these pages you'll find all those familiar characters you've encountered in exploring American Orthodoxy—but with a hilarious twist: the Orthodox Christian anarchist, the Orthodox white boy, and that incomparable superhero, Ortho-Man. You'll be introduced to the lighter side of fasting, theosis, living a holy life in a secular world, and the struggle to understand those on the other side of the cradle/convert divide.

For those days when acquiring the mind of Christ seems impossibly serious and, well, just plain impossible, a quick dip into *We Came, We Saw, We Converted* will restore your sense of humor and help you get up and try again.
Paperback, 232 pages (ISBN: 978-0-9822770-8-9) CP Order No. 007729—$18.95*

Close to Home
One Orthodox mother's quest for patience, peace, and perseverance
by Molly Sabourin

Close to Home is for every young mother who's ever wished children came with an instruction manual; who's ever longed for just one quiet minute to finish a thought or utter a prayer; who's ever despaired of perfecting herself in time to become a good example for her children; who's ever wondered why "happily ever after" takes so darn much work.

With courage, humor, and unflinching honesty, Molly Sabourin addresses all these frustrations and more—offering not answers or solutions, but a new perspective, a pat on the shoulder, a reassuring "I've been there too, and there is hope." Those who share her "quest for patience, peace, and perseverance" will see themselves in these pages, laugh a little, cry a little, and close the book with new strength to continue the quest.

Paperback, 192 pages (ISBN: 978-1-888212-61-7) CP Order No. 007612—$15.95*

Surprised by Christ
My Journey from Judaism to Orthodox Christianity
by Rev. A. James Bernstein

Surprised by Christ is the story of a man searching for truth and unable to rest until he finds it. Raised in Queens, New York, by formerly Orthodox Jewish parents whose faith had been undermined by the Holocaust, Arnold Bernstein went on his own personal quest for spiritual meaning. He was ready to accept God in whatever form He chose to reveal Himself—and that form turned out to be Christ. But Bernstein soon perceived discrepancies in the various forms of Protestant belief that surrounded him, and so his quest continued—this time for the true Church.

Surprised by Christ combines an engrossing memoir of one man's life in historic times and situations with an examination of the distinctives of Orthodox theology that make the Orthodox Church the true home not only for Christian Jews, but for all who seek to know God as fully as He may be known.

Paperback, 335 pages (ISBN 978-1-888212-95-2) CP Order No. 007604—$18.95*

Thirsting for God in a Land of Shallow Wells
by Matthew Gallatin

Beginning in the street ministry days of the Jesus Movement, Matthew Gallatin devoted more than twenty years to evangelical Christian ministry. He was a singer/songwriter, worship leader, and Calvary Chapel pastor. Nevertheless, he eventually accepted a painful reality: no matter how hard he tried, he was never able to experience the God whom he longed to know. His was a great dream that could not find fulfillment, a deep question that could not answer itself, an eternal thirst dwelling in a land of shallow wells.

In *Thirsting for God*, Gallatin expresses many of the struggles that a Protestant will encounter in coming face to face with Orthodoxy: such things as Protestant relativism, rationalism versus the Orthodox sacramental path to God, and the unity of Scripture and Tradition. An outstanding book that will give Protestant readers a more thorough understanding of the Church.

Paperback, 192 pages (ISBN: 978-1-888212-28-0) CP Order No. 005216—$14.95*

✳ Bread & Water, Wine & Oil
An Orthodox Christian Experience of God
by Fr. Meletios Webber

Worry, despair, insecurity, fear of death . . . these are our daily companions, and even though we attempt to ignore them or try to crowd them out, they are there, waiting for us in our quieter moments. It is precisely where we hurt most that the experience of the Orthodox Church has much to offer. The remedy is not any simple admonitions to fight the good fight, cheer up, or think positively. Rather, the Orthodox method is to change the way we look at the human person (starting with ourselves). Orthodoxy shows us how to "be transformed by the renewing of our mind"—a process that is aided by participation in the traditional ascetic practices and Mysteries of the Church. In this unique and accessible book, Archimandrite Meletios Webber first explores the role of mystery in the Christian life, then walks the reader through the seven major Mysteries (or sacraments) of the Orthodox Church, showing the way to a richer, fuller life in Christ.

Paperback, 200 pages (ISBN: 978-1-888212-91-4) CP Order No. 006324—$15.95*

⚓ Let Us Attend!
A Journey Through the Orthodox Divine Liturgy
by Fr. Lawrence Farley

Esteemed author and Scripture commentator Fr. Lawrence Farley provides a guide to understanding the Divine Liturgy, and a vibrant reminder of the centrality of the Eucharist in living the Christian life.

Every Sunday morning we are literally taken on a journey into the Kingdom of God. Fr. Lawrence guides believers in a devotional and historical walk through the Orthodox Liturgy. Examining the Liturgy section by section, he provides both historical explanations of how the Liturgy evolved, and devotional insights aimed at helping us pray the Liturgy in the way the Fathers intended. In better understanding the depth of the Liturgy's meaning and purpose, we can pray it properly. If you would like a deeper understanding of your Sunday morning experience so that you can draw closer to God, then this book is for you.

Paperback, 104 pages (ISBN: 978-1-888212-87-7) CP Order No. 007295—$10.95*

⚓ A Beginner's Guide to Prayer
The Orthodox Way to Draw Closer to God
by Fr. Michael Keiser

This is a book for those struggling to establish an effective life of prayer. Written neither for seasoned monastic nor lofty scholar, A Beginner's Guide to Prayer speaks to the average man or woman on the street who desires a deeper relationship with God but is unsure how or where to begin. Drawing from nearly 2000 years of Orthodox spiritual wisdom, the author offers warm, practical, pastoral advice whose genius is to be found in its homespun simplicity and straightforwardness of style. If you've been desiring to make prayer a meaningful and regular part of your life, this book will help set you on your way. But be careful! Prayer can be habit forming! In fact, the advice offered in this book may just change the course of the rest of your life. So, in the words of the author, "What are you waiting for? Start to pray!"

Paperback, 104 pages (ISBN: 978-1-888212-64-8) CP Order No. 006077—$10.95*

*Plus applicable tax and postage & handling charges. Prices current as of 4/2010. Please call Conciliar Press at 800-967-7377 for complete ordering information, or order online at www.conciliarpress.com.